JACQUES PAUW

THE PRESIDENT'S KEEPERS

THOSE KEEPING ZUMA IN POWER
AND OUT OF PRISON

TAFELBERG

Also by Jacques Pauw

Nonfiction
In the Heart of the Whore
Into the Heart of Darkness
Dances with Devils
Rat Roads

Fiction
Little Ice Cream Boy

Tafelberg, an imprint of NB Publishers,
a division of Media24 Boeke Pty (Ltd),
40 Heerengracht, Cape Town, South Africa
www.tafelberg.com

Set in 11 on 16 pt Chaparral
Cover by Fuel Design
Cover picture by Spencer Platt/Getty Images
Book design by Nazli Jacobs
Edited by Russell Martin
Proof read by Lisa Compton
Index by Mirie van Rooyen
Commissioning editor: Gill Moodie

Printed and bound by CTP Printers, Cape Town
First edition, sixth impression 2017

ISBN: 978-0-624-08303-0
Epub: 978-0-624-08304-7
Mobi: 978-0-624-08305-4

Contents

Abbreviations and acronyms

AFU	Asset Forfeiture Unit
ANC	African National Congress
ATM	Amalgamated Tobacco Manufacturing
BAT	British American Tobacco
CSU	Covert Support Unit
DA	Democratic Alliance
DDPP	deputy director of public prosecutions
DPCI	Directorate for Priority Crime Investigation (the Hawks)
DSO	Directorate of Special Operations (the Scorpions)
FIC	Financial Intelligence Centre
FITA	Fair-Trade Independent Tobacco Association
FUL	Freedom Under Law
HRIU	High-Risk Investigation Unit
IG/IGI	inspector-general of intelligence
IPID	Independent Police Investigative Directorate
JSCI	Joint Standing Committee on Intelligence
JvL	Johann van Loggerenberg
M&G	*Mail & Guardian*
MK	Umkhonto we Sizwe
MKMVA	Umkhonto we Sizwe Military Veterans' Association
MP	member of Parliament
NDPP	national director of public prosecutions
NEC	National Executive Committee (of the ANC)
NIA	National Intelligence Agency
NPA	National Prosecuting Authority
PAN	Principal Agent Network
Prasa	Passenger Rail Agency of South Africa
SARS	South African Revenue Service

SASSA	South Africa Social Security Agency
SCCU	Specialised Commercial Crimes Unit
Scopa	standing committee on public accounts
SIU	Special Investigating Unit
SOE	state-owned enterprise
SOU	Special Operations Unit
SSA	State Security Agency
TRC	Truth and Reconciliation Commission

Introduction

⸻•⸻

On Sunday night, 27 August 2017, my laptop and cellphone were stolen from my office at our restaurant and guesthouse in Riebeek-Kasteel in the Western Cape. Despondency and dread engulfed me when I walked into the room and was confronted by a computer cable and nothing more. A small window bordering Van Riebeek Street stood open.

I was initially calm, and walked to the bar and poured myself a stiff brandy and Coke. Then I went back to the office and phoned one of my sources.

"What was on the laptop?"

"Everything."

"How do you mean, everything?"

"Everything. The whole book. And notes, documents, reports, names, telephone numbers, everything."

"Is it password-protected?"

"Not really."

"Have you backed it up?"

"Some. Not everything."

"Is my name somewhere there?"

"I don't think so but I'm not sure."

Moments of silence before the source spoke: "You realise we're fucked."

"Do you think it's them?"

"Without a doubt."

"How can you be so sure?"

"This is exactly how they do it. It's a warning."

Composure gave way to panic and horror. I was convinced that someone from crime intelligence, the Hawks or the State Security Agency had nicked my laptop and cellphone. My sources would be exposed. I would be arrested. State lawyers would try to stop the book.

But my wife, Sam Rogers, was not convinced. She pointed at the window and said: "Look at that little hole. Only a child can get through it. It's not the baddies; it's children."

Riebeek-Kasteel and some of the farms surrounding the village are home to a throng of neglected, desperate children. They roam the streets, and some of the older children have been apprehended for petty crimes. Sam knows them by name; she feeds them every Friday.

The next morning, two of my staff members and waitresses from another restaurant took to the streets, telling locals about a reward for the return of my laptop and cellphone.

Twenty-four hours later, I bought my laptop back on the streets of Esterhof, the "coloured" residential area in Riebeek-Kasteel. I have no idea who the culprits were but they were not the baddies I had feared. My book was back on track.

Why am I telling you this? Because there were times during the writing of this book when I felt as though I was back in the late 1980s at the anti-apartheid newspaper *Vrye Weekblad*, where we exposed the police death squad at Vlakplaas. Then we lived under a white dictatorship, which banned, imprisoned and killed opponents of the regime. *Vrye Weekblad*'s editor, Max du Preez, became one of the most persecuted editors in South Africa. Our office was bombed.

Almost three decades on, we are the children of a constitutional democracy with freedom of speech, association and movement. We shouldn't fear anything from the state except when we commit a crime or don't pay our taxes.

And yet, once again, I was speaking to sources in a hushed voice, changing venues at the very last minute and exchanging encrypted messages. At meetings, some told me to switch my phone off and take the battery out. They reminded me that sensitive state institutions were the victims of mysterious break-ins. We were back in the era of dirty tricks.

Many of the whistleblowers I spoke to were scared. They came from our law enforcement agencies: SARS, state and police intelligence, the prosecuting authority and the Hawks. These were the "good guys" – officials who wanted to do the right thing – but they had seen what had happened to colleagues such as Anwa Dramat, Shadrack Sibiya, Johann van Loggerenberg, Ivan Pillay, Glynnis Breytenbach, Robert McBride, Mxolisi Nxasana, Gibson Njenje and Johan Booysen. They had all lived through the upheaval of the purges that drove these people from their offices.

Many of my sources have families, and need their jobs. They feel cornered, and are carrying the brunt of President Jacob Zuma's devastating administration.

Zuma and his small band have managed not only to capture our law enforcement agencies – put their pals in charge, make cases disappear, dismantle structures that worked effectively – but also use these institutions to eliminate their opponents through trumped-up charges and harassment.

The whistleblowers came to me because they felt that things had gone horribly wrong and that maybe, just maybe, a book like this would make a difference. I warned them that there was no guarantee of any significant or positive outcome.

My sources will remain anonymous but they are the heroes of this book. One day, when we emerge from this mess – and I have no doubt we will – they should be honoured for revealing the true colours of Jacob Zuma, and also of people such as Richard Mdluli, Nomgcobo Jiba, Lawrence Mrwebi, Berning Ntlemeza, Arthur Fraser, Prince Mokotedi and Tom Moyane. These latter folk will not be remembered for contributing positively to state institutions. Under their reign, crime has spiralled, thugs have walked free, prosecutions and convictions of organised criminals have disintegrated, tax collection has dropped and state revenue has decreased.

Instead of strengthening our democracy, they will go down in history as people who were prepared to sell their souls, to sup with the devil, to keep Zuma out of prison and in power. These are Jacob Zuma's keepers: the people who have brought our beautiful country to the brink of a mafia state.

ONE

The spy in the cold

———•———

How the hell do you track down a spy in Moscow, a metropolis of 14 million residents, 7 million cars and 203 metro stations? It might have been the stamping ground of spying and counter-intelligence during the Cold War but these days it's a city on steroids where super-rich oligarchs buy Greek islands and London football clubs and commission Jennifer Lopez to perform at the weddings of their offspring. Soaring skyscrapers stand side by side with granite feats of Stalinist architecture, and Mercedes-Maybachs and Aston Martins roar past the remnants of boxy Ladas on six-lane highways.

What has happened to the armies of snoops and spooks who floated like ghouls across Red Square with bulges in their pockets and poison-tipped umbrellas in their hands; and who concocted conspiracies in hushed voices in *stolovayas* – Soviet government canteens – while gulping down stinky kolbasa sausages with Moskovskaya vodka?

I had just spent a substantial amount of money on an air ticket, subjected myself to a torturous flight across three continents and abandoned my new life as a chef and restaurateur in the hope of tracking down a former South African spy who I believed had a hell of a story to tell. I was like a rehabilitated drug addict who after two years of abstinence was about to stick a needle in my arm and propel heroin through my veins. I was attempting to do exactly what I had vowed never to do again: immerse myself in the seamy world and fortunes of low-lifes and charlatans, fraudsters and crooks, conmen and swindlers.

I was beset by a mixture of guilt, doubt and apprehension when we approached Moscow's Domodedovo International Airport. Under the belly of the Emirates Airbus was mounted a camera that beamed pictures of the landscape to the television screen on the back of the seat in front of me. We had flown for hundreds of kilometres over a patchwork blanket of white fields and dark woodland. I realised there is no colour in an iced landscape; it's all shades of white, grey and black. The airport was way out of the city and was surrounded by farmland and tiny villages that stood frozen in the face of daily blizzards. Cars were buried under snow and there were no signs of life except for grey smoke belching from tall, thin chimneys.

Domodedovo is an unfriendly place. After we had disembarked, I stood in a queue that snaked around silver-coloured metallic dividers. A sense of paranoia permeated the air. Border policemen clutching Kalashnikovs eyeballed arrivals with looks that could kill. I was anxious. It is notoriously difficult to get a Russian visa, especially for an independent traveller (visas have since been scrapped for South Africans). You require what is called a "visa invitation", an official document issued by an accredited Russian travel company that confirms that you have submitted a full itinerary and that your accommodation and travel have been prepaid. I didn't have time to go through the formal channels and instead bought papers for £30 from a London-based company. I had within half an hour a bogus document in Russian, confirming a full (false) itinerary and containing a host of stamps and signatures. The Russian consulate in Cape Town accepted the invitation, but I had to take copies of my documents with me because customs in Moscow might require them.

Moscow has recently been named as the most tourist-unfriendly city in the world. There are no welcoming signs at the airport or any indication that the authorities want foreigners in their country. A blue-uniformed immigration commissar awaited me in a booth at the front of my queue. She probably came to work every day in one of those fucked-up Ladas and had a permanent frown on her forehead that was partly covered by a peroxided fringe. A set of glasses that Lenin's Bolshevik Republic issued to her grandmother balanced on her nose. She asked the passenger in front of me for a document. He scratched frantically in his bag. He was of Middle Eastern origin and I hoped that that was the reason why his documents were scrutinised. Russia was bombing Islamic State in Syria and was in the organisation's cross-hairs.

When my turn came, she studied my passport – page for page – under a magnifying glass. News might have reached the expanse between the Great Steppe and the Baltic that South African travel documents were easy to obtain on the black market. She then looked up at me, down at the passport and up at me again. Come on, comrade, I thought, it's a new passport! She scribbled for a long time and stamped many papers. Without uttering a word, she waved me through with a slapping action to face customs – an equally frightening and inquisitive lot. Outside the building I was greeted by sharp blades of icy wind that threatened to cut my face open. It was also a perplexing English-less world because every signpost, nameplate or noticeboard was in Cyrillic script. It left you bewildered, like a rudderless ship with a spinning compass in an open and hostile ocean.

It was just past three in the afternoon and a dingily bilious sun was seeping through a tent of black clouds, their bellies heavy with snow. Moscow's taxi brigades are notorious for ripping off foreigners. I approached one that wanted 8,000 rubles (about R1,700) for the journey to the hotel. He shoved a map in front of me and pointed at the distance between the airport and my hotel. I waved my hands, protested loudly in English and walked away. We settled on 3,000 rubles. He shook my hand, babbled incessantly and took swigs from a flask while swerving through the traffic and negotiating the icy roads.

Moscow's frenzied traffic was almost the only audible sound at the height of winter. Birds had long since headed south for sunnier pastures, the city's café society had emigrated indoors, playgrounds and parks were empty, and Muscovites themselves were like dark ghosts, clad in fur, wool or leather with scarves wrapped around their necks and *ushanka* caps on their heads and over their ears. They floated effortlessly and silently over the snowy brown sludge and cut like blades through the Arctic breeze. It was impossible to walk at their pace – as futile as trying to keep up with a Masai in the scrub and savannah of southern Kenya.

Moscow and Russia have always been high on my bucket list and I have throughout my journalism career submitted story proposals that included a trip to Russia. They were all shot down, and when I left the profession at the end of 2014, I had given up hope of ever strolling on Red Square or downing a shot of vodka in a Russian bar.

This was until November 2016, when I received a phone call from a former employee of the State Security Agency (SSA). I had last spoken to him when I was still a journalist and did a story on major corruption in the agency.

"Do you remember Arthur Fraser?" he asked me.

"The new guy at State Security?"

"That's the bugger! Well, I've got a name for you. And an e-mail address."

"Who are you talking about?"

"The guy that did the corruption investigation into Fraser. He knows everything. His name is Paul Engelke."

"I'm not a journalist any longer," I told him. "I'm a chef!"

"I know," he said. "But I thought you'd be interested. I've also been told that he might be willing to talk."

"Why would Engelke talk?" I wanted to know. "It's dangerous for him."

"I've been told that he had left the service and is bitter."

"Interesting," I said. Journalists feast on the disgruntled and those that are intent on revenge. But I wasn't a journalist any longer. I was now the owner of a 60-seater restaurant, bar and guesthouse. It was the onset of summer and the establishment was packed over weekends as Capetonians flocked to the Swartland to get married, sample award-winning wines or feast on our olives and lamb. I was also about to launch my new summer menu.

"You must send Engelke an e-mail and ask him if he will talk to you," said the contact.

"Hmm," I said. "And where is he?"

"Unfortunately, he's a bit far away."

"How far?"

"He lives in Moscow."

*   *   *

In October 2014, as I was about to close the chapter on my journalism life, I wrote a story for *City Press* under the headline "Spies plunder R1bn slush fund". It chronicled an orgy of fraud and corruption; of how a top intelligence officer by the name of Arthur Fraser had allegedly squandered hundreds of millions of rand of taxpayers' money. Fraser, then second in command at the National Intelligence Agency (NIA, which later became the SSA), had embarked on a project to expand South Africa's intelligence capabilities. It was known as the Principal Agent Network (PAN) and had a limitless budget. Millions of rand in cash were transported in suitcases from a state money depot in Pretoria central to "the Farm" – the nickname for the agency's headquarters, otherwise known as Musanda, on the shores of the Rietvlei Dam, south of Pretoria. Much of the money in the PAN slush fund was squandered.

I had never met the bald-headed Fraser and he seldom appears in public. He was described to me as a broody, burly and soft-spoken man – he was apparently a bouncer in his younger days – who was the archetypal spy. What is the typical spy? To start with, they think that they are on a mission to save the world. The worlds of Matt Damon and Daniel Craig are slick, fast-paced and sexy. Their suits never crinkle, women always say yes, and their cars shoot missiles. Real-life spy sagas unfold with far less panache. Overseas research has shown intelligence agents at the CIA to be often college graduates with low-value degrees; they are outsiders or loners, they have family or friends in the intelligence or armed services, they can't work with money and love firearms. Much of a spy's work these days is sifting through data.

Spies and assassins are akin in that they have their own unique phrases and slang that only they understand. An assassin never kills but "eliminates", "permanently removes a subject from society" or "makes a plan" with him. In spy lingo, a bodyguard is a babysitter, a dead drop is a secret location where material can be left, and a person can be a target, an asset or a sleeper.

Fraser remained defiant throughout the two-year investigation into him and boasted that he would never be charged. He set up a string of businesses after he resigned from the intelligence service and concluded multimillion-rand contracts with government.

There was little reaction to my exposé in *City Press*, which I attributed to corruption fatigue. Readers had simply had enough of the daily barrage of news of state pillage. It didn't bother me because I was about to embark on a new chapter in my life.

* * *

I was a journalist for thirty years. A columnist for a Sunday newspaper once wrote that if journalists were the "*nagkardrywers*" (sewage car drivers) of society, I'm grubbier than any of them. She said it is probably because I've encountered my fair share of loonies and psychos, civil war and genocide, warmongers and cut-throats, scammers and tricksters.

Hunter S. Thompson once said that journalism is a "cheap catch-all for fuckoffs and misfits – a false doorway to the backside of life, a filthy piss-ridden little hole nailed off by the building inspector, but just deep enough for a wino to curl up from the sidewalk and masturbate like a chimp in a zoo-cage". I think he exaggerated, but my mother till her death wanted to know when I was going to get a "real job" and was convinced that there are far worthier things to do. I'm not sure if baking milktarts and cooking *waterblommetjiebredie* would have met her expectations either.

I left journalism as the head of investigations at Media24 newspapers. When I wrote the Fraser exposé for *City Press*, I was already the proud owner of a neglected guesthouse, restaurant and bar in Riebeek-Kasteel in the Western Cape. The village is a mere eighty kilometres from Cape Town and one of the province's "happening" country spots and getaways. The guesthouse cum restaurant was once one of the grande old dames of the valley; a 150-year-old manor house that guarded Riebeek-Kasteel's south-eastern entrance on Hermon Road. She had been sleeping guests, feeding strangers and quenching thirsts for two decades.

Journalist and friend Chris Marais said of me and Sam in a magazine article: "Gone, for these two, are the days of flitting through Africa with a cameraman, a notebook and a notion of a good story to be told. No more killing fields of Rwanda, drinking sessions with death squads, TV production deadlines, dodgy spaza preachers, chasing junkies through the back streets of Maputo and sailing down the Congo River on a stinky market boat. Gone, too, are the days of the generous expense account, the top-end media awards dinners, the acclaim and the sweet result of seeing the bad guy brought to book after being exposed on air."

Riebeek-Kasteel, surrounded by tanned cornfields and green vineyards, feels as though it is thousands of miles from Gauteng. It is wall-less, tractors full of grapes roar through the village, children play in the streets, and in winter the mist tumbles and tosses down Kasteelberg. The locals are engaging and gentle, and it is the kind of place where Sam and I can live forever.

We threw all our savings and pension into our new venture. We gave her a complete facelift and rechristened her Red Tin Roof. We donned her in new colours and enlarged the bar – and then added another one. We revamped her from head to toe and decorated her with our eclectic mixture of art and collectibles that we have accumulated from around the world.

Sam and I moved into the roof of the manor house, which was used by the previous owners as a conference venue. "You know what," Sam said to me, "we live like white trash." We've done so ever since.

The first few months were tumultuous and at times Red Tin Roof resembled a madhouse. The whole village descended on the place on opening night. Our credit card machine didn't work and we collected wads of cash in plastic bags. I grabbed friends and shoved them behind the bar to serve customers. Others were elevated to chefs to braai *sosaties* and *skilpadjies* (a Swartland delicacy of chopped lamb's liver wrapped in stomach fat). Then Eskom switched off the electricity.

Whether by choice or not, I have since then been banned to the kitchen. I had early on proved that I lacked the social finesse to deal with customers when I told a Spanish guest to fuck off when he complained about his Dom Pedro. Problem was that he had just sat down with his extended family for a long and boozy lunch. They stormed out. The Spaniard returned the next morning and demanded an apology. He got one, but after that Sam dragged me to the kitchen and ordered me to stay there.

I think I'm a bit of a feeder, and in Ann Patchett's essay "Dinner for One, Please, James" she says: "I love to feed other people. Cooking gives me the means to make other people feel better, which in a very simple equation makes me feel better. I believe that food can be a profound means of communication, allowing me to express myself in a way that seems much deeper and more sincere than words."

Chris Marais writes: "It's a Sunday afternoon in Riebeek-Kasteel and we've just arrived to see Jacques and Sam and get a first-hand progress report on this, their latest adventure. We sat outside in the quietening courtyard. Lunch is a distant memory, and only the last few drinkers remain with what's left in their wine bottles. It's clear to see who is 'front of house' and who is 'engine room'. Sam is all smiles, elegance and welcome. Jacques is all kitchen confidential, a bit like the mad genius you had to drag out of the lab and into the sunlight."

* * *

For the first year of my self-imposed exile I happily slaved away in the Red Tin Roof kitchen. That was until December 2015, when President Jacob Zuma fired his minister of finance, Nhlanhla Nene, and replaced him with ANC backbencher Des van Rooyen. Nene was a proponent of stern fiscal discipline and cutting government spending to allow for growth and poverty alleviation. That was not the priority for Zuma. He wanted control of the state purse.

Although Van Rooyen has a postgraduate degree in economics, he had no experience in Treasury matters. He was the mayor of Merafong in 2009, but residents chased him out of the township after burning his house. He was reportedly the preferred choirboy for an Indian immigrant family known as the Guptas. Brothers Ajay, Atul and Rajesh relocated to South Africa from India's northern state of Uttar Pradesh in 1993, just as white minority rule was ending and the country was opening up to the rest of the world. They control a vast business empire (Atul is South Africa's richest black businessman) and have become notorious for the "capture" of Zuma, some of his cabinet ministers and important elements of the state.

Prior to his appointment as finance minister, Van Rooyen visited the Saxonwold, Johannesburg, compound of the Guptas seven times and made 17 phone calls to the brothers. Hours after his appointment the Guptas sent two of their business associates to be appointed as advisers to Van Rooyen. The ascendancy of an ill-qualified Gupta stooge to the most sensitive cabinet position in South Africa sent the rand into a tailspin, stocks slid and bond prices tumbled. The country lost billions of rand within 24 hours. Four days later and under enormous pressure, Zuma made an astonishing U-turn by removing Van Rooyen and reappointing the respected Pravin Gordhan as finance minister.

I was watching the spell-binding political drama with anticipation from my kitchen at Red Tin Roof. Before starting to cook and bake at five or six every morning, I scoured news sites for more information on Zuma's attempts to capture the Treasury. Like most South Africans, I realised that should a man accused of fraud and his henchmen lay their hands on the state's coffers, it would be as fatal as handing an alcoholic the keys to his local Liquor City.

Several former and current politicians and journalists visited me at Red Tin Roof, and old security and intelligence sources contacted me again. In the meantime Max du Preez, journalist, author and *gabba* for twenty-five years, was providing analysis and spurring me on to start writing again. He lives a stone's throw from me in Riebeek-Kasteel.

Max and I had co-founded three significant events in print and television journalism: the Afrikaans anti-apartheid newspaper *Vrye Weekblad* in 1988, the *Truth Commission Special Report* at the SABC in 1996, and the public broadcaster's premier current affairs and investigative show, *Special Assignment*, in 1999. We started the SABC ventures before the likes of ANC commissar Snuki Zikalala and Zuma clown Hlaudi Motsoeneng destroyed the broadcaster and turned it into a propaganda tool for the ANC.

"You have to write another book," said Max. We were sitting in a quirky restaurant called Eve's Eatery in the heart of the village when he added: "You know more about guys like this than anyone else."

"And what should the book be about?" I asked Max.

"About the people that Zuma surrounds himself with. The Shauns and the Mdlulis and the Ntlemezas and the Jibas and the Nhlekos and the Hlaudis and the Zwanes. But also about the faceless, nameless bunch behind them that play a vital role to keep him in power."

"And out of prison," I added.

"Precisely," he said.

"And don't forget that they also enable him and the family to make money," I said. "Just think about his son's links to the Guptas and illegal tobacco smugglers."

"There you have it," said Max. "It's a book."

Shortly after this lunch with Max, Arthur Fraser was appointed as the new director-general of the State Security Agency (SSA). The man implicated in a two-year forensic investigation for misappropriating hundreds of millions of rand and fingered as a possible treason suspect was now South Africa's top spy boss.

I was horrified at Fraser's appointment but neither shocked nor surprised. It was clearly payback time in return for the favour he had done the embattled Zuma almost a decade previously. Fraser had, at the very least, taken out a political insurance policy.

Fraser's rise to the top of the intelligence hierarchy must be seen against the backdrop of what I regard as the primary objective of Zuma's presidency: to stay out of prison. In order to avoid spending his last days behind bars, he has to cling to power in order to prepare an exit strategy that will guarantee his freedom. This is closely followed by his greed to fill his and his family's pockets. Cronies are welcome to help themselves but their priority is to assist him to retain his freedom. Only after Zuma has looked after himself comes the small little problem of governing the Republic and its millions and millions of hungry, uneducated and jobless voters who are looking to him for salvation and deliverance.

When I saw Max again, he said to me: "Remember what we spoke about the other day? Our conversation about the people that protect Zuma?"

"Of course I do," I said. "I think about it often."

"And now you have Fraser as well. There is now a Zuma person in virtually every crucial position in government."

I told Max about the phone call from the former spook who had told me about Paul Engelke in Moscow.

"I haven't contacted him yet," I said. "I don't know if he will speak to me."

"Find out and if he says yes, go! Go as soon as possible," he said. "*Ek weet mos dat as jy eers daar is, gaan jy met sy kop smokkel.* [I know that once there, you will get into his head.]"

*   *   *

I e-mailed Paul Engelke in Moscow and said who I was and that I wanted to talk to him about his investigation into Arthur Fraser. Would you see me if I come to Russia? He replied almost immediately – always a good sign – and agreed to meet me but added that he was bound by the constraints of the Intelligence Act and couldn't talk to me about anything he did as a senior SSA employee. The investigation into Fraser, he added, was top secret.

I replied that I already knew a lot about his investigation and maybe he could just confirm a few things. He said that if I came to Moscow, I had to bring a bottle of Rust en Vrede red wine, a plastic tub of Mrs Ball's and dried fruit. Russian food is bland, he complained. They add salt and nothing else. I smiled as I had just read a quote about the Russian capital that said: "You don't come to Moscow to get fat."

"I want to write a book again," I said to Sam on a blazingly hot afternoon on the veranda of the Red Tin Roof. Next to us bursts of white petals adorned the roses while on the other side of the fence heat waves danced on Hermon Road. She fell silent and stared at me. She had lived through the last three books and said that they had been the loneliest times of her life.

"And who is going to cook while you sit in your cosy little corner week in and week out and talk to no one?" she demanded to know.

"Fiona will cook. I'll keep an eye on the kitchen." I said. Fiona Snyders is

Red Tin Roof's chef and the heart of the kitchen. Large, gregarious and loud, Fiona has been with us from day one. When it is busy and the heat rises into the forties, Fiona is a sight to behold: a battle tank on a mission, her head perched forward and her mouth going off. She has a braai tong in one hand while a pudgy finger on the other presses against an Angus steak to determine if it is medium-rare or medium.

Sam finally conceded that I should write the book and that she would support me. "It's in you and you can't get rid of it. Go for it, otherwise you'll never be happy."

I then bowled her my googly: "I have to go Russia. Maybe next week already."

"To do what?"

"To see someone."

"Who is he?"

"A former spook. He was high up in State Security and knows a hell of a lot. He lives in Moscow. I think he might talk to me. His name is Paul Engelke."

"And for how long are you going?"

"Twelve days; maybe two weeks. I'm not sure yet."

"Do you need two weeks to speak to one person?"

"I might need time to persuade him."

Sam gave me one of *those* looks. "And don't forget to bring Olga back," she snarled. "We can do with another waitress."

*   *   *

In the drab twilight of a Russian winter with an ash-coloured sky blotting out the sun, I strolled along Red Square and past the Kremlin while waiting for Paul Engelke to contact me. Communism was long gone but the cobbles of the square still carry the echo of vast Red Army parades that rolled past Leonid Brezhnev with intercontinental ballistic missiles armed with nuclear heads that could obliterate the world. This was the core of Moscow and the square is surrounded by a series of concentric ring roads. It is almost as though power oozes from the Kremlin down the ring roads to every suburb in Moscow and beyond to every city, town and outpost in the Federation – as far as Vladivostok, nine time zones and 6,500 kilometres to the east. It is much quicker to fly from Johannesburg to Lagos than from Moscow to Vladivostok. I couldn't help thinking: can you imagine Jacob Zuma also ruling Nigeria, 4,600 kilometres to the north-west? The chaos and madness!

Every dynasty, order and ruler has added to the Kremlin. The grand dukes replaced the oak walls with a strong citadel of white limestone. The tsars imported Italian architects to reconstruct much of the Kremlin while Catherine the Great built a new palace. The communists destroyed a monastery, convent and cathedral and ultimately erected a mausoleum for Vladimir Lenin, the founder of the Russian Communist Party, after his death in 1924. Lenin's head still rests softly on a black pillow, his waxy hair and neatly trimmed ginger beard coiffed into a sharp point. He's dead but not forgotten.

Today, communist austerity, ancient history, devout orthodoxy and Russia's new capitalist indulgence live side by side on Red Square. Under communist rule, there was nothing to buy; now everything is for sale. If there was ever a capitalist finger up Lenin's waxy ass, it was the opening of the ultra-luxurious GUM store on the eastern border of the square, just a stone's throw from the mausoleum. It has become a playground for the ultra-rich and hosts brands such as Louis Vuitton, Zara, Calvin Klein and Dior.

I stumbled and slid in the snow from bar to bar, where I ordered a vodka and started compiling lists of those that keep Jacob Zuma in power and out of prison. I also noted those that keep the family's purse bulging.

Whether you have to get to the top of the Kremlin or clamber up Jacob Zuma's slithery and gangrenous pole, politics is a messy business. Everyone on that pole, from the lowest to the highest, is vying for position and trying to hoist himself or herself a little higher. In the process they make deals, stab one another in the back, plot the downfall of rivals, create alliances and latch onto those who they think will move them up the pole.

There is only one certainty in life on JZ's pole: his survival is your survival and the fact that you are on the pole is only because he is at the top.

TWO

Projects Vodka, Pack and Psycho

——•——

Two days after I arrived in Moscow, Paul Engelke agreed to see me. "Meet me at Arbatskaya station. It's close to Red Square. I will wait for you in the middle of the platform," he said. It's near impossible to meet someone in a bar or restaurant because names are displayed in the Cyrillic alphabet and are impossible to decipher. When you ask for help, most people simply ignore you or shrug their shoulders.

Moscow metro stations are astonishing feats of engineering, construction and art. On the instructions of Joseph Stalin, their architects created a subterranean and opulent communist paradise. When I walked off the train, I was standing in one of the most beautiful of all Moscow metro stations: a baroque celebration of Stalinism with white arched ceilings, bronze chandeliers, ceramic bouquets of flowers, red marble decorations and glazed tiles.

I recognised Engelke from his Facebook profile picture, which shows him standing on Red Square. He stood a few metres away from me, glancing up and down the pinkish granite floor. Around seven million Muscovites use the metro every day – more than London and New York combined.

Engelke is a stocky man with genial features and a boyish expression. He rushed me out of Arbatskaya, across Red Square, past the GUM shopping palace and down a side street. Underfoot was slippery and I must have looked like a drunkard trying to skate for the first time. It's an art to negotiate the iced pavement and brown sludge, and Engelke had lived in Moscow for long enough to have mastered the art.

Minutes later we stopped at an underground bar and restaurant. Bouncers the size and shape of Lenin's mausoleum searched my bag before we were escorted downstairs. The restaurant was packed with Russia's new young and rich; brash and cocky, assured and refined. They were decked in designer attire from GUM and several had their own bodyguards scouring the establishment.

When communism died, it was replaced by something far more alluring: money. It is said that never had so much money flowed into a place in so short a time. This gave rise to the so-called oligarchs: businessmen, senior civil servants and army generals of the former Soviet republics who rapidly accumulated wealth during the era of *Russian* privatisation in the aftermath of the dissolution of the USSR in the 1990s. It looked as though it was their offspring that had gathered in the bar.

"Do you come here often?" I asked Engelke. A waitress with booty shorts that flaunted her endless legs drifted on high heels towards our table. She had a bottle of iced vodka in each hand.

"I've been here once to watch the rugby," he said. "I think the owner is British and they show the rugby. But it's not really my kind of place."

Fifty years old, Engelke was an advocate before joining the old South African Defence Force as a legal officer in 1992. He left ten years later as a colonel and the head of the School of Military Law. He was also a prosecutor at the National Prosecuting Authority (NPA) before being recruited into the National Intelligence Agency (NIA).

He was initially an undercover agent and tasked to work on the Boeremag. This gang of Afrikaner separatist right-wingers had conspired to overthrow the ANC government and to reinstate a Boer-administered republic. Engelke was given a false identity and a cover as a member of an army commando (a Defence Force civil unit) who ostensibly had to investigate the high rate of farm murders. He soon made contact with Boeremag members and started gathering intelligence. He was in regular contact with former police death squad commander Colonel Eugene de Kock. After bombs exploded in Soweto in 2002, more than twenty right-wingers were arrested and charged with high treason and murder. More than a thousand kilograms of explosives were found in their possession.

Towards the end of 2015, Engelke left the State Security Agency (which is what the NIA became in 2009) as a senior law adviser. He had been offered a year-long contract to teach forensic law at the prestigious Moscow State University. He was getting divorced at the time and was looking for "something different".

Engelke's sense of adventure had also paid off on a personal level: he was engaged to a Russian woman, about ten years younger and also recently divorced. He faced a most pressing predicament in that he had to ask for her hand. Her old man was a formidable retired army general in both the old and new Russia. I later met her; she was no "Russian bride" but educated and independent with an iron will. She spoke English fluently.

Engelke was hungry for news from home; about the dismal antics of the Springboks and whether Allister Coetzee was going to be sacked; the stellar performance of the Proteas against Australia; and the latest episode of state capture by Zuma and his cronies. He didn't know any other South Africans in Moscow and hadn't spoken Afrikaans in several months. He said he was homesick.

It was late at night and after several vodkas that I prodded Engelke about the SSA and Fraser. "With that man," Engelke said and looked around him, "you don't mess. He's far too powerful."

"Why is he so powerful?" I wanted to know.

"He's very close to Zuma," said Engelke as he leaned forward and dropped his voice. "I've got two children back home. If I talk to you I might never see them again."

"What can you tell me about him?"

"I have to be very careful. I'm bound by an oath of secrecy. I'm afraid I cannot say much."

"I understand," I said and put my hand in the air to signal to the high-heeled and leggy waitress. "Why don't we have another vodka and discuss this?"

* * *

Towards the end of 2009, internal State Security Agency (SSA) auditors descended on the Route 21 office complex near Irene, south of Pretoria. The NIA had just been restructured by security minister Siyabonga Cwele and was now known as the SSA. The target of the auditors was the operational headquarters of the Principal Agent Network (PAN) programme, a top-secret state intelligence programme that had guzzled as much as a billion rand of taxpayers' money in just three years.

When the auditors arrived, expenditure files were stacked in the boardroom, at the ready for their scrutiny. What the auditors didn't know was that the boardroom was bugged and kitted out with concealed cameras. In the room next door, PAN agents and managers were surveying the auditors as they sifted through invoices, contracts, payment requests and much, much more.

The PAN agents had much to lose. For three years, they had almost carte blanche to throw public money at a range of gagged-up projects, which they named "Easimix" (concerned with the "old guard"), "Émigré" (concerned with immigrants), "Media Production" (the influence of the media), "Vodka" (Russian activities), "Pack" (Pakistani nationals), "Psycho" ("concerned with psychological assistance to PAN"), the ominous-sounding "Crims" (working on "political intelligence"), "Kwababisa" (Alexandra township mafia, Gauteng provincial government and corruption) and the ominous "SO" (political intelligence and organised crime).

The only project that was probably worth anything was "Mechanic", because PAN had purchased 293 cars – ranging from BMWs, Audis and Golf GTIs to smaller sedans – for their 72 agents, which they stored in three warehouses across the country that had been leased for R24 million. They also leased and purchased properties for R48 million and imported three "technical surveillance vehicles" from the UK for more than R40 million. And this was just a drop in the ocean.

The auditors at Route 21 had hit upon enough discrepancies and scams to report back to their superiors that the PAN programme was riddled with wastage, corruption and nepotism and warranted a full-scale investigation. One of the reasons why the PAN spooks were caught with their pants on their knees was that they had done a dismal job at covering their tracks.

Sometime later, a disgruntled PAN agent handed the auditors CCTV camera footage of their audit. A PAN surveillance technician who had been instructed to plant cameras in the boardroom to monitor the audit installed them the previous night but forgot to switch them off after he'd tested the system. The footage showed how agents worked through the night in order to generate invoices and documentation for the audit the next day. They also shredded records they didn't want the auditors to see. Agents manufactured documents by copying and pasting signatures. In their haste to deceive the auditors and with the clock ticking away, they put documents in the wrong files, accidentally shredded some of the manufactured papers and got everything all mixed up.

The auditors found devastating evidence in the files and were at the PAN offices for four days. When they left to report back to their director-general, the lid had been lifted on corruption and wasteful expenditure that far exceeded the shenanigans at President Zuma's private homestead of Nkandla.

But this was, after all, the hazy world of smoke and mirrors that they call state security, where the Intelligence Act is manipulated to shield marauders and veil miscreants.

* * *

A few days after the audit, the SSA's head of domestic intelligence, Gibson Njenje, called a meeting of his legal advisers in his plush office at the agency's headquarters. The complex, known as Musanda, is top secret and the public is not allowed to know how many people work there or how much money those in pursuit of state security drain from the fiscus every year. To the public, all that is visible of Musanda – affectionately known as "the Farm" by those who have basked in her veiled glory – is a sprawl of buildings with an array of satellite ears that point skywards.

Among those who attended Njenje's meeting were the head of the agency's legal department, Kobus Meiring, and SSA advocate Paul Engelke.

Meiring was an intelligence old-timer with an impeccable record and more than thirty years in the service. Engelke had vast experience as a prosecutor at the NPA, was an advocate in private practice and had served seven years at state intelligence. Both Meiring and Engelke had a top-secret clearance.

Njenje had only recently assumed leadership of the domestic branch of the SSA and was largely unaware of PAN, which resided under the Covert Support Unit (CSU) and ultimately under the director of operations. The first warning that public money was being shovelled into a black hole emerged when the CSU overspent its budget and PAN agents threatened the agency with legal action for not getting paid.

The polite and reserved Njenje was an intelligence legend, albeit a controversial one. An Umkhonto we Sizwe veteran, he was appointed by President Thabo Mbeki as NIA head of operations but was then suspended, along with spy boss Billy Masetlha, in 2005. This followed an investigation by the inspector-general of intelligence, who found that Njenje had acted inappropriately after spying on Saki Macozoma, ANC National Executive Committee member and Mbeki confidant, as part of a political intelligence-gathering exercise called Project Avani. It included hoax e-mails designed to suggest a plot against Zuma to prevent him from running for the presidency.

Njenje initially tried to challenge the suspension, but resigned after reaching a settlement with intelligence minister Ronnie Kasrils. When Zuma became president in 2009, it was payback time and he appointed Njenje as the director-general for domestic intelligence at the SSA. There was unhappiness in some government and ANC quarters about Njenje's appointment. He was prior to his official posting a founder member and director of Bosasa, a facilities management company that, according to a Special Investigating Unit report, was corruptly awarded multimillion-rand tenders by the prisons department.

Njenje told Meiring and Engelke that he wanted them to investigate the PAN programme as it might have gone rogue, misappropriated millions and even endangered the safety of the state. He said that security minister Siyabonga Cwele had given the go-ahead for a full investigation.

Engelke was appointed team leader and was joined by a senior auditor and a human resources official. They in turn reported to Meiring. The investigation was top secret and on a strictly "need-to-know" basis.

The PAN programme was the brainchild of Njenje's predecessor, the director-general Manala Manzini, and his deputy and national operations director, Arthur Fraser. Manzini was eager to expand and enhance the NIA's covert collection capacity. He shared this with Fraser, who concocted the PAN programme.

Fraser suggested that PAN employ NIA members who would resign or take severance packages, former NIA members, members from other government departments who would resign, and new recruits from the private sector. They submitted their plan to the minister of intelligence, Ronnie Kasrils, who agreed with the concept of the network as it was traditionally understood. A principal agent network is intelligence jargon for spy handlers (the principals) who engage, manage and deploy spies (agents) to perform specific services or functions on behalf of the agency. There was nothing cutting-edge about Fraser's proposal and it should simply have meant the employment of more spies and handlers.

As it later turned out, he may have had something completely different in mind: a parallel and detached intelligence network that operated independently of the NIA. In doing so, Meiring and Engelke later found, Fraser may have committed treason.

Jane Duncan says in her book *The Rise of the Securocrats* that intelligence services ballooned in the early 2000s under the ministerial direction of Lindiwe Sisulu, Kasrils's predecessor. She contended that NIA needed more resources and capabilities and should be expanded. This proliferation coincided with the issuing of a directive by the Presidency requiring an expansion of the NIA's mandate in 2003 to include political and economic intelligence. A host of new spies and agents were appointed.

The ministry of intelligence concluded in 2007 that there were no serious threats to the country's constitutional order, although organised crime remained a concern, as did the need to secure major events such as the upcoming 2010 World Cup. There was also no indication that South

Africa was either a major target of or safe haven for terrorists or religious fanatics. Why, then, was there a need for a further expansion of the NIA? Was the PAN programme truly to the benefit of national security, or did its architects and proponents have ulterior motives?

*   *   *

One of the first breakthroughs the PAN investigators made was when they discovered that the signature of Ronnie Kasrils had been copied and pasted onto a document that gave birth to the programme. The document was co-signed by director-general Manala Manzini, operations director Arthur Fraser, Covert Support Unit (CSU) operations manager Prince Makhwathana, and CSU financial officer Martie Wallace. It authorised the PAN top structure to identify projects and targets of national interest, appoint assets (agents and spies), purchase cars, lease safe houses and incur whatever cost was necessary to get the venture off the ground.

When Engelke unearthed the document, he said to his co-investigators: "This is it. This was their passport to do whatever they wanted."

Their first stop was Kasrils, who had resigned in September 2008. He has always been to his detractors a leftist rabble-rouser; to his devotees the archetypal counter-revolutionary. He confirmed that he hadn't signed the document. He also made it clear that he had only approved the concept of a PAN and did not authorise the implementation of the programme.

When the investigators confronted Manzini (then retired), he retorted that he had complete trust in his former operations director, Arthur Fraser. He looked at Engelke and added: "I don't like your tone, my boy. I will sort you out."

In the end, all roads led back to Fraser. Little is known about him, but he was born on the Cape Flats, one of six children of a factory worker mother and a teacher father. The SSA website simply states that he "joined the ANC underground structures early in his life", was an investigator at the Truth and Reconciliation Commission, headed the immigration branch of the Department of Home Affairs, and has an honours degree in video and film production from London University. He is the brother of former cabinet minister Geraldine Fraser-Moleketi.

When the team confronted Fraser, he refused to offer any explanation but was surprised when shown the copy-and-paste attempt of Kasrils's signature and said he knew nothing about it. A few days later, he was suspended, after which he offered his resignation – certainly not the action of an innocent man. PAN was shut down and the SSA, which had replaced the NIA, was compelled to integrate the programme's agents into the agency. The manager of the CSU, Prince Makhwathana, and most of the PAN mangers were also suspended.

Njenje accepted Fraser's resignation. With Fraser being history, the investigators broke PAN open and bared a gluttony of depravity that permeated right to the top. One of the first to confess her connivance in wrongdoing was Martie Wallace, the financial officer at the CSU (Wallace was her "agent" name). She made an affidavit and said that both her brother and her husband were appointed as PAN agents. She admitted that she had taken R1.2 million in cash, bought a townhouse and registered the property in her brother's name. The property was then leased back to PAN – for R1.2 million!

With Wallace on board and singing, skeletons tumbled out. Several SSA officials had resigned and were reappointed as PAN agents at a much higher salary. One of them registered a company and got R18 million in cash to buy six upmarket properties – including in Waterkloof in Pretoria – and leased them back to PAN.

This practice was repeated several times across the country. An invoice for nearly R6 million was forged for a leased property and the money was then paid into a private bank account. The investigators found that agents had committed forgery, fraud and various offences in terms of the Prevention and Combating of Corrupt Activities Act.

As far as the appointment of agents was concerned, the investigators found "wide-scale financial mismanagement, fruitless expenditure, nepotism and corruption". Makhwathana had signed the employment contracts of the 72 PAN agents, although he did not have the authority to do so. The salary bill came to R33 million annually, which amounted to almost R40,000 per agent per month.

After PAN had purchased 293 vehicles for their 72 agents, they needed warehouses to store them. They entered into an agreement with a private company that belonged to Arthur Fraser's brother, Barry. PAN paid him R24 million for the rental of the warehouse. Some of cars had been unused for almost four years. There were other Fraser family members working for PAN. Arthur's son Lyle became the floor manager at the warehouse while his mother, Ms C.F. Fraser, was also a PAN agent. Both Barry Fraser and Ms Fraser were board members of a community-based organisation that dealt with conflict resolution at schools. PAN contributed R10 million towards the organisation although it had nothing to do with national security.

PAN imported state-of-the-art surveillance vans from the British-based Gamma Group for an amount of R45.7 million. Gamma is a high-tech manufacturer that counts the world's foremost intelligence agencies among its clients. Their surveillance vehicles contain equipment for the "video and audio processing of targets", "grabber" surveillance machines and "command and control software". Engelke found that the "correct supply chain management procedures" were not followed in their purchase. The vehicles were also registered in the name of the agency, which created the danger that should anyone check their number plates, their cover would be blown.

The investigators found that Fraser had told an NIA agent, John Galloway, to resign and start a security company to supply PAN with high-tech equipment. Galloway was paid R11 million while he was still an NIA employee and before the company was set up. This already amounted to fraud. He left the service in March 2008, set up G-Tech and was paid another R47 million. He conducted his business from home, had no employees and provided services that the investigators said were of "poor quality". Galloway purchased within a span of 20 months property worth R11 million.

Wallace revealed to the investigators that enormous amounts of cash – up to R10 million at a time – were delivered to the PAN offices on a regular basis. Packets of money were wrapped in tinfoil and packed in bags. The investigators produced an internal audit report that revealed that there were discrepancies on temporary advances to the amount of R85 million. More than R200 million was unaccounted for.

Both Manzini and Fraser were fingered as having "forced" the chief financial officer of the NIA to release millions of rand to the Covert Support Unit by way of verbal approvals, which was in complete contradiction with the regulatory framework.

When the investigators evaluated the projects, they found little of value. Two drug addicts were, for example, recruited to work on Project Émigré and spy on immigrants. They did nothing. Project Kagee was supposed to focus on "counter-terrorism". PAN paid an informant R12 million for information that "could have been obtained through open sources". The informant used his hard-earned dosh to buy a stake in a BMW dealership.

The investigators said the projects were badly planned, managed and conducted and were costly to the NIA because any agent could have gathered the information. None of the projects had individual authorisation, operational plans or budgets as required. They were often initiated on the verbal instruction of Fraser and wads of money were thrown at them.

The investigators did lifestyle audits of the PAN managers and found that several seemed to have won the Lotto. Their personal wealth had increased dramatically during the lifespan of PAN. One of the managers who lived in a townhouse upgraded to a three-storey mansion and bought his wife a Range Rover Evoque for almost a million rand.

One of the most damning findings of the PAN investigation was about Fraser himself. The investigators stated there was "an intention to create an alternative intelligence capacity". Said the report: "An expensive communication system was put in place at Mr Fraser's private residence and he has been the sole recipient of information gathered by the PANs."

PAN agents had sent their intelligence reports in an encrypted electronic format to Fraser's personal server instead of submitting them to the NIA mainframe where they could be checked, analysed and verified, and then disseminated and integrated into the agency's information management system.

The SSA removed the server from Fraser's house. When they analysed the device, they found 800 intel reports that he had failed to send to the agency's mainframe. The investigators said this was in contradiction of the internal regulatory framework and transgressed the Protection of Information Act. As a result, the investigators concluded, Fraser could probably be charged with treason. "It also gives clear indications of the intent to establish an alternative intelligence structure for purposes unknown."

When Engelke challenged Fraser about the server, he refused to discuss it. Speculation was rife that Fraser was a double agent or that PAN had an ulterior motive: to keep the Western Cape in ANC hands.

Engelke and his team confronted one manager after the other, most of them in the presence of their lawyers. The manager of PAN's operational coordination unit, Graham Engel, allegedly said to Engelke: "Somebody is going to get hurt here, and that one is not me. Do you know who you are dealing with? This goes right to the top."

When Paul Engelke and Kobus Meiring handed their report to Njenje, they concluded that there was "wide-scale financial mismanagement, fruitless expenditure, nepotism and corruption". In their view, there was sufficient proof to prosecute Manzini, Fraser, Makhwathana, Wallace, Engel and ten other managers and agents for a host of alleged crimes.

*   *   *

Arthur Fraser was bulletproof. This was because he had probably saved Jacob Zuma from prosecution and thereby enabled the ANC leader to ascend to the highest office in the land. In the mid-2000s Zuma was fighting for his political survival and standing trial on 783 charges of fraud, racketeering and corruption. The case emanated from bribes that he had received from arms manufacturers during South Africa's controversial arms deal of the 1990s and 2000s. The money was paid to Zuma's financier and banker, Schabir Shaik, who in turn paid it over to JZ.

In 2005 Shaik was convicted of similar charges and sentenced to 15 years' imprisonment. This gave President Mbeki an excuse to fire Zuma as deputy president, thereby burying his ambitions for highest office. Zuma, in turn, was on his knees and holding on for dear life. The contest between the two was South Africa's Cold War: the political landscape was littered with skulduggery, hatchet jobs, sleights of hand and smear campaigns. Both sides were sneaking and snooping on one another.

In 1999 Mbeki and NPA boss Bulelani Ngcuka established a new, crack crime-fighting unit called the Directorate of Special Operations, widely known as the Scorpions, in the NPA. The Scorpions had to combat organised crime, taxi violence, politically motivated violence and drug-related crimes. There was from the outset bad blood and turf wars between the police and the Scorpions. The unit achieved a tremendous conviction rate but was accused of cherry-picking and pursuing only winnable cases. The Scorpions had a reputation for going after dodgy politicians and senior civil servants – like police commissioner Jackie Selebi and Jacob Zuma.

The Mbeki camp unleashed what should have been the killer blow. In May 2007, a top-secret report was leaked that purported to prove that Zuma's presidential ambitions were fuelled and funded by corrupt African leaders, among them Angola's Eduardo dos Santos and Libya's Muammar Gaddafi. Marked 'top secret' and known as the Browse Mole report, it alleged that Zuma had travelled to Libya on at least three occasions to meet with senior Libyan figures. Browse Mole also alleged that the Zuma backers had met at the Great Lakes in April 2006 to discuss military intervention to unseat Thabo Mbeki. If true, the report implicated Zuma in treason.

Mbeki agreed to institute an investigation into the report and appointed Arthur Fraser, who was then operations head of the NIA. The *Mail & Guardian* said that Fraser's initial investigation into Browse Mole was widely regarded in the NPA as "flimsy and one-sided", and one of its key conclusions, that a Scorpions special investigator was responsible for the leak, was never substantiated. A second probe by the Special Investigating Unit cleared the investigator.

Parliament's Joint Standing Committee on Intelligence found that the report was a hoax and drawn up by the Scorpions in a bid to discredit

Zuma. The committee said it was "extremely inflammatory" and "very dangerous" for South Africa's national interests.

The revelations in the report had backfired. Jacob Zuma's political career was finally saved by the very report that was designed to destroy him. Zuma supporters argued that it was evident that there was a political conspiracy against him and therefore the charges against him were also fabricated. As Martin Plaut said in his book *Who Rules South Africa?*, it was proof that "somewhere in the bowels of the security apparatus, somebody was watching Zuma's back".

That "somebody" could well have been Arthur Fraser. During Fraser's investigation into the Browse Mole report, the NIA tapped the phones of several high-ranking officials mentioned in the report, including those of Ngcuka and Leonard McCarthy, the Scorpions boss. On the tapes, they discussed when would be the most politically damaging time to charge Zuma. Fraser had unearthed what amounted to gold for Zuma.

What is astonishing about these recordings is that they were, according to the inspector-general of intelligence, legally made, but the intelligence minister knew nothing about them. Ronnie Kasrils said afterwards: "The NIA were obliged to report this to me as minister. They never did. I knew nothing about it."

But the Zuma camp did know about the tapes. Enter Moe Shaik, a man who has been integral to getting Zuma off the hook and into the Union Buildings. Shaik has been many things: he served under Zuma as an underground MK operative, was an ANC negotiator during the talks of the early 1990s, an ambassador to Algeria, and an intelligence and foreign affairs ministerial adviser. When his brother Schabir went to prison, Moe took charge of his businesses.

Moe Shaik was involved in the Zuma camp's own dirty tricks campaign. Two weeks after the state had announced that the NPA was about to hurl Schabir Shaik before a judge, Moe Shaik identified prosecutions boss Bulelani Ngcuka as apartheid spy RS452. He later said he'd made the allegations in order "to defend the honour of the deputy president of this country" – Jacob Zuma.

Moe Shaik's revelations were later exposed as a smear campaign when Eastern Cape human rights lawyer Vanessa Brereton admitted that she was agent RS452. Shaik had, however, guaranteed himself a plum position in the future Zuma administration.

When Shaik heard that Fraser had stumbled upon evidence that could help Zuma in his corruption trial, he went to see him to persuade him to part with the tapes. The two already knew each other by then. Shaik, today an executive at the Development Bank of Southern Africa, confirmed the meeting with Fraser to me. I asked him what he told Fraser. This was his response: "I told him to do the right thing. I said to him that you are sitting on these things and that it is in the national interest."

"And what did you tell him to do with it?"

"I told him to do the right thing and give the tapes to the National Prosecuting Authority."

"And did he?"

"As far as I know, yes."

There were two sets of tapes at the time: those of the police's crime intelligence unit and the NIA. I asked Shaik about the police spy tapes. "I don't know about the crime intelligence tapes. I don't think they were of good quality and NIA had more tapes."

The NIA tapes reportedly found their way to the deputy national director of the NPA, Willie Hofmeyr, who was a key defender of the conspiracy theory and a central character in the decision to withdraw the charges against Zuma. Again, Fraser failed to inform the intelligence minister.

The *Mail & Guardian* said they had evidence that Fraser also handed tapes to Zuma's attorney, Michael Hulley, although he has denied the allegation. According to the newspaper: "Fraser did a political flip-flop and handed the NIA recordings to Zuma's legal team. We understand Fraser felt the need to ingratiate himself with the new administration of Zuma and handed the NIA tapes over."

In April 2009, the new NPA boss Mokotedi Mpshe said the evidence on the tapes amounted to an "intolerable abuse" and abandoned the case against Zuma. Zuma's road to the presidency – barring a small legal predicament or two – was now paved in gold.

THREE

The shadow state

————•————

Cabinet – and therefore Jacob Zuma – must have been informed about the PAN investigation. Paul Engelke saw security minister Siyabonga Cwele at least ten times during the two years that he investigated the PAN project. The minister was initially shocked and in disbelief and instructed the investigators to get to the bottom of the rot. At a meeting at OR Tambo International Airport in November 2010, Cwele agreed that the PAN matter should be referred to the relevant authorities for possible prosecution.

The investigators also made a presentation to the minister of justice, Jeff Radebe, in his office in Cape Town. Cwele was also present. The investigators said in their report that even before the conclusion of their presentation, Radebe indicated that he had "heard and seen enough and that it is a *prima facie* case that must be dealt with by law enforcement".

In January 2011, Lieutenant-General Anwa Dramat, the head of the Hawks (which by then had replaced the Scorpions), arranged a meeting for the investigators with Major-General Hans Meiring, in charge of the Hawks' commercial crimes unit. Meiring allocated a Hawks colonel to evaluate the evidence. He concluded that the case was "too big for us" and recommended that the matter be taken further by a multidisciplinary task team comprising the police's commercial crimes unit, the Crimes Against the State unit of the Hawks, the Asset Forfeiture Unit (AFU) and the Special Investigating Unit (SIU). It was agreed that the SIU was best suited for the investigation.

Two months later, the SIU presented a "business plan" to the State Security Agency (SSA) that included an independent forensic investigation by PricewaterhouseCoopers that would cost R15 million. Gibson Njenje, head of domestic intelligence, personally entered the negotiations and later told the investigators that he had managed to bring down the cost of the audit to R6 million.

Although Engelke believed there was already enough evidence to charge and convict the PAN top structure, he realised that nobody, except for Njenje, had the stomach to take on the might of the SSA. Can you imagine charging one of the most powerful people in the country with treason and those around him with fraud and corruption?

Such trials had the potential to rip open the underbelly of the SSA and unmask those we entrust to guard the Republic as nothing but a coterie of thieving and squandering thugs. Although the state could cite national security to hold prosecutions behind closed doors, details of the debauchery would leak to the media and prompt uncomfortable questions about the antics at "the Farm". Spooks prefer to skulk in the shadows of anonymity for as long as possible.

Engelke refused to capitulate and turned to the only law enforcement agency that at the time would have the guts to cross swords with the SSA: the South African Revenue Service (SARS). The service was by far the most efficient law enforcement agency in the country and had pursued the like of Julius Malema, Radovan Krejčíř and Lolly Jackson with a hyena-like relentlessness and would have gone where the Hawks and the SIU feared to tread.

Furthermore, NIA and SARS had signed a cooperation agreement whereby they would share information and engage in joint operations. In April 2011, Engelke wrote to the SARS forensic service investigations and requested them to probe nine senior PAN managers and agents and several companies for their declared income and the taxes they had paid. Among them were Fraser, Engel, Makhwathana and Wallace.

SARS investigators and analysts compiled profiles of the managers/ agents as well as their spouses and connected the dots between the companies and their directors. Although most of the PAN transactions and payments were done in cash, it was clear that several of the "persons of interest" had feasted greedily during their terms at PAN.

One of the PAN agents who acted as a service provider had eight vehicles registered in his name, including a R1.3 million Mercedes-Benz, a Range Rover Sport, an Audi A4, a Pajero and a Harley-Davidson. He was an active and former director of more than twenty companies. One of these companies received 27 government payments worth R5.6 million; another 57 government payments worth R10 million. The latter company still owed R5.6 million in unpaid taxes.

The profiles of the other persons of interest showed how millions of rand of taxpayers' money flowed into the bank accounts of their companies, which had service provider contracts with PAN. They bought farms, jet skis, imported motorcycles and 4x4s.

The profile of Arthur Fraser, however, didn't show excessive wealth. He owned two BMWs and a house in Observatory in Johannesburg and was a director of a couple of companies. He did, though, receive two government tenders of R81,000 while he was the operations director of the NIA. But the profile of his wife, Natasha Fraser, made for more interesting reading. She became a director of a security company by using her maiden name of Taylor. After she resigned from the company, it received 240 government payments between 2005 and 2010 to the value of R7.4 million. It also owed SARS almost R4 million in unpaid taxes.

I have no doubt that there was great anxiety in the security agency around the SARS investigation. It had to be stopped.

* * *

When Zuma came to power, he was dealt an enviable hand because he had vacancies to fill in most of the key criminal justice institutions, which meant he could appoint his allies and cronies to them. He had to select a new police chief, a new national director of public prosecutions, a new intelligence chief and the head of the Hawks.

A former intelligence hand himself, Zuma has always relied on his intelligence and security chieftains to infiltrate the state apparatus while at the same time safeguarding him from revolt and overthrow. These stooges have little regard for law and order and for keeping the Republic safe. Instead, they have mostly been reduced to squads of hooligans that are prepared to harass and hound any Zuma adversary into submission.

A pattern of appointing cronies and loyalists in key positions emerged at the outset of Zuma's presidency. He was mindful that he could still be brought to book for corruption in the future, and set in motion a shadow security state that would undermine the independence of the police and the National Prosecuting Authority (NPA).

After Siyabonga Cwele became state security minister, Zuma appointed three loyalists as his intelligence chiefs: Gibson Njenje as head of domestic intelligence, Moe Shaik as head of foreign intelligence, and Jeff Maqetuka as so-called super-director-general. Unexpectedly, the trio soon showed an alarming sense of independence when they became intent on investigating the influence of the Gupta family on the government and the state. This was after press reports that the family had offered former ANC Youth League leader Fikile Mbalula a ministerial post. Cwele flew his three administrative heads to Cape Town and ordered them to halt the project. They refused and he ordered them to resign.

With Njenje gone, Engelke had lost one of his only allies. He wasn't ready yet to throw in the towel. He had a further appointment with the SIU, who told him that they were awaiting authorisation from the new spy boss, acting SSA director-general Dennis Dhlomo, to request the audit. Nothing was forthcoming.

Cwele also began to change his attitude towards the investigators during the latter half of their probe. He told Paul Engelke that he didn't trust him any longer and that he held a vendetta against Fraser. The investigation was on the rocks. At the time Cwele himself was under siege. His wife, Sheryl, was convicted of drug smuggling and sentenced to 12 years' imprisonment, later increased by the Appeal Court to 20 years. Opposition parties called for Cwele to step down, arguing that if he was not aware of his wife's illegal activities, he should no longer oversee the country's intelligence-gathering. There were also reports that the minister ordered that his wife be afforded intelligence protection for the duration of her trial. She was transported to and from court in official vehicles and protected by intelligence agency officers.

When Cwele received the final PAN report, he referred it to the inspector-general of intelligence (IGI) for "further investigation". This made no sense. PAN was already being investigated by the best legal brains in the SSA. What more was there to uncover? By doing so, Cwele ensured that the mire of PAN would be entombed in Musanda's boneyard and would ultimately disappear in the hidden workings of the inspector-general. This included the SARS investigation into the tax affairs of the PAN beneficiaries.

Only two bodies have oversight over the intelligence agencies: the Office of the Inspector-General of Intelligence and Parliament's Joint Standing Committee on Intelligence. The IGI is constitutionally mandated to protect the public from abuses by the intelligence services. Its activities are cloaked in secrecy, however; its reports are not made public and it doesn't engage with the media.

Engelke and Meiring had stored their evidence in an office at Musanda which they referred to as the "war room". The IGI never interrogated this evidence. Engelke appeared before inspector-general Faith Radebe and Jay Govender, the IGI's legal adviser, and was grilled about his apparent feud with Fraser and whether it had clouded his forensic appraisal.

The Office of the IGI has for many years been a blunt constitutional tool. The IGI investigates complaints against the SSA, the police's crime intelligence unit and the Defence Force's defence intelligence division. The IGI must also monitor their compliance with the Constitution, especially section 198, which states that national security must "reflect the resolve of South Africans, as individuals and as a nation, to live as equals, to live in peace and harmony, to be free from fear and want and to seek a better life".

The choice of IGIs since 1994 has not evoked any confidence in the office. Faith Radebe, appointed in April 2010, was a former spook herself. A trained lawyer, she was also a special projects manager at the NIA. This alone should have disqualified her from the job.

A glance at the IGI's website is indicative of the dismal state of affairs during Radebe's reign. She hadn't released or declassified a single report after her appointment in 2010. In fact, the last declassified report on the website dated to March 2006. The last speech of Radebe was posted on the website in August 2010 and the last press release in April 2010, when she was sworn in. Radebe's term expired in March 2015 and her successor was only appointed at the end of 2016. For almost two years there was no oversight over the intelligence services and the IGI's office barely functioned. It meant in practice that the country's intelligence agencies accounted to no one.

IGI legal adviser Advocate Jay Govender, who was one of the candidates for IG after Radebe left, admitted at the parliamentary hearings that the office "was clearly not without its problems" and was operational only "to a certain extent". Her colleague, Mampogoane Nchabeleng, who also sat on the executive committee, reported that they had been "managing the office as a collective" but could not say what they had been doing in the past year.

Setlhomamaru Dintwe, an associate professor of forensics at the University of South Africa, was appointed as IGI in March 2017. Five months later, the IGI website still stated that the process of appointing someone was under way. Dintwe said during his interview that the "role of the oversight officer is that you have to become a snake that eats the other snakes. That is the role of the inspector general of intelligence."

Security and intelligence expert Professor Laurie Nathan commented to *Daily Maverick* that the IG has the potential for great oversight because he or she is not answerable to the minister or the intelligence services. They can walk into any building and open any file or attach any computer. It is a criminal offence not to comply. There is incredible power in the position but it has unfortunately been squandered over the years. Said Nathan: "We have no idea what they do. The IG has no sense of accountability to Parliament or the people. It is every bit as secret as intelligence and is in fact in thrall of secrecy."

During the writing of this book, I sat down with a top-level intelligence guru who has intimate knowledge of the major role players in this saga: Jacob Zuma, Siyabonga Cwele and Arthur Fraser. "Did you really think that anything was ever going to happen to Arthur?" he said to me. "Did you think that JZ was going to sacrifice him? No way! There is something that you must understand about the president: it is all about how useful you are to him. And Arthur is very useful. I think he was always going to be JZ's intelligence chief, and PAN was just a *klein fokôppie* [little fuck-up] that had to be handled."

He reckoned that initially Cwele had no idea about the relationship between Zuma and Fraser, which dated back to the "Spy Tapes" saga. That was why he spurred on his investigators to sniff out the culpable and bring them to book. He then lost his appetite because he was instructed "to make a plan".

As my source said: "Fraser went to Zuma and said, 'Sir, there is big trouble here; lots of secret things are going to be compromised.' Zuma instructed Cwele to look after Fraser. A strategy was devised to circumvent other law enforcement agencies and to deliver the findings of Engelke and Meiring to Faith Radebe, who they knew would kill everything."

* * *

As Zuma's first term ended in 2014, none of his original justice and security appointees remained in their jobs. Zuma made two loyal lieutenants, Bheki Cele and Menzi Simelane, national police commissioner and national director of public prosecutions, respectively. They were both controversial, Cele because of his "shoot-to-kill" policy and Simelane because his evidence before the Ginwala inquiry was branded "contradictory and without basis in fact or in law".

It didn't take long for both to become toast. The Constitutional Court found that Zuma didn't apply his mind when he decided Simelane was "fit and proper" and declared his appointment invalid. A board of inquiry found Cele unfit for office and recommended his firing after he became embroiled in a R1.7 billion police lease deals scandal. Zuma's choice as head of the Special Investigating Unit, Willem Heath, was also forced to resign.

Zuma's selection of ministers didn't do much better. Justice minister Jeff Radebe was a mere onlooker at the destruction of the NPA, police minister Nathi Mthethwa was exposed as a beneficiary of a dodgy crime intelligence slush fund, and Cwele oversaw a divided and fragmented intelligence structure.

As political challenges against Zuma intensified, he obviously felt the need for new blood and in May 2014 announced a cabinet reshuffle. He demoted Siyabonga Cwele to the telecommunications portfolio and elevated a Mpumalanga departmental head, David Mahlobo, to take over one of the most crucial cabinet positions: that of state security minister.

Nobody outside the province had ever heard of Mahlobo, a 40-something-year-old trained biochemist with no intelligence experience. It later turned out that he loves "regime change" conspiracies and Thai pedicures.

Shortly after his appointment, IGI head Faith Radebe handed him her PAN investigation report. It inexplicably took her almost three years to produce her findings. I was told that one of the reasons why her investigation took so long was that the agency asked for more time to find the required documentation, invoices, contracts and authorisations. I have little doubt that much of it was manufactured in the Musanda war rooms.

I have never seen the report, but the SSA claimed that it exonerated Fraser and his cronies of wrongdoing. Your guess is as good as mine as to how the spy boss managed to wriggle himself out of the problem of having had a secret server in his house, explained the employment of family members as agents, and justified a host of unlawful contracts, claims, appointments and payments that carried his signature.

By the time Radebe handed her report to Mahlobo, the only other law enforcement agency that had the potential to upset the apple cart, SARS, had already been successfully dealt with.

Towards the beginning of 2012, the IGI's Jay Govender made an appointment with the head of tax and customs investigations at the revenue service, Gene Ravele. She explained to him that since the IG was conducting her own investigation, all other law enforcers should put their inquisitions on hold. Convinced that the SSA and the IGI were on top of their investigation, Ravele relented and the SARS audit was put on ice. Govender left with much of the SARS evidence under her arm.

At the end of 2014, the *Sunday Times* exposed the existence of a so-called rogue unit in SARS – the very unit that was targeting organised criminals and big-time tax evaders and money launderers. A few months later, many of SARS's most successful executives and managers were either suspended or resigned. Among them was Gene Ravele, who resigned in May 2015.

The campaign against the SARS "rogue unit" was driven by elements in the SSA, and you will read much more about it later in this book. Suffice it to say for now that the stories in the *Sunday Times* were bullshit, but they were integral to the destruction of the most effective law enforcement organisation in the country.

There was no rogue unit and the campaign was unleashed to stop SARS from investigating Jacob Zuma and his cronies, among others. I have little doubt that SARS's new rulers would have ensured that the audit profiles that Ravele's investigators had compiled against Arthur Fraser, John Galloway, Prince Makhwathana and several others were erased from the SARS mainframe.

*   *   *

Several PAN agents took the SSA to court for dishonouring the contracts and agreements that Fraser and his managers had entered into with them. One of them was John Galloway, the former NIA employee who formed a security company to supply equipment to PAN. According to the court papers, Galloway had to install sophisticated monitoring equipment in "25 secret bases" across the country. Galloway said in his submission that he hadn't been paid for work in Johannesburg, Polokwane, Durban and Mbombela. Fraser's brother, Barry Fraser, was a director in the Galloway company.

Although PAN had already paid Galloway R58 million for what the investigators branded "poor quality" work, he wanted another R6.7 million. He had already obtained a default judgment against the NIA front company that had entered into the agreement with him but the agency ignored his requests for payment. A court sheriff tried to seize the assets of the company but was chased away by intelligence officials.

Following the visit of the sheriff, Galloway received a threatening lawyer's letter from SSA which accused him of breaking the law and said if he pursued his claim he would be charged and his farm attached. The farm they referred to was in the Swartland in the Western Cape, which he purchased with the proceeds of PAN for R4.25 million in 2008. The SSA eventually settled with Galloway and most of the other agents and paid them out rather than risk negative publicity.

The IG did recommend disciplinary action against a handful of managers and agents and commented on various "operational shortcomings" of PAN. As far as I can gather, no disciplinary action ever took place against any agent.

The former manager of the Covert Support Unit, Prince Makhwathana, was suspended in July 2010 for misconduct but was never supplied with a charge sheet. Makhwathana, a Fraser confidant, had entered into employment contracts with the 72 PAN agents. Paul Engelke and Kobus Meiring found that he did not have the authority to sign these contracts and that he was probably also complicit in financial misconduct. When SARS investigators commenced with audits of the PAN managers, they discovered that Makhwathana and his wife owned seven properties, four of which were purchased during the PAN programme period.

While on suspension, Makhwathana sat at home receiving his full pay and full benefits. He approached the courts in September 2013 after having written to SSA director-general Sonto Kudjoe a month earlier demanding that he be allowed to return to work. The High Court ruled in his favour, but he was recharged in January 2015 with more than a hundred violations, including illegal bugging and the promotion of several agency employees to salary levels that he was not authorised to approve.

The legal services manager of the SSA advised, however, that Makhwathana had no case to answer. David Mahlobo intervened and lifted his suspension. All charges against Makhwathana were dropped, and almost six years after being suspended and at an estimated cost of R6 million to the taxpayer, he returned to "the Farm".

The last glimmer of hope – albeit a very small one – is the parliamentary Joint Standing Committee on Intelligence (JSCI). The committee is an oversight body composed of members of the largest political parties. They all undergo top-secret security clearances and intelligence "training" and are bound by an oath of secrecy. They cannot talk about anything discussed during committee meetings.

The JSCI has probably an even worse credibility record than the IGI. Laurie Nathan says the committee has to take the blame for the failure of the country's intelligence services to be held accountable. One of the reasons for the malfunctioning of the JSCI was that it was chaired by a Zuma acolyte and security hawk, Cecil Burgess. He also chaired the ad hoc committee that dealt with the so-called Secrecy Bill (the Protection of State Information Bill), of which he was a champion. In addition, Burgess was appointed to the ad hoc committee that considered the spending of taxpayers' money on upgrading Zuma's Nkandla compound. That committee saw no wrong on Zuma's part or in the way in which he benefited from the upgrades. Under Burgess's watch, the JSCI repeatedly failed to publish its annual reports by the stipulated deadline and hardly ever met.

The Democratic Alliance (DA) has three members on the JSCI. They had got scent of the PAN investigation and had been asking questions ever since. The IG briefed the committee in 2015 about the results of her investigation. Committee members are not allowed to talk about the briefing but, from what I heard, it was short and to the point. The committee was informed that Arthur Fraser was not criminally liable and there would not be any prosecutions.

Since then, the DA members of the committee have insisted that they want access to the full report of Paul Engelke and Kobus Meiring. At the time of the writing of this book, David Mahlobo was considering their application. But don't hold your breath.

* * *

On Wednesday, 23 September 2015, Her Excellency Faith Doreen Radebe, draped in an exquisite red Xhosa garb, was ushered in a horse-drawn carriage to the Royal Palace in Stockholm to present her letter of credence to King Carl XVI Gustav as South Africa's new ambassador to Sweden. Radebe wasn't the only one who was looked after following the undermining of Paul Engelke's PAN investigation. Shortly after Arthur Fraser's resignation, he went into business with Manala Manzini, his director-general, who had concocted the PAN scheme with him. Manzini's contract at the NIA had expired in September 2009.

The *Sunday Times* reported in August 2014 that the South Africa Social Security Agency (SASSA) had blown millions in public funds on a suspect deal with Resurgent Risk Managers, a company that belonged to Fraser and Manzini. SASSA paid them R14.6 million to conduct a "threat assessment", devise "mitigation strategies" and provide "strategic advice on security". According to Fraser, Resurgent had followed all due processes in contracting with government.

The Post Office also made use of Fraser's intelligence expertise. *Business Day* reported that CEO Chris Hlekane hired Fraser to spy on senior executives who apparently posed a threat to his position.

City Press revealed in October 2016 that Resurgent Risk Managers had scored a R90 million contract from the embattled Passenger Rail Agency of South Africa (Prasa) to provide security and risk advisory services for a period of two years. Resurgent also had to review and analyse Prasa's security strategy and provide training for security personnel. Prasa has been mired in controversy since it was revealed in 2015 that mismanagement led to the loss of billions of rand, through the acquisition of Spanish trains which were unsuitable for South African rails. Public protector Thuli Madonsela released a report, *Derailed,* which found evidence of widespread maladministration and impropriety in the awarding of tenders at Prasa. A Treasury probe revealed that only 13 out of 216 contracts awarded by Prasa between 2012 and 2015, all with a value exceeding R10 million, were above board.

According to *Daily Maverick*, the Treasury investigation found that Resurgent might have used a false tax certificate to score the contract, although Resurgent denied the claims. The forensic company that did the investigation for Treasury recommended that Resurgent's contract should be reported to the police for contravening the country's corruption laws.

The contract with Fraser and Manzini was awarded on the basis of a "confinement", which refers to deals that are awarded without a tender, but only if they can be justified by factors such as urgency or a lack of competitors in the market. *City Press* said Resurgent had apparently invoiced Prasa on a monthly basis and had received about R30 million before the contract was put on ice. Their services were halted by Prasa in the wake of the damning public protector's report.

Fraser said that he had resigned from Resurgent by September 2016. He was, however, a co-signatory to the Prasa contract and many millions flowed to him and Manzini prior to his resignation.

City Press reported that the tender awarded to Resurgent was among a host of contracts that Treasury was investigating at the request of the public protector. Treasury might at some point release a report and claim the money back.

*　　*　　*

The year 2016 hammered Jacob Zuma with remorseless savagery. It was what political commentator Max du Preez described as his *annus maximus horribilis*. By the middle of the year, Zuma was in a political maelstrom. The Constitutional Court ruled that he had failed to uphold, defend and respect the Constitution; the ANC had lost control of the country's biggest metros; and the rating agencies were yapping at his heels.

Zuma had to chortle his way through Parliament; a rebellion was brewing in his own ranks; and more evidence was emerging of his lovey-dovey relationship with his main benefactors, the Guptas. Journalist Richard Poplak remarked at the time that Zuma "looked as grey and wrinkled as an exsanguinated tortoise, and it did seem as if the end was nigh". Even on a personal level, Zuma behaved increasingly like a Don Vito Corleone in Mario Puzo's celebrated novel *The Godfather*.

He was at all times surrounded by at least 22 armed bodyguards. Stern-faced with squawking earpieces, steel-rimmed sunglasses and bulging pockets, they were drawn from a team of 88 members of the presidential close-protection unit. Nobody knew if the intelligence services had detected any threat against the president, except from one of his own wives, Nompumelelo Ntuli-Zuma, who was banished from Nkandla after she allegedly tried to kill him. The *Sunday Times* said that Russian intelligence agents had discovered that MaNtuli had been involved in a plot to poison Zuma. She has rejected the allegations against her and has never been charged with any wrongdoing.

It is at times like this that besieged leaders surround themselves with those they trust the most. In Zuma's case, it was his Rottweilers: his security cluster that had infiltrated almost every aspect of the state apparatus. One crucial piece on his political chessboard was still missing, however: a trusted and dependable spy boss.

That person was not the director-general of the SSA, Sonto Kudjoe. A former ambassador to Sweden and Egypt and educated in the Soviet Union, she was appointed as spy boss in 2013 but reportedly had a tense and unhappy relationship with David Mahlobo. In August 2016, the SSA declared that her contract had been terminated by "mutual agreement" and that she would pursue opportunities "elsewhere". She was probably asked to resign and given a bag of money to keep her happy.

A month later, Mahlobo announced that Arthur Joseph Peter Fraser had been appointed the director-general of the SSA. The ministry said in a statement that Fraser had extensive experience in the intelligence community and had "astute managerial experience". His complicity in a calamitous enterprise that had squandered hundreds of millions of rand of taxpayers' money was hardly mentioned by any newspaper, despite my story in *City Press* about PAN two years earlier.

When the *Sunday Times* asked the SSA for comment about Fraser and PAN, spokesperson Brian Dube said that Mahlobo was "concerned by the unlawful disclosure and possession of classified information that is flawed and inaccurate to unauthorized persons and or parties". He threatened the newspaper that the possession of classified material was a "contravention of the provisions of the Intelligence Services Act and the Protection of Information Act" and that this conduct "undermines the integrity, objectivity and fairness and violates the rights of individuals". Dube added that the IG did not make any findings against Fraser but recommended that the agency deal with his "non-compliance with some operational directives". He said the matter was "considered closed". The *Sunday Times* didn't publish the story.

It will not be the first or the last time that the SSA has abused security legislation in order to keep their dirty linen under wraps. Laurie Nathan says the intelligence services suffer from an "unreconstructed apartheid mentality" and remain "immersed in obsessive secrecy" which precludes accountability and oversight. They believe they are above the Constitution and think it is legitimate to break the rules. He says they are close to "rogue".

I can basically go to prison or at least be prosecuted for what I have revealed to you about the PAN programme investigation. The SSA will argue that I have jeopardised national security and endangered the lives of agents. This is, of course, nonsense. I have not revealed any state secrets and have not endangered any operations that are genuinely in the interest of national security.

What I have revealed is an orgy of depravity and venality, and if there is any attempt to stop the publishing of this book, it will be because they do not want you to know about it.

*   *   *

One of the first things that director-general Arthur Fraser did after taking office was to embark on a "roadshow" around the country to address staff and agents. He told them that the allegations against him in the media – the story that I had written in *City Press* – were nonsense. He reiterated that the IGI had found no criminal evidence against him and warned employees that the gossip must stop.

At the end of February 2017, he held a telephone conference with staff during which he announced a complete overhaul and restructuring of the agency. All the departmental heads would report directly to him. Staff refer to him as the "super-DG".

One of his first appointments was that of his right-hand man at PAN and his brother-in-law, Graham Engel, as his second in command. Engel was for three years on suspension with full pay pending the outcome of the PAN investigation. He is referred to as "CE10" – the head of all internal intelligence and operations. Married to Fraser's sister, he is in the all-powerful position as the national coordinator of all intelligence.

Insiders said they are concerned that so many of the former PAN managers and operatives have been brought back by Fraser. This group – and it includes Fraser and Engel – commanded and directed a failed intelligence structure and therefore they elicit no confidence.

When Fraser assumed his new role, an intelligence source warned me that it would just be a matter of time before the SSA exposed a tremendous threat to our national security. New spy bosses have to put their stamp of authority on the agency, and what better way than to sniff out a menace to the country's well-being.

Indeed. At the beginning of March 2017, David Mahlobo called a press briefing and said that South Africa was not an exception when it came to being a target of terrorists. He announced: "Attempts at regime change are happening. We know who does what." He didn't give any further detail but assured the nation that counter-intelligence was dealing with the matter. "We do that work quietly because at the end of the day South Africa should never be a failed state. Our duty is to protect its sovereignty. We are committed to ensure that our country remains relatively safe and free of any attempts to destabilise it."

Mahlobo repeated his claims in July 2017 when he said that talk of a regime change was not a scare tactic because South Africa already displayed some of the elements of a "colour revolution" – which in common parlance refers to non-violent or civil resistance such as protests and strikes.

My sources tell me that one of the "colour revolutions" that the SSA identified as promoting "regime change" was the Fees Must Fall student protests which spread across South African universities in 2016. Fraser and his analysts have concluded that these might at some stage deteriorate into an attempted coup d'état.

The SSA has also concluded that there are "foreign forces and their agents" that are attempting to destabilise the Zuma regime. Mahlobo has said that civil society is collaborating with foreign agents to subvert and undermine government. According to him, they had funding and surveillance equipment and some even had "funny names".

Following Mahlobo's most recent "regime change" speech, an SSA source contacted me and said: "Haven't I told you? The message they are trying to convey is that we are in safe hands and should be grateful for a man like Arthur Fraser at the helm of our intelligence services."

There is tremendous paranoia at the top. When, for instance, Zuma arrived at the ANC policy conference at the highly secured Nasrec show-grounds in Johannesburg in July 2017, he came with a cavalcade of 11 vehicles and 18 bodyguards. The president feels threatened, and his paranoia has filtered down through the ranks. Mahlobo showed clear signs of this, and at the same time insulted the intelligence of the nation, when he announced in a statement that the SSA was investigating allegations that public protector Thuli Madonsela and Economic Freedom Fighters leader Julius Malema were CIA agents. The claims were originally made by an American blog on the lunatic fringe with less than a hundred followers. Malema retorted: "This is a joke man, who belongs in a pre-school. There is no State Security in South Africa, we've got a group of clowns that call themselves Intelligence, with an intelligence-illiterate minister leading them."

In September 2017, *City Press, Rapport* and *News24* reported that the SSA had allegedly spent more than a billion rand in irregular expenditure over the past five years – but refused to account for it because its operations were "classified". The newspapers said seven sources had confirmed that between the 2012/13 and 2015/16 financial years, Treasury repeatedly asked the SSA for clarity on its expenditure. But, according to the same sources, the SSA wouldn't say how this money was spent because its activities were "secret".

It seems that old habits die hard.

* * *

The 16th of December 2016 was my last day in Moscow. A snowstorm had been raging since early morning, and when I peered from my window on the third floor of the legendary Hotel Sovietsky, a flurry of white powder swirled around trees that balanced a mantle of snow on their elongated branches. The winter light was pale and watery; the sky ashen and pasty.

I waited for Paul Engelke in the foyer of the Sovietsky, a throwback to Politburo times. The hotel was constructed in 1952 on the personal order of Joseph Stalin to accommodate government dignitaries. It still oozes Bolshevism from every nook and cranny with its faded red carpets, a life-size portrait of the Red Tsar (Stalin's nickname) and decor that represents the height of Soviet sophistication and opulence.

We eventually landed in a dreadful *ryumochnaya*, a Russian basement bar that serves alcohol and food on the cheap. The decor hovered between the old, the new and the kitsch: nylon window curtains, football memorabilia and the odd Lenin banner. The waitresses were gruff and crusty with brash lipstick and powdered cheeks, who slammed shots of nameless vodka and a bowl of pickles in front of us.

I'd decided by then that I really liked Engelke. He had limitless energy and tackled life with an exuberance and vigour that I admired. His Russian adventure had netted him a gorgeous woman and we had endless discussions about how he was going to navigate the general-dad dilemma and whether he should seek a life and future in Russia.

The frozen country had set Paul Engelke free. It didn't matter how cold or inhospitable it was; he was his own man in his own skin with his own destiny. He had broken free from the mental incarceration of the SSA, where he thought he was doing the right thing by busting reprobates but was in fact setting his own demise in motion. I realised in Moscow what a great loss Paul Engelke was to our fledgling democracy and our quest to inculcate a culture of justice and accountability. If he decides to settle permanently in Russia, that loss will be forever.

He seems to have had an unfortunate departure from the SSA. In 2015, he enrolled for a master's degree in law at the University of Pretoria. He met a Russian guest lecturer and they discussed the possibility of his doing a similar stint at Moscow State University. The Russians were interested in utilising his experience in forensic law. He then quit the SSA but soon afterwards had second thoughts and withdrew his resignation. He was allegedly fetched by guards in his office, told to pack his personal belongings and escorted out of Musanda.

Throughout my stay in Russia there was one subject he refused to talk about: the SSA and his PAN project investigation. He told me from the outset that he was bound by his oath of secrecy and that he has children back home in South Africa whom he might never see again if he opened his heart to me. By then I already had studied two of his reports and reckoned that so many people knew about the PAN programme that its details would ultimately be blown open. I had gone to Russia in order to start writing this book as much as to see and talk to him.

I have stayed in contact with Engelke, and in one of his last messages, he said to me: "And how is the book going? I shudder when I think about it! In the meantime, I've asked Diana to get married and she has said yes. You are of course invited. I'm also getting along very nicely with the general. We are thinking of getting married in Cape Town. What do you think?"

FOUR

Glimmers of horror

———•———

I have only seen Jacob Zuma twice, the last time towards the end of 2007 behind the soaring walls and electric fence of his home in the leafy suburb of Forest Hill in Johannesburg. He was under siege: he had been fired as deputy president and his rancorous rival, Thabo Mbeki, was going for his jugular.

The president's hit men, the elite crime-busting Scorpions, had reintroduced corruption, fraud and money-laundering charges against Zuma, which could have sent him to prison for a long time. But Zuma showed no hints of his legal predicaments. After security guards had searched our bags, they ushered us into a study, where a minute or two later Zuma sauntered in. A smile covered the width of his face.

Zuma's residence was hardly the sanctuary it should have been. It was exposed to the outside world by two dramatic legal events that marked the run-up to his appointment as South Africa's fourth democratically elected president in May 2009.

We sat in a study at a polished wooden desk, the very same room the Scorpions had searched for computer hard drives and documents to support their criminal case that Zuma had taken bribes from his financial adviser, Schabir Shaik. Prosecutors eventually formulated 783 charges of corruption, fraud and racketeering against Zuma.

A year earlier, the world was taken on a sordid journey through Zuma's guest bedroom where he had unprotected sex with an HIV-positive woman. She was the daughter of a struggle comrade who was imprisoned with

Zuma on Robben Island. She called him "Uncle" and regarded him as a substitute father after her own had died in a car accident. She became known to the world as Khwezi and claimed that Zuma had forced himself on her; his defence was that the act was consensual. He testified that Khwezi was wearing a "kanga" – a brightly coloured, wrap-around cloth – which he interpreted as an invitation for sex. He afterwards took a shower to protect himself against the Aids virus. In a country ravaged by Aids, he said: "A shower would minimise the risk of contracting the disease." Zuma was found not guilty, but the trial exposed his archaic and almost feudal perception of women, sex and HIV/Aids.

Quoting from Rudyard Kipling during his judgment, Judge Willem van der Merwe said: "And if you can control your body and your sexual urges, then you are a man, my son."

Although Zuma afterwards apologised for his defilement of a comrade's offspring, a few years later he procreated with another friend's daughter. The father was soccer boss Irvin Khoza and his 39-year-old daughter was carrying Zuma's 20th (known) child. Zuma had to pay customary damages to the Khoza family, known as "inhlawulo" in Zulu.

The rape trial should have spelled the end of Zuma's political ambitions but instead set in motion a political tsunami as comrades and cadres flooded to the Johannesburg High Court with posters that said "Burn the bitch" and "100% Zulu boy". They believed that the rape accusation was part of a Thabo Mbeki-driven political conspiracy to hammer the last nail in his deputy's political coffin. Khwezi, they argued, got what she deserved. Khwezi and her mother were subsequently hounded out of the country after Zuma supporters burned down their home. She died in October 2016 and was named as Fezekile Ntsukela Kuzwayo.

When I saw Zuma, it was a few months before he was elected as ANC president. I was a researcher for a foreign journalist and had managed to arrange an interview with him. Dressed in a loose, casual shirt, he flaunted a perfect row of white teeth and said: "Maybe you are talking to the wrong man, because I am just a cadre of the ANC. And I can tell you now that I have no desire to be the president."

Zuma laughed as he said it – not the *he-he-he-he-he* that later became his trademark in Parliament when he was in trouble or under siege, but a deep and genuine expression of merriment. It was difficult not to like him. His charm and geniality reminded me why he was often referred to as the "people's politician".

There are two public personae of Jacob Zuma. Think of him standing in Parliament delivering the State of the Nation address or answering questions from the opposition. Or even more daunting: think of him addressing the United Nations in New York. Gauche, bumbling, unworldly, clueless, fibbing, awkward. Long-*grump*-pauses-*grump*-between-*grump*-sentences. Zuma is one of the most lampooned and jeered heads of state in the world and can easily be brushed aside as an uneducated peasant – yet he is in fact a brilliant strategist.

But then there is the other Jacob Zuma, entering a township in a cloud of dust and flashing blue lights. There is no more effective politician than Zuma when he knocks on doors, pats babies and holds the hands of the elderly. He listens, he chuckles, he empathises, he connects, he brings hope, he says whatever people want to hear. He is living proof of how the ANC, for 75 years, built a party and a struggle movement from door to door and from comrade to comrade before winning the 1994 election.

* * *

The first time I saw Zuma, he was still banned and therefore regarded by the apartheid government as a terrorist and a communist – albeit for only one more day. It was 1 February 1990 and I was in Harare, Zimbabwe, for the first press conference of apartheid killer Dirk Coetzee.

Zuma was Coetzee's ANC keeper and protector. The story of Coetzee and how he got to the ANC is the subject of books but, in short, I was at the time a journalist at the Afrikaans anti-apartheid newspaper *Vrye Weekblad* (Free Weekly), which maverick editor Max du Preez, I and four other journalists had started.

Coetzee was once a golden boy in the police and a member of the feared Security Branch. In 1979, he set up a secret police unit on a farm called Vlakplaas, just west of Pretoria. The farm was manned by a few security policemen and so-called askaris – captured ANC and Pan Africanist Congress (PAC) guerrillas who were "turned" into killer cops. They were tortured until they agreed to work for the police. Once at Vlakplaas, they were dispatched to hunt down and assassinate their former comrades and ANC and PAC members.

After less than two years as commander of Vlakplaas, Coetzee had a falling-out with the generals and was transferred to the dog unit as a dog handler. He lamented at the time: "I don't even have a fucking dog!" Embittered and disillusioned, Coetzee embarked on a campaign to get back at the generals who had engineered his demise. He spoke to top Progressive Federal Party (PFP) politicians (the political party to the left of the ruling National Party) and a newspaper editor. He told them of his murderous missions; of how his unit had poisoned captured "terrorists" who refused to become askaris and then burned their bodies on pyres of wood and tyres – while gorging themselves on brandy and Coke at their own *braaivleis-vuur* (barbecue) a few metres away. He explained how they slit the throat of a well-known lawyer, Griffiths Mxenge, in 1981 because they suspected that the ANC was channelling money through his bank account. He mentioned the names of three generals and several brigadiers who ordered the assassinations. He also exposed a colonel who succeeded him at Vlakplaas: Eugene de Kock. De Kock acquired the nickname of Prime Evil and was eventually sentenced to several life sentences for a host of murders and other serious crimes.

Nobody believed Coetzee (or wanted to believe him) and he eventually found his way to me as a young reporter at an Afrikaans Sunday newspaper. The paper supported the government and would never have published the story. I kept in contact with Coetzee, and when we founded *Vrye Weekblad*, it was time to expose the existence of the police death squads.

Coetzee demanded that we arrange a haven overseas and look after his family back home. We didn't have money and decided there was only one option: Coetzee must join the ANC in exile and the organisation must undertake to protect him. In return, they could debrief him and use him for whatever propaganda purposes they chose.

Max du Preez and I embarked on secret negotiations with the ANC's head of intelligence, Jacob Zuma. His name meant nothing to me. A go-between flew between Lusaka and Johannesburg to deliver messages. Eventually the top command of the ANC agreed to our proposal, and in early November 1989 Coetzee and I flew to Mauritius, where I conducted the interview with him and took down a statement.

When he left the island to fly to London, where Zuma was waiting for him, he asked me: "So what do I call him when I greet him?" I wasn't sure myself and said: "Comrade, I suppose." From then on everyone was comrade.

Two weeks later, *Vrye Weekblad* pasted a big photograph of Coetzee on its front page with the words "I am Captain Dirk Johannes Coetzee. I was the commander of the SA Police death squad. I was in the heart of the whore."

Zuma, sporting a beard, endearingly greeted me in Harare and said: "Aha, so this is the unguided missile! You gave us almost as much trouble as that comrade sitting over there," he said, bursting out laughing and pointing to Coetzee.

After Coetzee was in ANC hands, Zuma tried to delay our publication of our article because the ANC wanted more time to debrief the killer cop. We ignored his request. Coetzee said afterwards that his interrogators wanted to know if he would be prepared to return to South Africa to conduct military operations for the ANC. That might be why Zuma wanted more time.

When I spoke to Coetzee in Harare, he predicted a big future for Zuma. "I'm telling you, he's going to be president one day. I've never seen anyone with such a sharp brain. He is a supreme strategist."

It was at the time a bizarre prediction. Nelson Mandela was in prison and the ANC was banned. That was until the next day when President F.W. de Klerk announced the release of the ANC leader and the unbanning of the organisation. Zuma scurried back to Lusaka and the host of journalists who had waited for Coetzee's appearance rushed to the airport to fly back to Johannesburg.

Coetzee added: "And I will be the new commissioner of police." I told him it was impossible.

"You are wrong," he said. "Zuma has promised me the commissioner's post." Coetzee frequently made lists of what his police top structure would look like. Most of his generals were white and from the old order. What about your new ANC comrades? I wanted to know. Where are they going? "To the army," he replied. "They will run the army. Leave the police to me."

I don't think Zuma ever made this promise. Coetzee's delusions of grandeur came to an end when he returned to South Africa in 1993. He got a lowly position at the National Intelligence Agency (NIA) and was dumped in the archives. "How many fucking newspapers a day can you read?" he bitterly lamented. He was also convicted of the murder of Griffiths Mxenge although the Truth and Reconciliation Commission (TRC) granted him amnesty and expunged his record.

Coetzee's hero worship of Zuma eventually turned into aversion and he blamed him for all his ills and misfortune. "Why do I have to stand in court but no other comrade is on trial for all the things they have done?"

After he retired from the NIA in the mid-2000s, he looked after security for an ANC-linked company, EduSolutions. He flew with the managing director to France in 2007 to attend the final of the rugby World Cup between the Springboks and England. Here he bumped into Zuma, who greeted him heartily.

Shortly before Coetzee's death in 2013 and on his sickbed, he said to me: "Can you believe that Zuma never even phoned to ask how I am? Not a word. Nothing. And to think I gave my life for them."

By then Coetzee had reverted to being a rabid racist. "That man is a snake. He's like all of them. You can never, ever trust any of them. Be very careful."

* * *

Little is known about Zuma's years in exile, but there are enough hints and evidence of a darker past that should have undermined his rise to the top. He doesn't talk about the 15 years he spent with the ANC in exile. He didn't even take his biographer, Jeremy Gordin, into his confidence. He is quoted as saying that details of the "operational events of those days" were the property of the ANC, not his to disclose.

It is often said that Zuma is proof that anyone, even from the humblest beginnings, can rise to the top. A son of a domestic worker mother and policeman father who died when he was a young boy, Zuma was chiselled from the land north of the Tugela River in KwaZulu-Natal. Called the land of hills, honey and cobras, it is an area tormented by poverty and stands in stark contrast to the rolling sugar estates and "white monopoly capital" on the other side of the Tugela.

Zuma had hardly any schooling because he had to support his mother by finding odd jobs. He taught himself to read and write. "I used to polish the veranda, you know, jobs like that," he said in an interview. He followed his brother into the ANC in the late 1950s and attended informal liberation schools which the organisation had set up across the country. A few years later, the apartheid government banned the ANC and PAC following the Sharpeville massacre. The ANC adopted the armed struggle and formed an armed wing, Umkhonto we Sizwe (MK) – the Spear of the Nation.

Zuma and a group of more than forty MK recruits were arrested in 1963 when attempting to skip the country for military training. He was convicted of conspiring to overthrow the government and sentenced to ten years' imprisonment. He served his sentence on Robben Island alongside leaders like Nelson Mandela, Walter Sisulu and Govan Mbeki.

He was released without ever receiving a single visitor. He returned to Nkandla, got married and worked in ANC underground structures. In 1975, he evaded arrest and went into exile. He returned to South Africa only in 1990 after the unbanning of the ANC.

Details are scant for these 15 years, and maybe for good reason. Zuma's predilection for secrecy might come from the need to conceal his alleged complicity in the deaths of MK cadres Thami Zulu and Cyril Raymond, who were tortured and murdered while in Zuma's care.

Zuma lived for 12 years in Mozambique, where he commanded the training of recruits and plotted armed incursions into South Africa. He was appointed to the National Executive Committee (NEC) of the ANC in 1977 and served as its chief representative in Mozambique. In 1987 the ANC called him back to headquarters in Lusaka as head of intelligence and the

commander – alongside Joe Nhlanhla – of the dreaded security department. It was known among cadres as the Mbokodo – isiXhosa for "the stone
that crushes".

Life in exile was perilous and lethal. Apartheid spies – known as *impim-*
pis – infiltrated the ANC and the movement was subverted by fear and
insecurity. Mbokodo attempted to snuff them out, put them on trial and
meted out punishment – often execution. Dissent in the ANC's training
camps was equally harshly dealt with and brutally quashed.

Mbokodo's headquarters in Lusaka was known as "Green House" and
the department held the same meaning for ANC cadres as the Cheka or
KGB did to Russian dissidents in the old Soviet Union. It was occupied by
a paranoid, violent and ruthless coterie of brutes.

In 1989, Thami Zulu or TZ (his real name was Mzwakhe Ngwenya) was
ordered to report to Green House. TZ was a popular MK commander and
head of the "Natal machinery". He stepped up MK attacks in KwaZulu-
Natal, but his campaign turned disastrous in 1988 when a Vlakplaas death
squad ambushed and killed nine MK infiltrators. There must have been a
police spy in ANC ranks who betrayed their operational plans to Vlakplaas.

Zulu's deputy, Cyril Raymond (or Ralph Mgcina), was also summoned to
Lusaka. According to the evidence, both men were detained and tortured.
Raymond died in detention, reportedly drowning in his own vomit after
refusing to sign a confession admitting that he was a spy.

When Thami Zulu's parents heard he was detained, his father, Philemon
Ngwenya, travelled to Lusaka to see him. He met Zuma, who denied that
Thami was in detention. ANC security personnel eventually brought Thami
to Ngwenya's hotel, where they spoke in the presence of guards. Thami
said he was in good health and that nothing was wrong.

Although two months of interrogation failed to find any proof of Zulu's
collusion with the enemy, Mbokodo recommended that he should be "disciplined for criminal neglect" for the 1988 deaths of his cadres. He spent
14 months on a mattress in a cell.

Ngwenya then received a call from his son, who said he was in a cell
and being tortured. He returned to Lusaka, where he waited 18 days in

vain to see either Zuma or Thami. He later testified before the TRC: "Mr Zuma would not see me. He spoke to me through this gentleman Sindisiwayo and told me that he would send my son to the hotel, which thing they never did. Why was I not allowed by Mr Zuma to see my son for 18 days? Even under the most cruel regime, apartheid regime, people were allowed visitors."

ANC president Oliver Tambo eventually ordered Zulu's release. He was in an emaciated condition and died four days later in the house of a friend. Forensic examinations in Zambia and the UK concluded that he was probably poisoned with diazinon, an organic phosphorus pesticide.

Zulu's treatment was reminiscent of the most brutal travesties of justice that apartheid's death squads and security apparatus ever perpetrated. Jacob Zuma has never defended his role in Mbokodo and he failed to turn up for a TRC hearing that might have brought some answers. The commission nonetheless found that Mbokodo had been responsible for "gross violations of human rights . . . against suspected 'enemy agents' and mutineers". They found no evidence that Zulu had been a spy.

Philemon Ngwenya agonised with the TRC to find answers about his son's death. Yet the man who held the key to the puzzle couldn't bother to honour his appointment with the bereaved father. Neither did he make any effort to speak to or contact Ngwenya privately.

Why are the deaths of Zulu and Raymond and Zuma's leadership position in Mbokodo so important? The first reason is that Zuma illustrated that, if necessary, he is prepared to trample on the blood and bones of his own to achieve his goals. It is one thing to cuddle babies when the cameras zoom in. It is another to stand up and admit error and wrongdoing – something Zuma has never done. His life has been marked by denial upon denial upon denial.

But there is another reason why this incident is important. The skills and skulduggery Zuma learned as ANC intelligence chief have helped him to endure as president. As the head of intelligence, Zuma became skilled in the art of neutralising traitors and incapacitating opponents. He hasn't lost his touch.

He has promoted obscure, inexperienced and, in some cases, incompetent officials to powerful positions within the security, intelligence and justice portfolios. On merit alone, they would never have achieved such high office. The compromise is unspoken and undocumented: you look after me, and I will look after you.

*   *   *

When I met Jacob Zuma for the second time, he had been a "kept politician" for more than a decade. He was a financial leech and sycophant who extracted money and favours on a habitual basis from a host of benefactors who included not just his financial adviser and a host of business people, but even Nelson Mandela.

At the basis of his dark journey into patronage was Zuma's inability to handle his financial affairs. Polygamy and serial philandering come at a price, and both the taxpayer and his financial benefactors had to dig deep to sustain his lavish lifestyle and to sponsor the design, construction, expansion and upgrading of his Nkandla homestead.

All indications are that Zuma led a frugal lifestyle as a dedicated ANC cadre but that this changed soon after 1994 when he was appointed as a provincial minister in the KwaZulu-Natal government. When Zuma returned to the country he was – at least in KZN – the local boy made good and was expected to flaunt money and bestow influence to help his impoverished people. He was literally the *umuntu omkhulu* – the Big Man – and was expected to have a household and lifestyle befitting his status. Zuma had, however, returned from exile with nothing and was – to put it mildly – in a "debt trap".

Badly in need of cash to sustain his image and ever-increasing household, Zuma turned to an old comrade from the struggle, Schabir Shaik, to give him a series of "interest-free loans". In return, Zuma would use his influence to allegedly divert business to Shaik. Shaik was one of a band of brothers who had worked for the ANC underground during apartheid and were involved in the covert management of ANC funds. His brother Chippy became the director of arms procurement for the post-apartheid defence force.

Zuma's financial affairs were laid bare in a 2006 forensic report that the auditors KPMG prepared on the instruction of the Scorpions. Running to about five hundred pages, the report was based on tens of thousands of documents Scorpions investigators had seized from Shaik, Zuma and others. After the decision to withdraw charges of corruption against Zuma, the report was buried for several years until the *Mail & Guardian* dug it up.

The report exposed in the finest detail the financial recklessness of Zuma, which should have raised a host of red flags about his fitness for office. He opened bank accounts left, right and centre (at ABSA, Nedbank, Standard Bank and First National Bank), entered into hire purchase agreements, signed for loans and acquired overdrafts without having the means to repay them. According to the report, Zuma wrote 140 dud cheques with a collective value of R477,766.67 between 1996 and 2003.

Zuma merrily incurred large debts without bothering to consider where the money would come from. There were times when he couldn't even honour the first payment on a purchase because there was no money in the bank. Despite his terrible credit profile, banks bent over backwards to indulge Zuma because of his political clout. In many instances, Zuma didn't even respond to their queries about his overdrawn accounts.

Enter Shaik, Mandela and a host of benefactors. Shaik's payments to Zuma totalled more than R4 million over ten years and ended with his fraud conviction and imprisonment in June 2005. Zuma's accounts were at times so overdrawn that Shaik didn't dare to make deposits. Zuma would collect the money – as little as R700 at a time – in envelopes.

Zuma bought his Nkandla homestead in the early 2000s – when it was, according to a bank valuation, worth around R700,000 – and was granted a loan by First National Bank. His KZN business friend Vivian Reddy signed surety for the loan and serviced the payments for the first year. Zuma started construction on the first phase of the homestead shortly afterwards – without having any money to do so.

Benefactors showered Zuma with white envelopes while banks were at his feet. When the cash-starved politician approached ABSA in the late 1990s to open an account, his bad credit record with Standard Bank and

Nedbank should have disqualified him. But the business centre manager wrote in a memorandum that Zuma was likely to be elected South Africa's deputy president soon and that his "bank balance was the last item on his mind, with more important matters regarding the country and the province to focus on".

Within three months, Zuma's account was heavily overdrawn.

* * *

The decision by the post-1994 ANC government to re-equip the new South African National Defence Force led to the controversial multi-billion-rand arms deal. Without facing any external threat, the government embarked on a mission to buy corvettes, submarines and fighter aircraft. Arms deals are notorious for bribing corrupt politicians. The South African arms deal was no different and was from the outset riddled with fraud, bribes and kickbacks to the ANC. The serial debtor Jacob Zuma was in the front of the line for his slice of the pie.

The *Sunday Times* and *M&G* revealed that in 2000 Zuma allegedly accepted a R500,000-a-year bribe from the French arms company Thales. Thales's South African subsidiary, Thint, had won a R2.6 billion contract in 1997 to fit four new navy frigates with its weapons systems. Thales also generously contributed to the ANC coffers. In April 2006, Thales wrote a cheque for €1 million (about R15 million at today's exchange rate) for the ANC to be paid from a Dubai bank account into an "ANC-aligned trust".

Another Zuma benefactor was former president Nelson Mandela, who came to Zuma's rescue in June 2005 with a R1 million payment. This was made just nine days after President Mbeki had fired Zuma as his deputy and shortly after the NPA announced Zuma's prosecution. Zuma was at the time overdrawn by more than R400,000. The *M&G* reported that Mandela had identified Zuma early on as a financial "problem child" and had attempted to "discipline" him about his financial conduct.

KPMG said in their report that Zuma profited from a host of meal tickets other than those given by Shaik and Mandela. These payments amounted to at least another R3 million. According to the *M&G*, it appeared that Zuma might also have benefited from another arms deal company, Ferrostaal, which clinched the submarine contract.

In May 2005, Schabir Shaik was convicted of fraud and corruption in the Durban High Court. He alleged that he gave Zuma loans and didn't charge interest because it "offended his religious conviction". Judge Hilary Squires would have none of it and sentenced Shaik to 15 years' imprisonment. The trial court found in the context of the corruption charges that the evidence established a "mutually beneficial symbiosis" between Shaik and Zuma.

Shaik tried his luck in the Supreme Court of Appeal (SCA) but a full bench confirmed the sentence and said Shaik "subverted his friendship with Zuma into a relationship of patronage designed to achieve power and wealth". Shaik used Zuma's name to intimidate people, and particularly potential business partners, into submitting to his will. The SCA concluded: "In our view, the sustained corrupt relationship over the years had the effect that Shaik could use one of the most powerful politicians in the country when it suited him."

You don't have to be a lawyer to grasp the significance of the court's judgment: that there was a crooked, conniving and reciprocal relationship between Zuma and his benefactor, and they therefore shared equal guilt.

Books have been written and newspapers have been filled with revelations around Zuma's alleged corruption (the only reason why I use the word "alleged" is that he has not yet been convicted). The evidence is compelling and devastating, yet when asked in an interview whether he is crooked, Zuma said: "Me? Well, I don't know, I must go to a dictionary and learn what a crook is. I've never been a crook."

*　*　*

They were once closer than brothers; once described as being like "tongue and saliva". But when they tasted the lure of power, the gloves came off and the camaraderie broke apart. Much has been written about this period in South Africa, and scholars and authors agree that Thabo Mbeki had a low opinion of the "poorly educated peasant". Mbeki's "imperial" and "removed" manner of governing was also light years away from Zuma's more "hands-on" and tribal approach to politics.

Mbeki was forced to tolerate Zuma, who was after all hand-picked by Mandela to be his successor's right-hand man. But once Mbeki was re-elected in 2004, he wanted to bury Zuma. Both leaders drew their daggers. Mbeki relied on his intelligence network, the Scorpions and the NPA to finish Zuma off.

Mbeki underestimated Zuma's access to an "alternative" intelligence network. To understand this, we must go back to the late 1980s to the exiled ANC's Operation Vula, in which Jacob Zuma played a leading role. Vula was arguably the most successful ANC intelligence operation ever, infiltrating extensive numbers of agents back into South Africa in heavy disguise. When it was uncovered in July 1990, Vula operated as a virtually distinct intelligence network within the ANC. The Shaik brothers played a key role in it and ran Operation Bible. Moe Shaik would later become Zuma's foreign intelligence chief. Other key operatives were Mac Maharaj (later Zuma's presidential spokesperson), Siphiwe Nyanda (later Zuma's communications minister), Nathi Mthethwa (Zuma's police minister) and Solly Shoke (Zuma's army chief).

By the mid-2000s, conspiracies and intrigues abounded. They were usually works of fiction with a splatter of truth and were leaked at strategic times, such as just before an ANC elective conference. The Zuma camp instigated its own dirty tricks campaign. Two weeks after the state had announced that the NPA was about to hurl Schabir Shaik before a judge, *City Press* ran an article that prosecutions boss Bulelani Ngcuka was an apartheid spy. As I have mentioned before, Moe Shaik later confirmed that he was behind the allegations in order "to defend the honour of the deputy president".

Then came the Browse Mole report (discussed in Chapter Two) and the hoax e-mails. In around 2005, e-mails started circulating among ANC NEC members and journalists that supporters of Mbeki were hatching a plot to permanently remove Zuma from the political scene. These fake e-mails seem to have been created and released by a pro-Zuma faction in the intelligence community to boost Zuma in the ANC succession battle.

These plots allowed Zuma to appear as a presidential hopeful under siege while Mbeki and his henchman were revealed as nothing but schemers and manipulators. Zuma said in an interview that it was his concern for "the masses and the poor" that prompted his political enemies to try to deny him the ANC leadership and the presidency.

*   *   *

Zuma is light on his feet. We have all seen him dancing: his fists clenched, his arms arched forward like the tusks of an elephant, and his body hunched while *"awuleth' umshini wami"* (bring me my machine gun) stirs from his mouth. In front of him are thousands of ecstatic and swaying followers, tooting on horns, blowing on whistles, and swaying back and forth to old anti-apartheid tunes.

If Zuma was a career boxer, he would have tiptoed around the ring, his gloves held high and his chin straight and square. Every time Zuma seems to be out on his feet and with his adversaries pummelling away at his bullet-shaped head, he is at his most dangerous. That is when he answers with nasty uppercuts and smashing right-handers, which have sent the likes of Thabo Mbeki staggering across the ring. He has an incredible ability to cheat political defeat and to emerge with his fists in the air.

On 16 December 2007, at the ANC's national conference in Polokwane, both Mbeki and Zuma allowed their names to be put forward for the party's presidency, the first time in half a century that the post had been contested. A curt-looking Mbeki, a short man with an elfin-like appearance and over-grown eyebrows, seemed startled to find himself in Zuma's company.

By the time the ANC delegates had settled in, Mbeki should have been assured of victory. Zuma was a tainted and divisive candidate with cor-ruption charges hanging over his head. He should have been finally counted out at Polokwane, but he brought with him the support of the trade unions, the Youth League, the South African Communist Party, his confidants in the ANC with whom he had worked over the years, and disgruntled and alienated former Mbeki supporters.

With ballots cast and votes counted, the result was announced. The comeback kid had thumped Mbeki by more than 800 votes. In his victory speech, Zuma described Mbeki as a "friend and a brother". He then buried him.

Mbeki had a year and a half left of his second term as president, but nine months later, the ANC's National Executive Committee decided to remove him from office. Zuma delivered the news to Mbeki, who promptly resigned. ANC secretary-general Kgalema Motlanthe became caretaker president until the May 2009 election.

* * *

On 6 April 2009, prosecutions boss Mokotedi Mpshe addressed the nation and said: "I stand before you today to announce the most difficult decision I ever made in my life. It was not an easy task at all." He said fresh evidence had emerged after the NPA studied the so-called spy tapes that were unearthed during Fraser's investigation of the Browse Mole report and those in the hands of Zuma's lawyer, Michael Hulley.

Mpshe said that the recordings showed political interference in the prosecution of Zuma, which amounted to an abuse of office. He concluded that it was "neither possible nor desirable for the NPA to continue with the prosecution of Mr Zuma". In justifying his decision, Mpshe emphasised there had been a valid case against Zuma. He added that the prosecution team itself believed the case should continue and that a court must decide whether to stop the prosecution because of political meddling.

It later emerged that part of Mpshe's legal justification had been lifted from a Hong Kong judgment. That judgment was, however, later overturned on appeal.

* * *

By the time Jacob Zuma took the oath of office in May 2009, the daughter of one of his friends was pregnant with his 20th child. The child was born three months before Zuma married for the fifth time. By then, he had been unmasked as a venal, kept and gluttonous politician who had scant control over his carnal urges.

South Africans had been alerted to an impending calamity, yet an ebullient mood pervaded large parts of the country as Zuma vowed at his inauguration: "This is a moment of renewal. I will devote myself to the well-being of the Republic and all of its people."

After the Mbeki era, when hundreds of thousands of Aids invalids wasted away before his very eyes while he denied them life-saving medication, South Africans opted for a "people's president": the man cuddling babies in the townships and arousing the hopes of those whose hands he clasped. What they didn't see (or want to see) was that, long before his rise to the presidency, Zuma had been infected by the most noxious disease of politics: greed. And we all know that greed is a fat demon with a small mouth, and whatever you feed it is never enough.

I urge Jacob Zuma to read *It's Our Turn to Eat: The Story of a Kenyan Whistle-blower*, written by the distinguished foreign correspondent Michela Wrong. It is a frightening tale of what happens when state corruption goes rogue and becomes endemic.

Kenyan president Daniel arap Moi presided over two decades of state pilfering and repression. He was succeeded by the country's first democratically elected president, Mwai Kibaki, who proclaimed at his inauguration in 2002: "Corruption would now cease to be a way of life in Kenya." In a country where ordinary citizens pay an estimated 16 bribes monthly to state and law enforcement officials, Kibaki promised the end of graft. He appointed veteran journalist and forensic investigator John Githongo as the head of the anti-corruption authority and gave him vast powers and an office in State House.

Githongo unearthed the existence of Anglo Leasing, a British-based company that had 18 contracts with the Kenyan government for the supply of everything from a forensic laboratory to a navy frigate and jeeps. Sixteen per cent of the government's expenditure in 2003 and 2004 was paid to this company – which turned out to be nothing more than a street address in Liverpool. The Anglo Leasing payments were siphoned off to Kibaki's associates and cronies. They repeatedly told Githongo to back off. After being shunned by previous regimes because of tribal differences, the Kibaki cabal was in power and it was their time to eat – much like the previous power cliques had done. Githongo initially pretended to ignore their graft while collecting evidence. He surreptitiously wore a recording device while colleagues discussed the details of the scam – only to have it malfunction and begin playing back their incriminating conversation.

His cover was blown. Kibaki refused to support Githongo, who received death threats and was tailed by Kenyan intelligence. He fled the country and blew the whistle in London. A few token officials and ministers lost their jobs, but Kibaki was exonerated and it was then back to business as usual.

In 2007, Kibaki stole the election from his challenger, Raila Odinga. They were from different tribes, and decades of suppressed ethnic resentment and anger at the government exploded when Kibaki had himself sworn in. Tribal killings swept through Kenya and scores of people died. Githongo had warned against manifestations like these unless the government truthfully addressed corruption.

Zuma's shenanigans are not unlike that of Kenya's Mwai Kibaki. And that is why Jacob Zuma should read *It's Our Turn to Eat*. Because he's eating, and those around him are also eating – while many have nothing to eat. That is why resentment at his rule is growing, leading to the ANC losing almost ten per cent of its support in the 2016 local elections and the Democratic Alliance controlling the biggest metros in the country. If the trend continues, the ANC will probably lose the 2019 general election, despite Zuma's July 2016 assurance that the ANC will rule until the coming of Christ.

On the very day that I write this paragraph, the statistician-general announced that unemployment has hit a 13-year high. Nearly 28 per cent of South Africans (9.3 million jobseekers) have no work, and very few of them will ever find a job. They are unemployed for life. Exports are falling, commodity prices are falling, growth rate forecasts are falling, business confidence is falling. We have become world leaders in income inequality, racial tension, rape and illicit financial outflows.

A few hours later, global ratings agencies S&P and Fitch confirmed South Africa's downgrading to junk status – which Treasury, under new finance minister Malusi Gigaba, welcomed. Yes, imagine a Trevor Manuel or Pravin Gordhan embracing junk.

There is no dispute: Jacob Zuma has ripped the society and state to shreds. He swore at his inauguration to be faithful to our country and that he would observe, uphold and maintain our beautiful Constitution. It was all bullshit. From the moment he became president, the Republic was in the market. Under his rule, South Africa has become a two-government country. There is an elected government, and there is a shadow government – a state within the state.

* * *

South Africa has many John Githongos – a growing list of dedicated and skilled civil servants, law enforcement officials and prosecutors who have been malevolently and deceitfully purged from the civil service. They have honed and polished South Africa's law enforcement capacity but they crossed swords with high offices when they stumbled upon corruption perpetrated by the politically connected cronies of the ruling party, powerful politicians, and Jacob Zuma and his family members.

This band of remarkable public servants are heroes of our democracy because in the face of injustice, corruption and nepotism, they have refused to let their voices lie silent. In most cases – despite their being experienced, skilled, reputable and independent-minded – the president's keepers drove them from their offices through discrediting campaigns, trumped-up charges, false allegations, malicious rumours and fake dossiers. Their careers were ruined, they were humiliated and shamed, persecuted and prosecuted, and had their life savings exhausted because of malicious litigation.

The most important among those in the law enforcement agencies who were hounded into submission were former SARS acting commissioner Ivan Pillay and three of his executives – Gene Ravele, Johann van Loggerenberg and Pete Richer. They were joined by former national director of public prosecutions Mxolisi Nxasana, former Hawks head Anwa Dramat, former

Gauteng Hawks head Major-General Shadrack Sibiya, former KwaZulu-Natal Hawks head Major-General Johan Booysen, former head of the NPA's Specialised Commercial Crimes Unit Glynnis Breytenbach, and former State Security Agency director-general Gibson Njenje.

Their demise triggered an exodus of competent government officials. For example, following the departure of the SARS top executives in late 2014 and early 2015, more than fifty managers resigned within a year. Many performed vital functions at South Africa's most crucial state institution but they rejected the leadership of Tom Moyane, a Zuma choirboy whose highest previous job in government was that of prisons boss.

"Dissident" politicians like former finance ministers Pravin Gordhan and Nhlanhla Nene, deputy finance minister Mcebisi Jonas, former tourism minister Derek Hanekom and former mining minister Ngoako Ramatlhodi were also axed for discharging false notes in the Zuma choir.

Business Day reminded us that by the end of March 2017, Zuma had made 11 cabinet reshuffles since coming to power in May 2009. He has made 126 changes to the national executive: 62 changes to ministerial positions, 63 changes to deputy ministerial positions, and one change to the deputy presidency. After his reshuffle in March 2017, the national executive (ministers and deputy ministers) stood at a bloated 74 people.

In getting rid of "troublemakers", Zuma and his keepers gutted the country's most crucial institutions by not just getting rid of top-level civil servants, but replacing them with hand-picked acting successors and low-level ANC apparatchiks who were in most cases nothing but lame ducks and weaklings.

* * *

The one institution that was untouched during Zuma's first term in office was the South African Revenue Service (SARS), the crown jewel in the civil service. Year after year, it didn't just meet its targets, it surpassed them, enabling government to pay social grants to millions upon millions of poor people. SARS was hailed internationally, and its systems were studied by business schools over the world.

Long before I set out to write this book, it was revealed how the top structure of SARS – comprising Ivan Pillay, Gene Ravele, Johann van Loggerenberg, Pete Picher – was purged after a series of articles in the *Sunday Times* that they had run a "rogue unit". The stories were fabrications but nonetheless saw the rise of Zuma acolyte Tom Moyane as the hatchet man who rid SARS of its tried and tested top executives.

Van Loggerenberg wrote a book, *Rogue: The Inside Story of SARS's Elite Crime-Busting Unit*, in which he chronicled how his affair with a Pretoria attorney became the trigger for the "capture" of SARS and the departure of its experienced and independent-thinking officials.

What I discovered in my research for this book adds another, untold layer to the SARS narrative. I gave a handful of friends the chapters on SARS to read before publication. It left them devastated and disillusioned, and they agreed that they had never imagined the Zuma regime would descend to these lows to preserve its survival.

FIVE

Little altar boy

————•————

Sometime in 2015, a tall, upright man with a brooding demeanour and piercing green eyes walked into the headquarters of the South African Revenue Service (SARS) in Brooklyn, Pretoria. His name was Johann van Loggerenberg, the former group executive for SARS's tax and customs enforcement investigations. He had by then, earlier in February 2015, resigned from SARS but was ordered to report to the Lehae la SARS head office to remove files from the safe in his old office.

The safe was armoured with a combination of electronic and mechanical locks. It was among the safest safes at SARS; the kind you expect to find at the State Security Agency, the Hawks or the Presidency. It had to be, because ensconced in its belly were top-secret files about highly sensitive tax investigations.

In his book, *Rogue*, Van Loggerenberg described this event: "Certain files were kept in the safe in my old office and I had to hand them over to this official. Basically, I was told we had to ensure that files concerning matters of national importance were safeguarded. I made very sure I had sufficient evidence to prove that I went to the SARS offices that day and met certain people."

Van Loggerenberg didn't say in his book who requested the tax dossiers and what the contents were. His former colleagues who walked in to greet him saw him sifting through a pile of files and, an hour or so later, leaving with a box of folders. He was accompanied by the personal assistant of the new SARS number two man, Jonas Makwakwa.

Everybody knew why Van Loggerenberg was at SARS that day. It was about files relating to politically sensitive cases and investigations. The visit was much talked about at the time in SARS. One of the files concerned President Jacob Zuma, his family and his Nkandla compound. It was an open secret where the files were going and who ordered them: newly appointed SARS commissioner Tom Moyane and Jonas Makwakwa.

One of the files contained the details of Azeem Amodcaram, residing at United House, Lilian Road, Fordsburg, Johannesburg. An alleged tobacco smuggler who had "turned" and confessed to Van Loggerenberg and his investigators, he provided devastating evidence about payments to Zuma family members, associates and Nkandla. And of course, and you may have guessed, some of the files dealt with Zuma's pals, the Gupta family.

Other files detailed the tax history of Jacob Zuma, whom one would expect to set an example to the citizenry by diligently submitting his tax returns every year. It should be a given that the president is tax compliant.

At the time, SARS was an institution in flux. Earlier, in October 2014, Zuma unexpectedly appointed Tom Moyane as the new commissioner for the tax service. When his predecessor, Oupa Magashula, resigned owing to an alleged jobs-for-pals controversy, Moyane wasn't one of the 104 candidates that applied for the job. Moyane was appointed unannounced, even to the SARS executive. When he was head of South Africa's prisons, he was implicated in a tender scandal of over R378 million. One would assume that he didn't qualify for the SARS job. Although the president appoints the tax commissioner, it was the practice that the finance minister selected his candidate of choice and presented the name to the president, who then concluded the formalities. Zuma bucked the system, ignored his finance minister and dispatched a crony to Lehae la SARS. As soon as Moyane arrived, all hell broke loose.

In Moyane's sights were four men that Pravin Gordhan had groomed during his reign as SARS commissioner to lead the service into the new millennium and enable it to collect enough money to meet South Africa's vast social grants needs and developmental requirements. They were acting commissioner Ivan Pillay, strategic planning risk group executive Peter

Richer, and tax and customs investigations heads Humbulani Gene Ravele-Singo – better known as Gene Ravele – and Johann van Loggerenberg.

The reconstruction of SARS is a post-apartheid success story. Once the inefficient and clumsy Inland Revenue Service and a separate Customs and Excise department, it was remodelled into a mean tax-collecting and customs machine to serve as the engine driving South Africa's social democracy, including the funding of over 17 million grants to more than 10 million people every month. Its transformation has been chronicled in at least two international business school journals.

One of Gordhan's strategies was to establish investigative units to penetrate the "illicit economy". Criminals and tax evaders laundered, concealed and smuggled billions every year and were a potential gold mine to SARS. Pillay and his team did their work with great aplomb, mortally wounding some of the biggest hoodlums in the country while tapping billions in taxes from them. In the process, however, they crossed swords with the first family and their cronies.

Enter Tom Moyane. Within months, he had rid SARS of the "Gordhan Four" and many others, and dismantled virtually every investigative unit. This band of officials were idols in SARS and, when they left, they were followed by a host of highly skilled officials, among them many of SARS's most experienced top tax practitioners. One example was chief operating officer Barry Hore, who was in 1999 selected as one of the World Economic Forum's "100 Global Leaders for Tomorrow".

By adopting a strategy of wild allegations, media leaks and subterfuge, Moyane eradicated the most effective law enforcement unit in the country. As a result, a host of executives, managers and other skilled tax collectors quit the service, leaving behind a mortally wounded animal that continues bleeding experienced staff.

To get rid of the four, Moyane, without a shred of credible evidence, accepted false evidence that the "Gordhan Four" were complicit in running a "rogue unit" that committed a host of unlawful activities, ranging from housebreaking, spying on Zuma and other politicians, illegal interception of communications and illegal tax settlements to victimisation and whore-keeping.

None of it was true. There was no logic or lucidity in what Moyane did. Why destroy something that worked? Why jeopardise the most important state institution in the country, the jewel in the civil service crown? Why cut a hole in the public purse? South Africans – especially the poor – will pluck the fruit of his actions for many years to come. If SARS is broken, South Africa is broken.

Tax collections have slowed down across all categories, except dividends tax. In the 2016/17 tax year, SARS reported a R30 billion shortfall, the first time since the worldwide recession in 2009. Parliament heard in September 2017 that for the first quarter of the 2017/18 tax year, SARS had already recorded a R13 billion shortfall. SARS was expected to miss its overall target for the tax year by about R50 billion.

SARS had over a decade beefed up revenue by targeting the underworld economy for unpaid taxes, and it did not shy away from tracking down powerful people to pay their taxes. But since Moyane took over, many cases have been put on ice and the service now lacks the capacity and capabilities it once boasted. Some analysts have said that SARS, as part of Treasury, has become a key battleground in the attempts by outsiders to capture the state. That makes Tom Moyane a vital player in the much greater state capture drama.

While that might well be true, I believe that the answer to Moyane's deployment to SARS lies in the files that were secreted in Van Loggerenberg's safe. They tell the tale of the depravity of Jacob Zuma, members of his family and their cronies. Under the "old" SARS regime, these people were facing the full wrath of the tax collector. In the case of Zuma, it could have spelled calamity for his presidency and his fitness to hold high office.

Nobody was ever supposed to have access to the files in Van Loggerenberg's safe. The tax executive himself was very circumspect about the files and he didn't discuss their existence with anyone except a select group of his colleagues and superiors.

I haven't seen every document or every file, but I have been shown enough by my sources to conclude that one of the reasons why Zuma sent

Moyane to SARS was to make sure that the putrid skeletons in Van Loggerenberg's safe were transferred to the one in his office and stayed there.

Much of this detail has never been revealed before, and you are going to read about it in the next few chapters. It will show Tom Moyane as the ultimate Zuma altar boy, the ever-loyal acolyte who stands accused of getting rid of his master's tax difficulties – and those of his son, his nephew and his cronies.

*   *   *

I've been witness before to the mayhem and uncertainty that follow dramatic intervention at an institution such as SARS. I had closely observed the upheaval in the security forces just before and after the unbanning of the ANC in 1990. Droves of disillusioned and nervous operatives came forward and put their trust in me. Some were assassins who hoped that confession would save them from prison. Others wanted to negotiate an arrangement with the new rulers and wanted me to advance their case. Others were intent on revenge against their former masters because they felt betrayed and left to face the music.

SARS is no different. I don't think even the apartheid police and defence force were subjected post-1994 to the level of upheaval that was inflicted on SARS. What Tom Moyane did at SARS must count as one of the most brutal institutional interventions in democratic South Africa.

It was an open secret at SARS that Van Loggerenberg and his investigators had discovered something explosive about Jacob Zuma and his family. The investigators, sworn to secrecy, sealed the information. Van Loggerenberg briefed Pillay and Ravele and locked the files in his safe. Despite these measures, by the end of 2013 news leaked out that SARS was investigating Zuma and the media asked questions. SARS spokesperson Adrian Lackay gave a standard response that taxpayers' affairs are confidential. The investigation stayed under wraps.

During the Zuma investigation, a SARS official made copies of documents in one of the files, which included official debriefing notes of Azeem Amodcaram and an associate, affidavits they compiled (but were never signed), a spreadsheet that showed payments from a front company's bank account, extractions of cellphone text messages, and several other SARS documents. These weren't all the documents in the file, but they were enough to show a web of intrigue, subterfuge and money laundering that implicated some very important people.

I don't know what motivated that person. At the time of the investigations, there was already an onslaught against Pillay, Van Loggerenberg and the others. Maybe the person made the copies as an insurance, or to ensure the information wasn't buried somewhere.

Tom Moyane underestimated the resentment that would follow when he shafted four of the most revered and respected executives in the service. Many officials who stayed behind were disillusioned and uncertain about the future. Is my job safe? Am I next on Moyane's list? Do I have a future at SARS?

When I set out to expose Zuma's keepers, the SARS story was foremost on my mind because I was the first journalist in August 2014 to reveal that the State Security Agency (SSA) played a crucial role in orchestrating and plotting the demise of Pillay and the others. (More about that later.)

I settled my hopes on Johann van Loggerenberg as my "deep throat" for this book. When I exposed the SSA plot to unseat Van Loggerenberg and the others in 2014, he briefed me, with permission from Pillay, about the campaign to discredit him. More than two years on, I thought he would be aggrieved and angry about his downfall. Maybe he wanted revenge, in which case I was his man.

Well prior to these events, I once persuaded him to meet me for lunch at a Cape Town waterfront restaurant. I wanted to extract information from him about Julius Malema's tax affairs. We ordered *moules-frites* and I asked for a bottle of wine. Van Loggerenberg said he didn't drink during office hours and wanted a Coke. I knew there was no way I was going to butter him up. There was not going to be a "splash" for Sunday: not for page one; not even for page 11. He insisted on paying for himself and said he couldn't accept any gift from me.

Van Loggerenberg – known as JvL – has a steely and impenetrable persona. When I contacted him at the beginning of 2017 to arrange a meeting, he declined and said he had put SARS behind him and started a new life. I tried my best. Phrases like "deep background" and "off the record" didn't help. He was polite but terse and to the point. "Come on, you know what I've been through. They're probably watching me. I can't be seen with you. Not now. Maybe one day. Sorry, I can't help you. SARS is behind me."

I had drinks with a journalist friend during a research trip to Johannesburg in February 2017. When we discussed the SARS story, he said he had a potentially great contact in the service, but that the official was scared and not forthcoming. You try, he said and gave me the number. I called the official a few days later, said who I was and what I was doing, but the person refused to speak to me.

The next day, someone called me from another number and said my phone was not safe. I had to get a new phone number, and not in my name. I must then SMS my new number to this person. An hour later, I texted my new number. I received an SMS a while later. What do you want to know? I texted back that I wanted to know the real reasons why Moyane booted Pillay, JvL and the others.

Even if we tell you, you won't be able to publish it.

Why not?

It's about the president.

Oh yes, I will publish it. Believe me.

I got an SMS to meet the person at the Wimpy Bar on the R21 highway between OR Tambo Airport and Pretoria. I wanted to SMS back: why the fuck do people like you always meet at a Wimpy Bar?

As I sat down, the person – I assumed it was the SARS official – sent an SMS that he/she couldn't get away from work. We made another appointment. Two days later, I met two SARS officials in a students' bar in Hatfield in Pretoria. We started talking about SARS. They had incisive and authoritative knowledge of the service and claimed to have evidence to back it up. Much of what you are going to read about SARS stemmed from this meeting and these two people. They later introduced me to two former officials.

At one point during the meeting, they asked me: "Do you know the name Azeem Amodcaram?"

I sat forward. A few weeks before, an investigative journalist had mentioned this name to me as a key player around a SARS investigation into Nkandla. The journalist had attempted to speak to Amodcaram about his involvement in payments to the Zuma family. He/she had seen spreadsheets of payments but didn't have enough evidence to publish.

"Yes, I've heard of him."

"What have you heard?"

"He's a tobacco smuggler who was involved in payments to Zuma family members. SARS has spreadsheets of these payments."

They were taken aback by my answer and looked at one another. "Where did you hear this?"

"I can't tell you," I said. "But maybe there is another SARS leak."

"He is very, very important to the story you want to tell."

"Why?"

"He worked with a guy called Yusuf Kajee and another guy, Faizal Hattia. They were all in on it. But Kajee ultimately screwed him and stole all his money."

"How do you know that?"

"We've got some documents."

"Will you give them to me?"

"We will show them to you. We've got stuff about other cases as well."

"Like what?"

"Lots of Zuma's cronies were taken on by SARS. We'll show it to you. Those investigations are now either dead or are stalling. There's the Guptas, Nkandla, Robert Huang, Mark Lifman, you name them . . . those cases are now as good as gone."

"How come?"

"Moyane and his people have killed them or are busy killing them."

We met a few days later at the same place again. My one source had a white envelope and pushed it across the table to me. It contained a spreadsheet, reports, link charts, bank statements, text messages, a statement and internal SARS evaluations of the information.

I greedily scanned them. One of the documents detailed text messages, one of which caught my eye because someone wanted to "do sumting into that account".

"Who is the sender?"

"Azeem."

"And who received the message?"

"Edward Zuma."

"We only have some of the documents," they said as they explained a spreadsheet to me. "These spreadsheets were their way of keeping track of payments; their kind of bookkeeping. We got a few, but there are many more spreadsheets and records in files that JvL kept in his safe. Moyane's got them now."

As I scribbled in my notebook, one said: "There is something very important you have to understand."

"And that is?"

"These payments were the proceeds of crime. It was income generated through tobacco smuggling. Any person who received that money became complicit in crime."

* * *

In or around September 2013, two alleged tobacco smugglers, Azeem Amodcaram and Faizal Hattia, reported to SARS headquarters in Pretoria. They were in trouble and wanted to come clean. According to them, another alleged tobacco smuggler, Yusuf Kajee, had hijacked their business and stolen their money. On top of that, SARS was onto them for fraud, money laundering and tax evasion, and they wanted to try and negotiate a way out of their predicament.

The High-Risk Investigation Unit (HRIU) was tasked to debrief them. The HRIU was a tiny division of six people who worked on matters that presented a risk to other investigators. They reported to Johann van Loggerenberg. This was Tom Moyane's illusory "rogue unit".

SARS was at war with tobacco smugglers, and the illegal trade in cigarettes had reached epidemic proportions. In 2015 South Africa was rated among the top five countries in the world with the highest incidence of trade in illicit cigarettes, referred to as the "new gold". Tobacco smuggling costs the fiscus an estimated R3 billion a year because of tax evasion, money laundering and corruption. Profit margins approach 1,000 per cent in an industry that has grown into one of the largest organised criminal enterprises. Tobacco smuggling doesn't just deprive the state of taxes and duties, but it often masks other crimes, including money laundering, fraud, drug smuggling and human trafficking.

A host of small local manufacturers, wholesalers and importers sprouted across South Africa, and they were raking in millions. SARS registered Project Honey Badger, which targeted both the smaller companies and multinationals like British American Tobacco (BAT).

Johann van Loggerenberg said in his book *Rogue* that when his units focused on tobacco smuggling, they came up against the "interests of people with more influence and power than we could dream of in our wildest dreams". It is world captured by the likes of apartheid assassin Craig Williamson, notorious Zimbabwean arms tycoon John Bredenkamp, an alleged genocide-financier in Rwanda, Tribert Ayabatwa, and Capeland gangsters. It was also a playground for Jacob Zuma's eldest son, Edward, who received vast amounts from the tobacco smugglers.

In coming clean with SARS, Amodcaram and Hattia were not motivated by guilt or a sense of doing the right thing; they were intent on saving their own asses. Their statements to SARS exposed a tangled web of bribery, corruption, back-stabbing, double-dealing and deceit.

There are a few people I need to introduce here. The first is Yusuf Kajee, a colourful cigarette manufacturer and alleged tobacco smuggler from Pietermaritzburg in KwaZulu-Natal. He was a business associate of Hattia and Amodcaram. He and they had frequent falling-outs, stabbed one another in the back and bad-mouthed each other, but in the end kissed, made up and smuggled again. That is, until the last occasion, when Kajee supposedly took everything from Amodcaram, who claimed to have "made" Kajee and that Kajee was "nothing" were it not for him.

Kajee is of crucial importance in the narrative of this book because of his proximity to the Zuma clan. He was for years the subject of SARS investigations into tax evasion, money laundering and fraud involving hundreds of millions of rand.

In 2008, Jacob Zuma's eldest son, Edward, became a shareholder and director of Kajee's Amalgamated Tobacco Manufacturing (ATM). Kajee had applied for a cigarette manufacturing licence and hoped that a politically connected director on his board would fast-track his application. Zuma was a director until the end of 2011, but stayed on afterwards as a shareholder. According to Amodcaram, after Zuma resigned as a director of ATM, he became a "silent partner because of continuous media attacks on him".

In 2013, Kajee, Edward Zuma and controversial Zimbabwe-born businessman, Paul de Robillard, became directors in a consortium that had a majority shareholding in a new low-cost airline, Easyjet Holdings.

The SARS investigation into Kajee covered a substantial period when Edward Zuma was a company director. SARS repeatedly raided ATM on suspicion that they stored contraband tobacco. SARS found evidence that ATM had produced nearly four times more cigarettes than it declared. Kajee said the raids were nothing but harassment and accused SARS of a smear campaign. Kajee had once before been forced to liquidate and close a tobacco company because of SARS's investigations.

Edward is the most controversial of Zuma's estimated 22 children and is fiercely loyal to his dad. He studied law at the University of Zululand (he didn't finish) and was reportedly arrested in 2000 for rape, but the woman withdrew the charges after allegedly receiving "*inhlawulo*" (damages).

He's often in the news for the wrong reasons. He defaulted on a multi-million-rand loan, failed to pay his wedding planner a million bucks (his marriage made it onto *Top Billing* but lasted just three years), reportedly avoided paying maintenance for his son, and allegedly dealt in contraband cigarettes.

Edward is best known for his rage against those attacking his father. He recently said that ANC stalwart Mathews Phosa made him want to vomit. Former tourism minister Derek Hanekom was a "vile dog trained to maul a black skin" while Pravin Gordhan was "one of the most corrupt cadres of the ANC who thinks African natives are no better than just being sugar cane cutters who must be forever subservient to a master like him for sustenance".

The last person that is important for our narrative is Lloyd Hill, a convicted gang boss known in the underworld as "the Enforcer". The *Mail & Guardian* reported that Hill was released from prison at roughly the same time as the ANC was unbanned. Hill and Jacob Zuma became acquainted because of the support Hill gave the ANC during their war with Inkatha in the 1990s. Hill has been a Zuma family associate ever since.

Hill's brushes with the law continued. He was arrested in December 1995 near Cape Town with thousands of poached abalone. The case disappeared. He was apprehended for murder in 2002 for being part of a gang that allegedly abducted and killed a state witness in a case against a Durban businessman. One of the killers turned state witness and implicated Hill and the others. He was found strangled in a cell in Durban's Westville prison. The case fell apart. In 2003, Hill survived a gang shootout but was wounded in the stomach, chest and hand.

According to the *Mail & Guardian*, he became a director of a company called Goldridge Trading, but resigned a month later when the company became part of the Gupta empire. Hattia told the SARS investigators that Hill "gets things done for Edward Zuma" and added: "Lloyd and Edward are very close together. If Kajee ever gets in trouble, the first person he will phone is Edward Zuma."

* * *

SARS separated Faizal Hattia and Azeem Amodcaram, and in October 2013 started debriefing them in detail. They were interviewed for hours at a time, and notes and recordings of the sessions were made.

Two other teams were brought onto the case. Their versions were compared with one another and verified against evidence independently obtained during the tax collector's nationwide tobacco investigations, known as Project Honey Badger. Both Hattia and Amodcaram were significant players in the illicit tobacco trade and opened a window into one of the most fascinating criminal enterprises in the country.

Their debriefing lasted three days and ran into tens of pages of notes. These detailed their cellphone numbers, their families, their financial histories, their associates, their smuggling activities, how they laundered money, evaded tax and much, much more. The debriefing notes would eventually have been converted into affidavits.

Amodcaram gave SARS text messages between himself, Edward Zuma and Lloyd Hill. He also gave them a spreadsheet that detailed payments from an account of a company named Royal Sonnic. This was Amodcaram and Kajee's "off-book" record of the payments. They allegedly washed and laundered money derived from smuggling through this company's bank account. The account of Royal Sonnic was used to pay and bribe a host of other smugglers and business associates, including Edward Zuma and Lloyd Hill.

"We smuggled cigarette stock into South Africa with transporters and people who were connected at the border. The smuggled cigarettes were delivered to Royal Sonnic's door," declared Amodcaram. He said that Kajee and he "simply used the existing business structures of Royal Sonnic to conduct our illegal cigarette businesses".

SARS launched a full-scale investigation into Amodcaram's allegations. They investigated his cellphone messages and records, the front company's bank account through which proceeds of the alleged smuggling enterprise were laundered, and the spreadsheets of the payments made. The findings corroborated what the smugglers had told them. There were payments to themselves and a host of tobacco smugglers. There were payouts in rands, US dollars and British pounds. They paid for overseas trips to Dubai and Mauritius, furniture, lawyers and a host of cars which included three Mercedes-Benzes, a Range Rover, three BMWs, a Ferrari and a Lamborghini. I have to mention in their defence that they donated R140,000 to "charitable causes".

Edward Zuma invited Amodcaram to his wedding. On 14 September 2011, Zuma SMSed him: "U r invited to my wedding on the 8th October 2011 in Nkandla at 11am yo presence will b appreciated."

On 5 October 2011 at 04:39:29AM, Amodcaram sent this message to

Edward Zuma: "Morning chief I need your bank details to do sumting into that account."

Zuma replied on the same day at 04:51:15AM and provided his account number and details: "e m zuma fnb florida branch".

A SARS analysis detailed payments to Edward Zuma, Hill and a person by the name of Thulani, who received smaller amounts. The spreadsheets also revealed payments for "Nthanthla". Amodcaram explained this was the code word for Nkandla and that the payments were destined for the upkeep of Jacob Zuma's compound. It was all paid in cash.

In January and February 2010, R66,880.81 was paid to Edward Zuma and Hill. This included a R20,000 cash payment to Zuma, an instalment of R14,547.48 on a BMW X5 and R1,283.33 for the vehicle's insurance. The BMW instalment was paid every month. Edward Zuma drove a black BMW X5 at the time. When he failed to pay his wedding bill, the sheriff of the court threatened to repossess the BMW and sell it on auction. He couldn't because it wasn't registered in Zuma's name.

In the following month, R76,278.81 was paid out and in April 2010 R75,830.81. This included a payment of R20,000 in cash for Edward Zuma and R10,000 for "Nthanthla".

In May 2010, an amount of R101,830.81 – again R10,000 for "Nthanthla" – was paid out, and in June and July a total of R35,830.81 for each month. The amount for August 2010 was R58,267.81. In September 2010, Edward Zuma took R30,000 in cash and there was also an instalment for R10,095.49 for a Mercedes CLK 500. In the following month, Edward Zuma was paid R60,000 in cash. Amodcaram and Kajee paid out altogether R140,708.47 in October 2010.

My SARS sources didn't have records of all the payments that Kajee and Amodcaram made to "Nthanthla", Edward Zuma and Hill, but said they continued until at least April 2012. According to a SARS report about the debriefing, "approximately R15,000 was paid on a monthly basis for the Nkandla home of President Zuma".

I do not have all the answers and details around the payments to Nkandla. There is no evidence that it was handed to Jacob Zuma. My SARS sources reckoned that Edward Zuma got the money and that he in turn delivered it to Nkandla.

The SARS enforcement unit was investigating the Royal Sonnic account in detail when Moyane arrived at SARS. The tax collector was building a case against Yusuf Kajee's Delta Tobacco – his first tobacco plant, which the tax collector had closed and liquidated. SARS now got information that Kajee was using Royal Sonnic to launder money.

The directors of Delta – which included Edward Zuma – would most likely have been charged with racketeering, tax evasion, money laundering and fraud. Edward Zuma was at the time already being investigated because of his directorship in ATM – Kajee's company which replaced Delta Tobacco when SARS shut it down. It is inconceivable that Edward Zuma could plead ignorance and say he didn't know where the money came from. A simple internet search would have enlightened him about Yusuf Kajee's alleged shenanigans.

SARS would have investigated the beneficiaries of the laundered money to determine if they had declared the Royal Sonnic "income" in their tax returns. This included the final recipient of the "Nthanthla" money. It is unlikely that the recipients would have disclosed these proceeds, because how would they have explained where the money came from? This would have unleashed a full tax audit on all the recipients.

My SARS sources said: "The bottom line is that Zuma's household, Edward and their gangster friends might all have benefited from the proceeds of crime. If so, that means racketeering, money laundering, tax evasion and customs fraud charges at the very least. They can spin it as they want, but they were probably the beneficiaries of the income of smuggled tobacco."

Another SARS internal note shows that Van Loggerenberg briefed Ivan Pillay and Gene Ravele about the revelations of Azeem Amodcaram and Faizal Hattia in January 2014. They ordered him to lock the file in his safe while SARS waited for Jacob Zuma to submit his outstanding tax returns.

* * *

In February 2014, a struggle stalwart greeted his former intelligence commander in the west wing of the Union Buildings in Pretoria. The one was the acting commissioner of SARS; the other the president of South Africa.

Ivan Pillay and Jacob Zuma suffered hardship and broke bread in exile in Mozambique while plotting the overthrow of the apartheid government. Pillay, born and bred in Durban, went into exile in the wake of the 1976 Soweto uprising. After receiving military training, he commanded Umkhonto we Sizwe's esteemed MJK (Mandla Judson Kuzwayo) unit, which infiltrated cadres back into South Africa.

Pillay was also a central committee member of the South African Communist Party. Pillay, alongside Zuma, was a central figure in Operation Vula. While Zuma was head of intelligence, Pillay reported directly to ANC president Oliver Tambo, oversaw logistics and had to set up an infrastructure to send people and weapons into South Africa as part of the operation.

When the two shook hands in February 2014, it wasn't to reminisce about the struggle years. Pillay was in the west wing on official business to brief the president about sensitive SARS projects and to inform him that SARS had stumbled upon what seemed to be illicit cash payments for both his son and his Nkandla homestead. Pillay was also there to plead with the president to comply with his tax obligations and submit his tax returns.

Pillay had much on his mind that day. SARS was under siege. Outside forces, which included SSA agents, law enforcement officials, and disgruntled current and former SARS officials, were waging a campaign to rid SARS of its top executives. Less than a year after speaking to the president, Pillay and three other SARS executives were suspended and eventually resigned. Many more followed in the wake of what unfolded then.

Pillay briefly referred to this meeting with Zuma in a 2015 affidavit to the Labour Court. Pillay said he had presented Zuma with a document titled "Common interests between SARS and SSA", an account of "attempts to malign and discredit SARS; and concerns about the role of SSA agents in the tobacco industry".

My SARS "deep throats" showed me a confidential memorandum about the meeting. It appears from the memo that it was at times an acrimonious episode that revealed Pillay as a virtuous and straight-shooting civil servant, while Zuma was entangled in his web of backers and benefactors. At one point, the president apparently even jumped from his chair to protest when Pillay confronted him with evidence that officials in the Presidency were digging for dirt against him and SARS.

This meeting is pivotal to the unfolding spectacle of Jacob Zuma, his clinging to power and desperate attempts by others to protect him at all cost – even if it meant the destruction of SARS.

When SARS came under the leadership of Pravin Gordhan, first as commissioner and later as finance minister, he instilled in his underlings the doctrine of the "higher purpose". This ethic imposed on the service the responsibility to act as a mechanism to help the state deliver on its social contract by collecting the revenue that would fund government programmes providing services to the citizenry.

Zuma himself has sung the praises of the tax collector. He said in a speech in August 2011: "It is no flattery or exaggeration to single out the South African Revenue Service as one of the most efficient, effective, highly regarded, fair and trusted institutions of state over a prolonged and sustained period. For without this faith and trust in SARS, our ability as a government to finance our programme of action in meeting the needs of our people would be seriously undermined. It is imperative for SARS to maintain its independence, its values, its moral authority and its objectivity."

These were empty words, uttered by a man who was – as you will come to learn – a serial tax offender and made little effort over a period spanning many years to settle his tax affairs.

*   *   *

Jacob Zuma is one of the world's highest-paid heads of state. In 2016, he earned R2.75 million annually (about R230,000 per month) – more than his counterparts in Russia, Brazil and Japan. South Africa's Number One falls into a new, super tax bracket announced by finance minister Pravin Gordhan in his 2017 budget speech. It means that he forfeits more than 40 per cent of his presidential income to the fiscus.

But the president is showered with fringe benefits. We feed him and his large, ever-expanding family, we dress them, we house them, we pay his ever-increasing legal bills (he mostly loses his cases, which means we also pay the legal costs of his opponents) and we ferry them around the world, always accompanied by large numbers of bodyguards and blue-light cavalcades.

The Times reported that the first five years of his presidency cost the taxpayer an estimated R517 million, which included his medical aid, helicopter flights, overseas allowances, hotels, private vehicles and spousal support. Polygamy comes at a cost and in 2016 the state bought 10 luxury cars for his four wives at a cost of R9 million. That was enough to fund 116 university students for a year or hire another 61 police officers.

With so many fringe benefits, one would expect Zuma to dutifully pay his taxes and submit his annual returns. He has several legal counsels at his beck and call, and SARS has a division, the VIP Taxpayer Unit, that deals with the taxes of prominent politicians, cabinet ministers and top civil servants.

One of the founding fathers of the United States, Benjamin Franklin, once said there are only two certainties in life: death and taxes. That is not the case if your name is Jacob Gedleyihlekisa Zuma. Political commentators and analysts often talk about his nine political lives and his uncanny ability to survive. One can almost speak of his nine SARS lives as well.

I divide Zuma's tax history in two parts: before he took high office in May 2009, and his rule as president since then. Before he was sworn in, his taxes were in a mess because of the alleged bribes and donations that everyone from Nelson Mandela to Schabir Shaik showered on him. Zuma and Shaik have maintained that the payments to him were nothing but donations to pay for, among other things, the education of the Zuma offspring.

For several years in the 2000s, the VIP Taxpayer Unit of SARS begged Zuma to submit his tax returns and become tax compliant. This unit doesn't do audits or investigations but assists "restricted taxpayers" to submit their returns and sort out their tax predicaments. Their records are sealed and not accessible except to a handful of top officials who have access to the unit's database.

This is how it was described to me: "They work softly with tax offenders to avoid embarrassment to government. They quietly inform a minister or director-general that his returns are outstanding and will assist him to become compliant. They don't make trouble; they help the top echelons of government to quietly settle their tax affairs if they are not compliant."

After the VIP unit finally received Zuma's returns, he was audited and assessed. The man in charge of his assessment was Ivan Pillay, who was then general manager of enforcement. Top SARS officials sat for days with Zuma's attorney, Michael Hulley, to sort out his taxes.

Public records show that SARS had a devil of a time to get Zuma to comply with his tax obligations. In February 2007, a summons to appear in court was served on Zuma by SARS because he had ignored a demand from the tax collector to provide further information and documentation to back up his tax returns.

On 11 April 2007 Hulley appeared on behalf of Zuma in court and paid a R500 admission of guilt fine for contravening the Income Tax Act. Court records reflect that Zuma admitted to contravening section 75 of the Income Tax Act of 1962 by failing to disclose information to SARS. A summons for Zuma's appearance before court was stayed by the prosecutor and the case was removed from the court roll. How exactly this worked was explained to me by a prosecutor.

One could say that Zuma has technically been convicted of a crime. But these offences are considered misdemeanours, much like a person not paying a traffic fine and then summonsed to appear before a court with the option to pay an additional fine to avoid doing so. At the time, prosecutors had the discretion to issue the option of an admission of guilt fine to people who were summonsed to appear before court for such offences. They are called "J175s". This discretion was intended to afford prosecutors the means to process matters through the system when people who were charged were prepared to accept guilt and save the court a lot of time.

It was incredibly difficult to confirm this information about Zuma and there is hardly any reference to it, maybe because it happened in Durban. Newspapers reported the issuing of the summons, but not the admission of guilt, probably because Hulley told them: "The matter has been resolved. We consider Mr Zuma's tax affairs to be private and so there is nothing to say."

This event is important for two reasons. The first is that Pillay and people under him did Zuma's audit and SARS showed that they were going to treat Zuma like any other taxpayer. Several years on, this knowledge would have lingered in his mind. The second is that it illustrates Zuma's total scorn for SARS and for his obligation to be tax compliant.

Zuma's pre-presidential tax affairs were laid bare when the National Prosecuting Authority (NPA) charged him with racketeering, corruption and tax evasion days after his election as ANC president in Polokwane in December 2007. According to the indictment filed in the Pietermaritzburg High Court, Zuma failed to submit tax returns for nine years from 1995 to 2003. The NPA alleged that he hadn't declared any of the 583 Shaik payments. He failed to declare taxable income of R2.7 million and evaded tax of R1.6 million.

Zuma filed a review application in response to the NPA indictment in June 2008. He didn't deny that he hadn't submitted his returns or that he owed R1.6 million, but said the NPA was on an "improper frolic of its own". He argued that it was "wholly improper and unlawful of the NPA" to prosecute him without the necessary consultations and go-ahead from SARS.

Zuma said that he wanted to sort out his tax problems because "it is the right thing to do for a person in my position and political role". He said he accepted SARS's assessment of his tax debt even though he disagreed with it. He said he didn't want "political enemies to have any reason to make political capital out of my income tax affairs". He added that the dispute between him and SARS was resolved and that he had paid his tax debt and that SARS's claim had been settled in full. In his judgment, Judge Chris Nicholson said the NPA had "thrown the book" at Zuma by including charges relating to tax evasion. He found that the charges against Zuma were invalid and set them aside.

At the time SARS would not comment on the indictment and said: "The confidentiality provisions contained in tax legislation prohibit SARS from publicly disclosing details pertaining to the tax affairs of particular tax-payers." Zuma and tax offenders like him have for years hidden behind this secrecy clause in the Income Tax Act. It prevents SARS from revealing or publishing the tax matters of any individual. It means that you are not allowed to know if Zuma – or any other senior public official – is tax compliant and has diligently paid his or her taxes, excises, duties and levies to the fiscus. This secrecy provision might well be unconstitutional in a modern democracy and is ripe for challenge in the Constitutional Court.

The disclosure of Zuma's tax affairs, especially where it relates to possible criminality and statutory non-compliance, is undoubtedly in the public's interest. We have a right to know if he has paid his taxes, and he should not be able to hide behind a secrecy clause to avoid exposure or censure. The secrecy clause hampers every honest taxpayer's and voter's ability to make an informed decision to vote for his or her choice for higher office. In fact, ideally the tax affairs of senior civil servants, public officials and political office-bearers should be public knowledge as a matter of course.

There are precedents in multiple instances in which newspapers and publications have revealed the tax affairs of individuals. To date, there is no record or instance known where SARS acted against any media house which published information of this kind.

SIX

President on a payroll

————•————

Once Jacob Zuma ascended to the highest office on 6 May 2009, one would have hoped that he had changed his ways and obeyed the laws of the land. He didn't, and failed to submit a tax return for his first year in office. This was no exception. He didn't submit a tax return for the second year, either. Or the third or the fourth.

By 2011, the VIP Taxpayer Unit was again begging the president to get his tax affairs in order. At the time, this unit reported directly to Ivan Pillay, who was concerned that Zuma's non-compliance would create a political fallout and cause people to pitch SARS against the president. He appointed Mark Kingon to handle this predicament. Kingon, Pillay and Ravele had meetings with both Hulley and Zuma – one was held in Durban – where the president's onus to submit his returns was (yet again) explained to him. The majority of subsequent meetings appear to have been between Kingon and Hulley.

At the time, ironically, Zuma addressed the SARS award ceremony in Johannesburg and said the tax service must "act without fear or favour in ensuring the full compliance with the law by every South African – irrespective of who they are or what office they may hold. SARS plays an important role in the fight against fraud and corruption, through working with enforcement agencies in rooting out non-compliance."

There are probably three reasons why Zuma didn't want to submit his tax returns. The first was more than likely the predicament of the Nkandla upgrades. Much has been written about Zuma's Versailles; this sprawling symbol of corruption and sleaze that will forever be a shrine to his calami-tous rule. As Richard Poplak has written in *Daily Maverick*: "Zuma's crib, regardless of its miserly vision and its relatively low sticker price, was always more powerful as a symbol – it reminded us that post-apartheid South Africa was a kleptocracy built on the ruins of a kleptocracy, a fact perfectly expressed by an architectural botch-job replete with remote-controlled chicken pens and a fire-pool."

After it was exposed by the *Mail & Guardian* for the first time in November 2009, it took a host of newspaper revelations, 12,000 pages of publicly released documents, dozens of parliamentary debates, millions in legal costs, the scalps of two ministers, a 400-page public protector report and a Constitutional Court ruling to force Zuma to make an insincere apology and pay for a small fraction of the upgrades.

Legally, Zuma owed millions of rand in tax on the fringe benefits that accrued to him because of these upgrades. He has always maintained that they were security-related and that he didn't ask for them. He argued he was therefore not responsible for any taxes. As the extent of the upgrades became more apparent in 2012, the tax effects on Zuma became equally clear.

Fringe benefits must be declared by taxpayers, who are then taxed on these annually as a matter of course by SARS. According to the seventh schedule of the Income Tax Act, there is no doubt that Zuma owed SARS for the benefits he derived from the upgrades to Nkandla. Whether the upgrades were security-related or not is irrelevant. The fact remains that he received significant fringe benefits. Tax law determines that tax is owed whether such benefit is "voluntary or otherwise".

It thus wouldn't have helped Zuma to argue that he didn't ask for the upgrades – this didn't matter either. He anyway discussed the details of the upgrades with his architect, and instructed that he take the lead on the project. He had also received correspondence relating to the upgrades. The public protector later found that not all the upgrades were security-related and that Zuma had to pay for those.

SARS determined that Zuma was probably liable for taxable fringe benefits of around R145,185,235 relating to the upgrades. Taxation of this amount at a rate of 40 per cent is R58,074,094. Because Zuma hadn't declared these fringe benefits, a penalty of 10 per cent – amounting to R5,807,409 – would have to be added, plus additional interest. This alone would have brought his tax bill for Nkandla to R63,881,503.

Even if Zuma were to repay the state for some of the Nkandla upgrades, it wouldn't automatically exempt him from having to pay tax on these fringe benefits. Income Tax Case 1346 44 SATC 31 established that even if an employee repays an amount that was determined to be a taxable income in a prior year, it may not be offset against the taxable income of the year in which it was repaid. It may also not be offset against the taxable income of the year in which the taxable amount was received.

By October 2013, SARS had completed its preliminary inquiries into the upgrades and other aspects of Zuma's non-compliance with tax laws. The file was kept with the VIP Taxpayer Unit and locked away while SARS waited for Zuma's tax submissions. Although Michael Hulley had promised that Zuma would submit his returns, nothing was forthcoming. SARS, mainly through Kingon, kept on nagging Hulley to comply, but Hulley just kept on giving SARS the runaround.

If SARS had received Zuma's returns, they would have examined his declarations to see, among other things, whether the fringe benefits were declared. If Zuma had declared the upgrades, the VIP Taxpayer Unit would have presented him with his tax bill, which would more than likely have been an amount of over R64 million, including penalties and interest for late submission and non-payment.

But let's play devil's advocate. Assuming Zuma had declared the benefits of Nkandla, his returns could potentially have included a motivation as to why he believed he shouldn't be held responsible for the upgrades and why he would not agree with such a tax assessment.

He could, if assessed, have objected to such an assessment and, if this was denied, he could also have appealed against the decision. Ultimately, he could have gone to a tax court to argue the matter, and if he was still unhappy, he could've gone to the Supreme Court of Appeal. If he was still unsatisfied with having to pay tax on the Nkandla fringe benefits, he could then have turned to the Constitutional Court.

Of course, all of this would've led to the entire matter becoming public, something one can guess he wouldn't want. The law stipulates that even in cases going on appeal in tax courts, the tax defaulter must still pay their tax. This is known as the "pay now, argue later" principle, which the Constitutional Court confirmed in the early 2000s. This rule makes sense because if every taxpayer in the country was to delay paying tax by simply objecting, appealing and tying up their cases in legal litigation – something Zuma has shown to be quite adept at – then the country's coffers would soon run dry. Clearly, whatever route Zuma might have chosen, he would have had to pay up.

But my sources tell me that by May 2015 Zuma had still not submitted his returns. He behaved as though he was above the law. His failure to submit his returns would have triggered a full-scale audit, which would have landed with one of SARS's penalty committees. Such a committee might have mandated further penalties and even criminal prosecution, which is hard to fathom.

Imagine if all taxpaying companies in the country upgraded the homes of their employees out of pre-tax profits, complete with swimming pool (call it a fire-pool if you like), security gates and electric fences, a couple of new additions to their dwellings, their own personal amphitheatres, a cattle kraal and a chicken pen. Imagine what would happen if all these companies and employees then decided not to, or failed to, declare this to SARS, and then declined to pay their fringe benefits tax on these home improvements. Our taxes would dry up in just one financial year.

One must question, once again, the quality of the legal advice that Zuma received. In theory, there was a way out of his Nkandla predicament. The Remuneration of Public Office Bearers Act 20 of 1998 specifically refers to the taxation of remuneration and allowances granted to the president. Section 2(2) provides that the National Assembly may by resolution decide what portion of the president's remuneration shall be exempt from tax as an allowance under section 8(1)(d) of the Income Tax Act. I have no doubt that Parliament would very happily have passed such a resolution, had Zuma been upfront and sincere about Nkandla. But of course, he couldn't ask for this at the time because it would have contradicted his own version he had put to Parliament and the country. His catch-22 situation had caught up with him.

But such a solution is of academic value, since it would have been of no avail to him if the National Assembly, at this late stage, had attempted to pass such a resolution in any event. The tax liability was incurred in an earlier year, so the passing of a resolution in a subsequent tax year would not have helped Zuma's tax predicament in any case.

My SARS "deep throats" told me how, on the occasion that Zuma met Pillay and others, he insisted that the upgrades were none of his business. At the time, an "alternative viewpoint" was floated in some circles within the service that Zuma was not liable for tax on the fringe benefits because the land on which the Nkandla homestead was built did not belong to him. This may have been a view put forward by Hulley and Zuma, but it was rejected because the president explained in Parliament that Nkandla was his homestead, was bonded with a commercial bank, and he and his family enjoyed the benefits of these upgrades.

Zuma told a crowd in Gugulethu in March 2014: "I did not use the public's money in Nkandla. What I'm saying is I'm not guilty. Even if they look for me under a tree they can't find me. I did nothing wrong. I did not do anything . . .They go around and say this fella used public money. I am not guilty, there is no case against me."

There might be another reason why Zuma was hesitant to submit his tax returns: "alternative" sources of income. There is, firstly, the "Nthanthla" payments that the alleged tobacco smugglers made from their Royal Sonnic bank account. I don't know what happened to the money or whether it was indeed delivered to Zuma and his Nkandla household. The president – via Edward Zuma – may have known that SARS was aware of some of these payments. What if he didn't declare them in his tax returns and SARS established that the money was indeed handed to the president?

I have heard during the writing of this book about other payments – especially in brown envelopes – that were delivered to Zuma and to Nkandla.

And let me not even start with the Gupta family and others like them. It is, however, impossible to substantiate any of these claims as a fact.

My SARS sources gave a fascinating account of an incident in early 2011 when a "donation for Nkandla" arrived on a private jet at King Shaka International Airport outside Durban. When customs inspected the cargo, they found, among other things, medical equipment on board. The shipment originated in Russia and the sender was a man by the name of Vladimir Strzhalkovsky.

An internet search revealed that Strzhalkovsky is a former KGB agent who joined the ranks of post-communist Russia's oligarchs and became one of the biggest businessmen in that country. He is the former CEO of Norilsk Nickel, the world's largest nickel and palladium producer. Strzhalkovsky received a R1.4 billion payout in 2012 to step down from Norilsk Nickel.

My sources told me that the medical equipment on board the aeroplane was a mobile clinic for Nkandla. SARS impounded the equipment because it didn't have the required clearance certificates and documents. Vivian Reddy, Zuma benefactor and friend, contacted SARS commissioner Oupa Magashula, insisting they release the shipment without following due process. Strzhalkovsky was due to visit South Africa where he would present the clinic to Zuma at Nkandla. Magashula refused to budge.

Enter the minister of state security, Siyabonga Cwele. He informed Magashula that the cargo on board Strzhalkovsky's plane concerned "state security" and that his agents were taking control of the shipment. Magashula relented because national security overrode the customs laws of SARS.

At the end of March 2011, the Russian multinational Norilsk Nickel said in a press statement that Vladimir Strzhalkovsky had visited Jacob Zuma and had handed the president a Russian mobile telemedicine laboratory at Nkandla. Siyabonga Cwele was present at the ceremony. Norilsk said in its statement: "Jakob [sic] Zuma expressed high opinion of the Company's current projects in the country. He emphasized that South Africa is ready to proceed with supporting the participation of Norilsk Nickel in new ore extraction and processing projects in South Africa."

"But that is not the end of it," said my source. "The medical equipment wasn't all that SARS detained on that day at the airport."

"What else?"

"There was also a lot of cash on that plane. A lot. SARS detained the entire plane with everything on board. When Cwele moved in, he took over the whole shipment, including the money. The money was also not declared and therefore illegally imported. Its origin and destination were never determined. But I think it makes sense that the clinic and the money had the same end destination."

*   *   *

What I discovered next was almost too fantastic: implausible and far-fetched. Have you ever heard of any head of state anywhere in the universe who was, while running the affairs of his country, also an employee of a private company?

In 2010, a SARS auditor in the Durban office of the revenue collector was doing a routine tax compliance check of a security company by the name of Royal Security. The company's founding member and director is Roy Moodley, who is a public friend of Jacob Zuma and an ANC benefactor. The company has offices and security personnel in at least six provinces and says on its website it has three thousand clients and contracts with the police, First National Bank, Engen, Transnet, MTN and Telkom.

Employers are by law required to deduct tax from employees monthly and pay this over to SARS. At the end of the year, they submit a payroll reconciliation to SARS and an IRP5 certificate to the employee, showing how much tax has been paid to SARS on the employee's behalf.

It was explained to me that SARS uses reconciliations to ensure that the tax which employers claim to have paid to SARS on behalf of their employees and the income declared by the same employees add up. It is a criminal offence for any employer to deduct tax from an employee and not pay this over to SARS. It seems a simple enough process: if employers and employees both declare the correct facts to SARS, then the numbers should balance.

The Royal Security payroll reconciliations that the SARS official scrutinised included the tax years 1 March 2009 to 28 February 2010. From what I could establish, Royal Security was not under SARS investigation and it seemed at face value to have been tax compliant.

However, one of the Royal Security employees on the reconciliation raised a red flag because the auditor was unable to determine whether tax had been deducted from his salary and paid to SARS. The employee was remunerated at an amount of R1 million per month. Income tax on that salary bracket would have been around R400,000 per month. The employee was J.G. Zuma, which didn't raise any unusual suspicions from the official until he searched for the details of the taxpayer on the SARS mainframe. Access to the employee's tax records and employment history was blocked because his affairs were being handled by the VIP Taxpayer Unit.

It dawned on the official: J.G. Zuma, employed by Royal Security, was none other than Jacob Gedleyihlekisa Zuma, the fourth president of democratic South Africa.

* * *

At his 60th birthday bash at Durban's International Convention Centre in February 2014, the son of the flamboyant security tycoon Chockalingam "Roy" Moodley told the attendees that his father was the most powerful man in the country. Nobody blinked, not even Jacob Zuma, who was the guest of honour and sat at Moodley's table.

When the president delivered the keynote address at the horseracing-themed bash, he said to Moodley: "You're a friend, comrade." He then bumbled in true Zuma style: "We have something to do with you during elections which we have discussed with you. It will be impacting on people in different ways. I want him to impact on certain people in a few months. Your friends and colleagues here vote well."

Zuma and Moodley come a long way. When the ANC leader was inaugurated as president in May 2009, Moodley was one of his VIP guests. He was, however, unhappy with his seat allocation, and when he registered for the event before the inauguration, he allegedly attempted to bribe a woman at the accreditation table with R100. He was arrested and charged. The case was later dropped after Moodley said the money was a mere "token of appreciation for efficient service rendered". The state dropped the case and said there was a "misunderstanding".

However insignificant this event might seem, it says something about Moodley's disposition, doesn't it? There have for years been rumours that he has been bankrolling both Zuma and his family. He is also reportedly a generous contributor to the ANC and was previously ward chairperson of the organisation's Umhlanga branch in KwaZulu-Natal.

When public protector Thuli Madonsela did her *State of Capture* report, she submitted a list of 42 questions to Zuma. One of the questions was about his relationship with Moodley. Zuma refused to answer her. Their friendship has nonetheless been public, warm and beneficial. Moodley is an avid racehorse owner (he had 51 winners in the 2014/15 season) and in 2010 Zuma famously won R15,000 at the Durban July and was pictured flaunting the cash alongside Moodley. The two were again pictured together at the 2016 Durban July.

News24 reported in 2016 that mystery surrounded payments of R550 million to Moodley by a tender-rich IT security company. Siyangena Technologies won disputed contracts from one of our many ailing and besieged parastatals, the Passenger Rail Agency of South Africa (Prasa), worth R4 billion, and in turn paid large sums of money to companies directly linked to Moodley.

The news site said that Siyangena is co-owned by soccer boss Mario Ferreira, whose relationship with Moodley seems to involve more than just business; they are co-owners of local racehorses.

The payments from Siyangena to Moodley were the third example of large, unexplained payments that Prasa contractors made to individuals closely linked to Zuma and his family.

* * *

The "J.G. Zuma" tax query from the Durban auditor at the regional office in Durban caused a minor consternation at head office in Pretoria. The auditor escalated the matter to SARS audit boss Jonas Makwakwa. He reported the matter to Oupa Magashula.

I want to pause for a moment at Makwakwa. He became Tom Moyane's number two after the departure of the "Gordhan Four" and has been described to me as an ambitious official who seized this opportunity to gain more influence and power. It was rumoured at SARS at the time that Makwakwa wanted to use the Royal Security/Zuma case to gain access to the president, and then somehow come to his "rescue". Makwakwa had no struggle background and apparently considered this a hindrance to his career at SARS. This case was perfect for him to achieve his ambitions.

Magashula reassigned the case, however, to Mark Kingon at the VIP Tax-payer Unit. This might have angered Makwakwa, because the next moment SARS received two media enquiries about the Royal Security payments to Zuma. The Presidency received similar enquiries and accused Magashula of undermining the president. SARS gave the usual "we do not discuss the affairs of taxpayers" and the allegations were never published.

My sources told me that Makwakwa underwent a polygraph test because he was considered the possible leak. They didn't know what the outcome of the polygraph was, but he kept a much lower profile afterwards. He had a chance to reimpose his lost authority with the arrival of Tom Moyane. He was the only executive committee member left with tax administration experience and the new SARS boss turned to him for advice and leadership.

My SARS sources mentioned this case at the outset of our relationship, but had little detail. I sent them back to scrounge for more information and they eventually gave me the names of the two journalists who sent the enquiries. I met one of them, and it was a tricky and uncomfortable occasion because I didn't want him/her to even sense that I had more information. I said I had been told about his/her enquiry to SARS and wanted to know if he/she had more. It turned out that the journalist had met the source only once, who gave a brief outline of the case. The source promised much more, but failed to pitch up for further meetings.

My SARS sources eventually reported back with as much as they could find. I was initially disappointed that they couldn't show me documents, but they said there were none. The records were interned at the VIP Tax-payer Unit and there was nothing on paper. All the employment details about J.G. Zuma, they said, must be on the system and are difficult to access.

My sources said that Royal Security ultimately paid the taxes due to SARS on behalf of the "employee" (J.G. Zuma) and the matter, at least from the company's perspective, was laid to rest. Moodley paid the tax via bank transfer.

They said – and this is the crux of the matter – that Zuma was employed at the security company for at least four months after becoming president. It means that for the first months of his presidency, Zuma's boss was Roy Moodley. These payments to Zuma must give Moodley an iron hold over Zuma.

What Zuma allegedly did was dishonest, unlawful and unconstitutional. He came close to losing his presidency after the Constitutional Court ruled in 2016 that he had failed to uphold the Constitution. But this is much worse.

* * *

If Zuma's only income since he took office in 2009 was his presidential salary, it would have been simple and straightforward to become tax compliant. But he didn't dare to submit his return because it could have opened him up for penalties, interest and even prosecution.

What's more is that while he may have been able to play with words in the public domain, he would have stood and fallen by what he declared in his return. He would have had to declare the Nkandla upgrades as fringe benefits, security-related or not, and he would have had to declare all other income that he may have received over the years from any number of sources, in cash, by way of gifts or as the additional salary he allegedly earned during his first few months as president. He would not have been given a second chance, because a tax declaration is cast in stone. You sign it and declare that what is stated is the truth, and you will be held to it.

Zuma was in deep trouble, because the officials that dealt with Zuma's tax affairs – Oupa Magashula before he left SARS, Ivan Pillay, Mark Kingon, Gene Ravele and Johann van Loggerenberg – would have treated Zuma no differently from any other taxpayer. And the president was in complete agreement with this, wasn't he?

During the meeting between Pillay and Zuma in February 2014, the SARS acting commissioner apparently stressed to the president that he could not continue to drag his feet on the Nkandla tax issue and that unless he submitted his tax returns and declared the fringe benefit, SARS would have no choice but to advance the case to the next level.

According to internal SARS notes of the meeting, Pillay told him that whatever his answer was to be regarding Nkandla, he needed to do his tax planning on the effects of the Nkandla benefits and do so properly and soon. Otherwise it would become a problem and SARS did not want to be drawn into political fights.

Zuma was once again noncommittal about his returns and undertook to give the matter his attention. There are several reasons why a full-scale probe of Zuma's tax affairs posed mortal danger to him. The first is that Zuma couldn't afford paying the taxes, which could ultimately have resulted in his sequestration – which would have spelt the end of his presidential reign. A South African president cannot be an unrehabilitated insolvent.

Secondly, had it come out that he was also an "employee" of a private company in the first few months of being president, he could have been "impeached" and removed from office.

Thirdly, there's also that question of his household allegedly receiving funds from third parties, some of which might well amount to the receipt of the proceeds of crime.

Even if a generous sponsor was prepared to settle Zuma's massive tax bill, it would have unleashed donations tax. If Zuma got a loan to pay his tax bill, he would have had to show how he was repaying the loan. Through a mixture of ignorance and arrogance, the president had spun himself into a cocoon from where there was no escape.

When the Constitutional Court ruled in 2016 that Zuma must repay R7.81 million for the non-security upgrades at Nkandla, he had to scrounge South Africa's northernmost outpost to find an institution that would lend him the money. VBS Mutual Bank was set up in the former "independent"

Republic of Venda and specialised in home loans for residents in the area. Zuma has a woeful credit record. Any credible financial institution would red-flag and reject his application.

My SARS sources said: "We know that Zuma fears the corruption charges. That's common knowledge. But that's nothing in comparison with his potentially huge tax bill, the fact that his household may have received proceeds of smuggled tobacco, and those payments allegedly made by Roy Moodley. And there are others too, the Guptas and so on. He would never have survived it. He could even have been sequestrated ultimately. That was his biggest fear. And he knew these guys hardly lost cases in court."

There was, of course, the last and final solution for Zuma; the ultimate way out of his tax problems. This is the one I am suggesting was the reason for the upheaval at SARS and the removal of the "Gordhan Four".

The first step for Zuma was to appoint his pal Tom Moyane as SARS commissioner. He, in turn, purged the place of anybody that could cause trouble. That, of course, wouldn't have been enough, because what if they talk, or what if they enter the system in another way? No, they had to be branded as dishonest, criminal even, crooks, untrustworthy – just in case any of them decided to say something nasty about Zuma.

* * *

Like father, like son. In 2013, SARS served notices on dozens of cigarette manufacturers, warning them of formal investigations and ordering them to ready their tax affairs for inspection. One of these was Yusuf Kajee and Edward Zuma's ATM/Delta. In addition, Johann van Loggeren berg, perhaps somewhat emboldened by the evidence of Azeem Amodcaram and Faizal Hattia, wrote a letter in which he gave them until 25 January 2014 to respond. He said that SARS had evidence that ATM manipulated processes and procedures and was at worst fraudulent and corrupt. Neither Zuma, Kajee nor any other director responded to SARS.

Edward Zuma had long attempted to use his political "clout" to get the heat off ATM. He approached Oupa Magashula in 2012 and requested him to intervene in the dispute. He got a cold shoulder. After a SARS raid in 2011, during which investigators seized goods and machinery and shut down the plant, he made an affidavit. According to the *Sunday Independent*, he accused SARS of racism, corruption, underhandedness and running a smear campaign against him. Nothing came of his affidavit.

If Yusuf Kajee had offered Edward Zuma a directorship in exchange for wielding his political influence, it was a lamentable business decision.

To add credence to this, my SARS sources tell me there is a recording of a conversation that Van Loggerenberg made while interviewing a number of people, including Kajee, sometime in late 2010. Van Loggerenberg and another SARS official featured in the conversation, with Van Loggerenberg mostly asking questions of Kajee. Apparently, in this recording, Kajee said that he now had "political cover" because he'd got "Edward Zuma on board".

* * *

Hold onto your seat for I'm going to take you on a short journey through gangsta land. And not just because it entails gaudy and lurid characters with high entertainment value, but because it relates directly to the events around tobacco smuggler Yusuf Kajee, Nkandla and Jacob Zuma. It highlights Kajee's relationship with the president and might explain how the "Nthanthla" payments worked.

Towards the end of 2013, four unsavoury characters met at the upmarket Serengeti golf estate near OR Tambo International Airport on Johannesburg's East Rand. They were convicted drug dealer Glenn Agliotti, Yusuf Kajee and a business associate, Paul de Robillard, as well as a fourth person by the name of Warren who never spoke. A magistrate once placed Agliotti among the "snitches, pimps and rats" who sold their soul to avoid spending time in the slammer. Called the "Landlord", he has for years been known in the underworld as a "fixer"; the go-to guy who sets up "connections", makes problems disappear and negotiates deals.

Agliotti's biggest feat has been his cunning ability to avoid prison time. He was the man who bribed police commissioner Jackie Selebi and then turned state witness against him. In the Selebi case, he was offered immunity from prosecution in exchange for his testimony against his friend. His evidence was poor, and the judge refused his application for immunity, but he was never charged.

As Selebi commenced his 15-year prison sentence, Agliotti was charged with the 2005 assassination of mining tycoon and ANC benefactor Brett Kebble. He wriggled himself out of that predicament as well. The actual trigger-pullers had lined the witness box to tell the court that Agliotti had masterminded the killing. Agliotti admitted in court that he had perjured himself about a host of things – but so had his accusers. Everyone had lied, and therefore Agliotti got off.

Days after the refusal of his indemnity, SARS laid criminal charges against him and eventually took him down when they found that he owed more than R70 million in unpaid taxes and penalties. He pleaded poverty and was in 2013 sequestrated by one of Van Loggerenberg's SARS units. The criminal charges have been languishing at the NPA ever since.

Two meetings between Agliotti, De Robillard, Kajee and "Warren" were digitally recorded by one of the men, who gave the recordings to Van Loggerenberg. He has stated publicly that he handed copies of the recordings to SARS, various investigative panels, the Hawks, the police, the NPA, the SSA, and the inspector-general of intelligence. I have dealt with both Agliotti and Kajee in my days as a journalist and the voices on the recordings are undoubtedly their own.

Much of the conversation between the men is nothing but gangster-banter-shit-chit-chat. Agliotti did most of the talking and puff, swagger and rant about his magnificent feats in gangsta-land.

Agliotti: *I play here and in Pecanwood. I live in Pecanwood and in Illovo. We terrible. We gangsters. I believe in the AGE. A in AGE stands for Arrogance. Most of us, we are arrogant. G for greed. E for Ego.*

Kajee steered the conversation towards their tax predicament and wanted to know: *How is JvL [Van Loggerenberg]? Is he a guy you can talk to?*

Agliotti: *He seems a nice guy. And then he will fuck you up. Van Loggerenberg did my case. They sequestrated me. They said 70 million. The sheriff: sit down, relax. I've got to take your stuff. He took all the kak [shit] from my garage. I am so fucking happy. R23,000 for all the stuff. That's what they got out of the 70 bar [R70 million].*

De Robillard: *What do I need to do?*

Agliotti: *Understand one thing. SARS will run you. For ten years. They will kill you. I'm your protection. Nobody will extort from you. I've been there. Speak to my partner if anybody approaches you. Give my number.*

Agliotti then banters about his friend, Czech mobster Radovan Krejčíř, who was in 2016 convicted of attempted murder, kidnapping and drug dealing and sentenced to 35 years' imprisonment. At the time of writing, Krejčíř was standing trial for the murder of Lebanese drug dealer Sam Issa, who was gunned down in October 2013. The murder happened just before this recording was made and long before Krejčíř's arrest for the killing.

Agliotti: *Radovan, he's gone, boy. And I warned him. Radovan's a fucking blast. The nicest guy. Brother, did you kill him? We talk like this. He would go after you till you pay him. For your protection, you will pay him. Sam Issa, we called him Penguin. We were having drinks with him. The night before. I had drinks with him. Him and Sam. Next morning, I get a call saying Sam has been shot. He and Radovan carried on drinking until one in the morning. Fuck let's have a drink on poor Sam. Radovan had him taken out.*

Kajee: *Why?*

Agliotti: *Because a drug deal went wrong.*

Agliotti had arranged the meeting because he needed cronies to be part of his state-sponsored cigarette smuggling operation.

It is easy to get overwhelmed by facts and names but I will attempt to keep it simple.

In August 2011, SSA agents and a police crime intelligence informant embarked on Project Robin to set up their own tobacco smuggling enterprise. Among them were SSA acting head of economic intelligence Ferdi Fryer; another SSA agent, Graham Minnaar; and SSA agent and Pretoria attorney Belinda Walter. Some of them would later greatly assist Tom Moyane – and, by implication, Jacob Zuma – by plotting to discredit SARS and specifically Van Loggerenberg.

The rationale behind the project was that they could eliminate tobacco smuggling by flooding the market with even cheaper cigarettes through smuggling their own, while making a lot of money for themselves in the process. They needed a "sponsor", someone who could set up the infra-structure and in return profit from the enterprise. They decided on Tribert Ayabatwa, who has an estimated personal fortune of about R2 billion. He is a Rwandan industrialist who owns a significant property portfolio in South Africa.

Ayabatwa was charged with R55 million tax fraud in 2009 and fled to the United Kingdom, where he was arrested and faced extradition. He entered into a plea agreement with the NPA and pleaded guilty to a range of crimes. He received a suspended sentence and had to pay a huge fine and settle his enormous tax bill.

Apparently, a clause in the plea bargain prohibited Ayabatwa from trading in cigarettes for several years. Project Robin flouted this condition, but Ayabatwa initially agreed to be the sponsor. Ayabatwa was going to invest R10 million and profits of R40 million were anticipated. Ayabatwa would receive back his initial investment of R10 million, leaving a halfway split of the remaining R30 million, which would've left the SSA agents with R15 million to share among themselves.

Whether Ayabatwa was aware of the fact that he was collaborating with SSA agents or whether he was being played by them is something which remains unanswered, because this matter has never been properly investigated.

A month after the launch of Project Robin, Graham Minnaar said in an e-mail addressed to the other agents that he was putting the project on ice for at least six months "to build a better relationship before implementing the commercial aspects of the story". It appears that at some point the SSA agents had problems with Ayabatwa and that he withdrew as a "sponsor". They had to find a new one – which might explain Agliotti's insistence that the project was approved by what he called the "NIA" – the National Intelligence Agency.

Agliotti: *I have been smuggling cigarettes for thirty years. I am a fucking gangster. Cigarette game is bigger than drugs. We are all smugglers. We can make money together. The government has asked me to run a smuggling operation ... From Zuma's office there is a team in place. I will appear nowhere because I know the game.*

De Robillard: *Why the fuck me?*

Agliotti: *Because you are successful. You are in the cigarette game. Indemnity to whoever I tell them. Three-year project. Smuggle as much as you want.*

De Robillard: *What do you need from us?*

Agliotti: *Get the product and we will run it. I will give you all the protection in writing. They know I am a gangster.*

Kajee: *Will it be with their blessings?*

Agliotti: *SAPS, Hawks, SARS all the way down. We already negotiated the whole thing. Three years. That is my retirement. I said Zuma you are going to pay. I helped you become president or you would have been arrested.*

Kajee: *But he is a genuine guy.*

Agliotti: *No, he is fine. He is a gangster like us.*

De Robillard: *How many do you have to shuffle a week?*

Agliotti: *As much as we want. It's our call. But I have three years. The best advice I can give is sell your Ferraris. I have fuck-all in my name. Not even a bank account. I have three things in my name. My three kids.*

Kajee: *Why did you choose us, Glenn?*

Agliotti: *I'll rather run with operators. You run it. I will give you the protection from the president's office.*

It appears from the tape that Kajee's biggest concern was his tax predicament. SARS was busy liquidating one of his companies.

Agliotti: *The only fucking department in this country that works is SARS. SARS will have you under surveillance. The tax enquiry on me was 11,593 pages to copy.*

Kajee: *They have done an audit. They have nothing.*

Agliotti: *Don't kid yourself. They will not play their hand. Van Loggerenberg is not a cunt. And the team around him is brilliant.*

Kajee: *I worry about Johann [Van Loggerenberg].*

Agliotti: *He will not even blink. He will fuck you up.*

The men parted but agreed to meet again in a few days' time. The next meeting took place in a noisy Johannesburg restaurant. It is clear from the conversation that Kajee was eager to bribe Van Loggerenberg. Agliotti played along and created the impression that he knew the SARS executive. He probably wanted to extort money from Kajee based on his claimed "direct access" to Van Loggerenberg. This was an old scam of Agliotti's, pretending to have influence and access to people, and then fleecing people for it.

Agliotti: *Thirteen of your companies are being investigated right now.*

Kajee: *What do they have? Is he just stressing us out, or does he want something for his pocket, or what does he want?*

Agliotti: *I'm not going to lie to you. They going to investigate. It is a project. But Johann will be on board with us.*

Kajee: *But what does Johann want? What are they going to attach?*

Agliotti: *But he can turn it around. Johann was saying I've got to arrest them. This is a major project for SARS.*

Kajee: *But you know it's going to risk all the businesses. All the transport. If we go that route then why cut a deal with him? Because we gonna lose all our contracts for cross-border business.*

Agliotti: *You must tell me what you want me to do.*

Kajee: *I thought we give him a parcel and call it a day.*

Agliotti: *Listen, he is a Dutchman. Leave him to me, boss. I can go back to him and say listen cunt, because this is the way I talk to him. You come back to me with a figure for Johann.*

Kajee: *He must tell us what he wants. How can we give him a figure?*

Agliotti: *I'll ask him.*

Kajee: *I can bring SARS to its knees with all the shit that we have. I'm meeting the old man* [Jacob Zuma] *this weekend. I'm going to tell him this fucking Dutchman is getting clever, he affects everybody. Not that we haven't played our part. Let me ask him. I will show you the message from Nkandla. Don't know if this is the right phone.*

There is silence on the tape as Kajee searched his phone for a message. He found it and read it to Agliotti.

Kajee: *"Boss hope all are well with SARS. I'm meeting the old man." See who this is from.*

Kajee showed the message to Agliotti. The message might have been from Edward Zuma. The "old man" is a common reference to Jacob Zuma, among those who revere him.

Agliotti: *Go and meet the old man. The bigger thing here is the project.*

Kajee: *Because if they going to fuck us up we can't do the project.*

Agliotti: *So I gave them the names. I said Yusuf Kajee, Paul de Robillard and Glenn Agliotti. And I said to him just register the names, cunt. Give us three years.*

De Robillard: *Who did you chat to, Glenn?*

Agliotti: *I met with them; NPA, NIA. I met with them in Erasmia [in Pretoria] yesterday. The NIA. They are on board. It's been approved.*

Kajee: *Edward Zuma is a shareholder with us in the factory . . . He is with the Guptas.*

Agliotti: *Dudu makes big money. He is the only one with the brains, the others are all . . .*

Kajee: *We going to get fucked by SARS.*

Agliotti: *That's how he [Van Loggerenberg] is. Understand the animal we dealing with?*

Kajee: *Don't waste my time. Pull the fucking trigger. I've got no problem. He must change his fucking ways.*

Agliotti: *I sat with him. He said he is going to arrest you.*

Kajee: *How many ice cubes does he want? One, two, three. That's the only game. Any other game I'm not interested. Then I will fight him in court.*

Fuck him. His mother's poes, man. He can take his granny through the motions, not me. You can tell him that.

Agliotti: *Fuck him.*

Kajee: *Politics is dirty.*

It is astonishing that despite the various law enforcement agencies having been placed in possession of this evidence since as early as 2014, none has ever investigated these serious allegations.

SEVEN

I beg you, Mr President

————•————

Mr President, I also regret to inform you that elements in your intelligence agency, law enforcement agencies and former SARS officials are waging war against SARS. They are undermining us. We have been warned that they want to discredit us and that they want us gone. Please, Mr President, we need your help. We need you to intervene.

I don't know if those were the exact words spoken by acting SARS commissioner Ivan Pillay at his February 2014 meeting with Jacob Zuma, but I have seen a SARS document on the briefing, and the State Security Agency (SSA) campaign to discredit SARS was high on the agenda.

Pillay presented extraordinary evidence to Zuma about "dossiers" that disgruntled former SARS employees, in conjunction with some existing officials, had compiled to discredit the service. Gordhan, Pillay and Van Loggerenberg were often the targets of these campaigns and the false allegations usually centred around them being racists, somehow linking them to the old apartheid security establishment, conducting illegal surveillance on taxpayers, abusing state funds and acting as an untouchable mafia. By the end of the 2000s, these claims were being regurgitated thick and fast as SARS, and especially Van Loggerenberg and his units, targeted organised criminal enterprises.

Over time, Pillay had briefed the president about Project Broken Arrow and Operation Snowman. In Pillay's Labour Court case in December 2015, annexed to his file were several documents which all explained not only how Pillay had informed Zuma about developments, but also how a desperate

SARS had tried to fend off these attacks by briefing members of Parliament, the police and the SSA as far back as 2010. The information always related to "intelligence dossiers" that disgruntled former and existing SARS employees had compiled to discredit the service. These "dossiers" were usually based on a host of falsehoods that were spiced with a smattering of truth to give them an air of credibility.

* * *

The most notorious of these aggrieved ex-hands was Michael Peega, a former special forces soldier who joined SARS. In December 2008, while on leave, Peega was stopped at a roadblock. When police searched the vehicle, they found an unlicensed hunting rifle, ammunition, poaching paraphernalia and a bloodied jacket. The blood turned out to be that of a rhino that had earlier been poached and its horn chopped off.

Peega made a confession to the arresting officer that he had been recruited by a rhino-poaching syndicate and paid an advance fee of R10,000, and admitted having shot at a baby rhino. He took the police to places where they had waited for rhino and revealed the location of an AK-47 rifle and .303 rifle and ammunition. The criminal case against Peega collapsed after the docket and a key piece of evidence, a cellphone with photos, mysteriously disappeared. SARS fired Peega after he was found guilty in a disciplinary hearing.

Peega was intent on revenge, and in late 2009 and early 2010 he released a "dossier" to the media and various politicians, including ANC Youth League leader Julius Malema. It made fantastic claims, including that the SARS unit had spied on politicians and conspired to overthrow the government. Peega claimed that the unit was given the names of "JZ sympathisers" to investigate for tax offences. Nowhere in the supporting documentation attached to his "dossier" was there any evidence supporting these claims. Minutes of team meetings referred only to six projects in which the unit was involved, none linked to the Zuma sympathisers he named.

Van Loggerenberg observes in his book *Rogue*: "Compiling 'dossiers' and distributing them to influential recipients became a veritable cottage industry for detractors of SARS over the years. Most of these dossiers contained similar elements, although they came in various guises. They were usually aimed at Gordhan and Pillay, and I would sometimes be dragged in. They often claimed anti-black sentiments, sometimes that there were 'apartheid spies' at work, most of the time alluding to a secret unit of some kind, and often claiming that we were intercepting communications or were scheming against politicians. From the mid-2000s they began to include the suggestion that we were conspiring against Zuma."

In response to Peega's allegations, SARS wrote several letters to the police, SSA, members of Parliament and ministry of finance, all which I have seen, from as early on as 2010, asking them to investigate the "dossiers" and the claims against the unit.

SARS released two very detailed rebuttals of the "dossier", which included annexing Peega's confession to the police, his disciplinary records when he was fired, his appeal, and details of the unit that he sought to slander, which set out its mandate and purpose. At the time, that seemed enough to stem the attack on SARS. The media, including the *Sunday Times* – which later regurgitated Peega's claims in its "rogue unit exposés" – were briefed about the ludicrousness of his claims, and all were given the documents to keep.

Another former SARS employee with strong links to the SSA who dished dirt on the tax collector was Dr Mandisa Mokwena. She was a former head of the SSA's economic intelligence unit before joining SARS, where she became the group executive of the SARS business intelligence unit, later renamed the risk, segmentation and research division. Her deputy at the SSA's economic intelligence unit was none other than Ferdi Fryer, whom we have already met and who, when she left, stepped into her shoes.

In 2009, Mokwena was arrested for allegedly defrauding SARS to the tune of R11 million by handing out training tenders to her friends. She resigned after internal charges were levelled against her. Mokwena and eight accused were charged and stood trial in the North Gauteng High Court on more than 40 counts of racketeering, corruption, money laundering and fraud.

At the time of writing this book, the case against Mokwena and her co-accused was still dragging on. The state had closed its arguments. At the start of the trial, Mokwena advanced the narrative that a "rogue unit" existed in SARS. She claimed that she was framed by Van Loggerenberg and this "rogue unit", which was intent on "destroying her career". Facts didn't seem to matter. Van Loggerenberg's units didn't even investigate her alleged wrongdoing; she was nailed by the SARS anti-corruption unit.

Mokwena was a business partner of one of Jacob Zuma's wives, Thobeka Madiba-Zuma. They shared a directorship in three companies. During an earlier interaction between Zuma and Pillay in 2012, the SARS acting commissioner warned the president to advise Madiba-Zuma to break ties with Mokwena. It seems Zuma followed Pillay's recommendation, because just a month later, in September 2012, when asked about this, Madiba-Zuma was quoted in *City Press* as saying that "she was unaware of her business partner's pending corruption case" when they went into business. She cut all ties with the alleged fraudster.

Pillay assured the president that the SARS investigation units were legally constituted, operated within the ambit of the law and didn't have the knowledge or expertise to expedite audits.

* * *

Sam Sole explained in an investigation: "The economic logic of cigarette smuggling is relentless. In South Africa, as elsewhere, steep sin taxes comprise the major part of the cost of a pack of cigarettes. Find a way of avoiding paying those duties and the profits are on a par with narcotics. But the risks are low: being caught smuggling earns little more than a fine. Combine this with a semi-lawless neighbour, Zimbabwe, which produces tobacco, and the economics have propelled a succession of small players to carve a niche in 'cheapies' – low-cost brands, often backed by creative ways of avoiding the prying attentions of SARS."

At the time, every state law enforcement agency probed illicit tobacco: the Tobacco Task Team (TTT), the police's crime intelligence unit, the Hawks, the SSA's economic intelligence unit and various SARS units. The TTT was a multi-agency initiative to combat the scourge of tobacco smuggling. While the Hawks, the SSA, the National Prosecuting Authority (NPA) and the Financial Intelligence Centre (FIC) had a seat on this team, SARS was excluded from it from its inception.

The only agency making progress in the tobacco war was SARS. By 2014, the service had instituted proceedings or was acting against 13 major tobacco manufacturers for crimes that involved corruption, bribery, attempted murder, money laundering, racketeering, tax evasion and fraud. Multinational British American Tobacco (BAT) was itself in the taxman's sights when in 2014 it was presented with a reported R1.79 billion tax bill, after its payments between 2006 and 2010 were reassessed.

SARS had achieved a 92 per cent conviction rate in the cases it handed over to the NPA for prosecution. An effective 555 years of imprisonment, 258 months of correctional supervision and 2,480 hours of community service were handed down to those convicted. In contrast, the Tobacco Task Team had made no significant arrests or convictions in their three years of existence (they were quietly disbanded at the end of 2014 during the unfolding saga at SARS). Instead, they seem to have been mostly involved in hampering SARS's efforts to curb the scourge.

By the beginning of 2014, Pillay and Van Loggerenberg realised SARS was under siege and they had an uneasy feeling that an upheaval was looming. As Pillay was meeting Zuma, Van Loggerenberg got a tip-off from an attorney that a member of the police crime intelligence unit and a member of the Tobacco Task Team, Lieutenant-Colonel Hennie Niemann, had met him to look for "dirt" on Van Loggerenberg.

SARS had nailed the attorney in the early 2000s for tax evasion and Niemann believed that he had an axe to grind with Van Loggerenberg. Niemann was accompanied by two people whom he introduced as Hawks officials. The attorney sent them packing and called Van Loggerenberg. He said he was willing to testify about the meeting and detailed who said what in an e-mail.

SARS reports show that at an interdepartmental meeting in early 2014 SSA officials warned Van Loggerenberg that they "were coming for him".

Officials working under him reported strange incidents of suspected surveillance, break-ins and thefts of computers and phones. A manager of SARS's High-Risk Investigation Unit, Johan de Waal, said in a report that investigators had been threatened, including himself. There were burglaries at the houses of two investigators, though only computers were stolen. Another's dog had been poisoned and there was an attempted burglary at his own house. Other investigators said they were convinced that they were being followed.

Van Loggerenberg and his investigators meticulously recorded these events in several reports during this period. Gene Ravele and other senior SARS officials met Hawks head Anwa Dramat to discuss these events. The records of these reports, I am told, are still in the archives at SARS.

When Pillay met Zuma in February 2014, he told him that SARS was being confronted by a "set of adversaries acting singly or in concert whose interests are to weaken its enforcement capability". The service was at the time the victim of a shark-feeding frenzy to bring it down at any cost. Among the sharks were competing state institutions such as the SSA, crime intelligence, Hawks, the illicit tobacco industry, the Tobacco Task Team, and disgruntled former and current staff members.

SARS and the SSA had long been at odds, and evidence mounted that the agency was targeting the tax collector. The evidence is compelling and is documented in several SARS memoranda and submissions that I have seen.

In 2010, spy boss Gibson Njenje called an extraordinary meeting of the heads of the law enforcement agencies, among them Hawks boss Anwa Dramat, the NPA's Willie Hofmeyr and Ivan Pillay. The *Mail & Guardian* reported that Njenje introduced a report, presented by Ferdi Fryer, which claimed to have evidence of corruption by senior members of SARS.

Pillay responded by saying that SARS had recordings which showed that the allegations were engineered by a group of individuals targeted by SARS for their involvement in tobacco smuggling. In one report, a whistleblower stated that more than half a million rand were made available to the NPA, Hawks and state intelligence to discredit SARS investigators.

In 2011, Njenje and an NPA advocate who formed part of the Tobacco

Task Team reportedly requested SARS to delay a raid on a transport company that was smuggling truckloads of illegal cigarettes across the border from Zimbabwe. Njenje apparently made the request on the advice of Fryer. When SARS eventually raided the company's premises, evidence had been removed and destroyed. The loss to SARS and the fiscus was an estimated R50 million. Evidence also shows how another SSA agent created a false paper trail to divert SARS's attention from their probe of the tobacco manufacturer Carnilinx. The estimated loss was more than R25 million.

Tobacco smugglers, in conjunction with their SSA cronies, collaborated to smear and remove a top SARS investigator, Marietjie van Wyk, who was tasked with probing four tobacco manufacturers. Among them were Carnilinx and Delta Tobacco. She was instrumental in raising civil liabilities against one of them for R86 million. In December 2013, SARS detained tobacco worth R300 million from Carnilinx.

Members of the Tobacco Task Team, including Belinda Walter – an attorney and spy of whom you will read a lot more later – and her SSA handler, Chris Burger, conspired to remove Van Wyk from the investigation by planting dirt on her. There is compelling evidence about Belinda Walter's role in this and the extent of the campaign. Walter complained to her SSA handler, Burger, that Van Wyk was too efficient in her work and was harassing her clients.

Burger: *Do you have any evidence, with the emphasis on evidence, that JvL*
    [Van Loggerenberg] is on the take?
Walter: *No. None . . . Tired of SARS's shit.*
Burger: *We are also tired of them.*

Walter and Burger appear to have contrived a story that Van Wyk had illegally purchased furniture from a sequestrated tobacco smuggler. Walter used another alleged tobacco smuggler, Luis Pestana, to sign an affidavit, which she had compiled on his behalf, to serve as a "complaint" against Van Wyk. Pestana would later, in 2016, confess that he had been manipulated and deceived by Walter to participate in this sham, and apologised to Van Wyk.

Walter: *All hell will break loose soon. What happens if we can show MvW [Marietjie van Wyk] took furniture and a fridge from Westhouse without paying for it? When it was being liquidated?*
Burger: *Anonymous to SARS anti-corruption?*

The two furnished the SARS anti-corruption unit with "evidence" – Pestana being their "star witness" – and as a result, Van Wyk was suspended and removed from the tobacco cases. She was found not guilty during a subsequent SARS disciplinary hearing, but as a result 11 criminal cases on which she had worked were never advanced and the fiscus lost an estimated R100 million because she was "compromised".

The memo I have seen doesn't say what Zuma's reaction was to this item on the agenda in his meeting with Ivan Pillay, but can you imagine that you are the president of a country and your tax commissioner presents you with evidence that your intelligence service is undermining his ability to efficiently and independently accumulate duties, excises and tariffs to fill the state's coffer?

It's a silly question, because we know the answer. But Zuma did nothing, and therefore the revenue service festered until Jacob's quack, Tom Moyane, splayed it on the operating table, amputated a limb and allowed it to bleed empty. He dispatched the goose that laid the golden eggs.

* * *

Nothing can illustrate the moral slippage of President Jacob Zuma more than the next item on the agenda of Ivan Pillay: his cavorting with the Western Cape's most notorious gangsters to win the province back for the ANC.

In 2013, a gangster under investigation for dodging the taxman told SARS – probably to win favour with the service – that Jacob Zuma had met gang bosses at his official Cape Town residence in May 2011. This was just more than two weeks before the local government election. The meeting was facilitated by none other than Lloyd Hill, the Durban mobster and Zuma family friend who was an alleged beneficiary of Amodcaram and

Kajee's laundered tobacco money. According to the gangster, some of the participants at the meeting told the president that they had problems with SARS and requested him to do something about it. As a result, Pillay put this item on the agenda for his own meeting with Zuma.

According to the *Mail & Guardian* – they picked up the story in November 2015 – the president's son Duduzane Zuma, who happens to be the Gupta family's favourite Zuma, met the delegation at the gates of the presidential estate in Cape Town and ensured that security guards did not record the identities of his father's visitors. Among the gangsters were two of the Cape's biggest criminal bosses, Quinton "Mr Big" Marinus and Americans gang leader Igshaan Davids. Marinus is reportedly the kingpin of one of South Africa's largest crime syndicates and has appeared in court on multiple charges of murder, robbery, fraud and abalone poaching – of which he was acquitted. Davids was convicted of five crimes between 1989 and 2014, including culpable homicide, for which he received a seven-year jail sentence.

The leader of the delegation to Zuma was reportedly Lloyd Hill. At the opening, Hill thanked the president for seeing them and said in Afrikaans: "*OK, ouens, hier's julle kans nou. Die ou ballie is 'n naai net soos ons* [OK, guys, this is your opportunity. This old fossil is a fucker just like us]."

Pillay raised this issue with Zuma because SARS was concluding its tax evasion case against Marinus. They had seized his belongings, including his home in the upmarket suburb of Plattekloof, to recover tax debts. He was eventually sequestrated after owing SARS R3.2 million in taxes.

Pillay told Zuma that SARS was concerned about what Marinus had said to the president during the meeting. This was: "We have our troops inside each community. We will mobilise them and we will swing the vote." He then added: "Sir, we're having big problems with SARS."

Zuma reportedly responded: "We will look into that."

Why didn't Zuma tell the mobster that SARS acts independently and in accordance with tax legislation and the Constitution? Neither the president nor anyone else can dictate to the tax collector who or what to investigate. What did Zuma mean when he told Marinus that he would attend to the matter?

Pillay requested Zuma not to get involved in SARS's tax investigations. SARS, he said, was guided by the Constitution and various tax Acts that guaranteed its autonomy.

* * *

Your good office wants me out, Mr President. If that is indeed the case and you support the notion, I request that you execute it in such a manner as not to harm the revenue service or the country.

Pillay presented Zuma with evidence that his legal adviser, Bonisiwe Makhene, had allegedly contacted selected SARS officials and requested them to "find dirt on Ivan [Pillay]". She wanted him replaced with Zuma's political adviser, Vuso Shabalala.

I have seen reports from two different sources that refer to Makhene and her inappropriate interference in the affairs of SARS. She is one of several advisers in Zuma's office and has earned around R1.7 million per year since taking up the job in 2009. An advocate, Makhene was previously a chief state law adviser at the Department of Justice. Advisers act as the president's emissaries in sounding out key players in civil society and business circles. They are not part of cabinet, but can demand information from cabinet ministers, and they prepare reports for the president.

Makhene has played a secondary role to Zuma's chief legal adviser, Michael Hulley. You and I pay him an annual retainer of R1.6 million and R800 per hour to keep Zuma's hyenas at bay. Hulley became Zuma's lawyer when, as deputy president, he battled corruption charges in 2005. He continued to provide Zuma with advice until he was appointed part-time presidential legal adviser in 2011. Hulley still runs his legal practice on the side, while advising Zuma both in his personal capacity and as president.

The president's legal team have been slammed for their dubious advice to Zuma, who has been battered in court time and time again. When the Constitutional Court mauled Zuma in their judgment about Nkandla and found that he had failed to uphold the Constitution, his excuse was that he acted on wrong legal advice.

In 2014, the *Mail & Guardian* reported that a meeting of irate security cluster ministers raised concerns about the quality of his legal advice. This was after Zuma's lawyers conceded in the Supreme Court of Appeal that they could not make an argument for refusing to hand over the "Spy Tapes" to the Democratic Alliance.

Zuma also acted on questionable legal advice when he bungled the appointment of Willem Heath as head of the Special Investigating Unit in 2011 and Menzi Simelane's appointment as national director of public prosecutions, which the Constitutional Court ruled was "inconsistent with the Constitution and invalid".

When Pillay confronted Zuma with Makhene's role in discrediting SARS and Pillay, the president's immediate response was: "I'm not behind this." Pillay informed him that several SARS employees had reported her efforts to discredit him. According to accounts of the meeting, Pillay said that she had told them that Shabalala was better qualified for the job.

Shabalala, the former customs boss at SARS, is a fervent defender of the Gupta family. He wrote in *Politicsweb* in February 2016 that "sewer journal-ism" was pursuing a "regime-change" agenda and that much of the reporting around the Guptas was nothing but "malicious innuendo". According to Shabalala: "What is the extent of the economic clout of the Guptas in the economy? It can be no more than a speck on the radar. That a handful of members of Zuma's family have or may have business connections with the Guptas is fact. The value of their assets from such relationship is at best fanciful . . . whatever wealth they may accumulate can barely impact on the extended family."

And then this beauty: "What do the Guptas have to give that outweighs what everybody else can give?" Really? How about money? Heard of it, Mr Shabalala? The stuff that greases the palms of politicians?

When four major South African banks closed Gupta company accounts in 2016, Shabalala said this "macabre tragicomedy" was a "brazen display of power by banking oligopolies" that were resisting "a radical socio-economic transformation programme". According to him, the idea that "democratic regime change will save South Africa belongs to Sterkfontein [a mental institution]".

When Pillay showed his evidence to Zuma, according to an impeccable SARS source, the president apparently jumped from his chair and exclaimed: "I didn't instruct her [Makhene] to do that. But leave it with me. I will deal with the issue." He purportedly said that if there was any crusade to install Shabalala as SARS commissioner it didn't have his support.

Pillay later heard that Makhene was allegedly raked over the coals and her campaigning in favour of Shabalala stopped. There is, however, a sting in the tale. Makhene's husband is a senior SSA agent, Yekani Monde Gadini. Gadini was exposed in *City Press* and its sister newspaper, *Rapport*, in 2016 as part of a "shadowy network of intelligence agents and contracted operatives closely linked to President Jacob Zuma".

Enter forensic investigator Paul O'Sullivan, who has been on a crusade to bust corrupt cops and state officials. He's famous for his role in bringing police commissioner Jackie Selebi to book for corruption. He has laid a host of criminal charges against the likes of then acting police commissioner Khomotso Phahlane and former Hawks head Berning Ntlemeza. In turn, they and their cronies have accused him of treason, espionage, conspiracy to commit murder, corruption, intimidation and harassment, defeating the ends of justice, tax evasion and contravention of the immigration laws.

Gadini drifted onto O'Sullivan's radar screen in April 2015. The latter wrote an e-mail to Gadini and said: "People like you belong under a magnifying glass. For the record, criminals don't take me down, I take them down. You will soon find out, and can expect a lot more scrutiny in the coming weeks, months and years."

An aerial photograph of a mansion on a walled estate allegedly belonging to Gadini and Makhene was attached to the e-mail, and O'Sullivan asked: "Who paid for this house? Where does the cash come from to pay bodyguards who drive around with you, sit in the corner whilst you're having your 3rd force meetings and protect you in your fortress? What's your relationship with Tom Moyani [sic]? Apart from getting Tom to neutralise No 1's tax bill on Nkandla and to shut down the SARS undercover unit that would have brought No 1 more headaches, what else have you got him to do?"

* * *

Just days after Pillay's meeting with Zuma, finance minister Pravin Gordhan said: "All South Africans pay tax on their income and fringe benefits. South Africa is one of the few democracies where we are all equal when it comes to taxation, in that we are all taxed, with the exact amount determined by our income and fringe benefits, minus any allowed exemptions and deductions."

Is it a coincidence that Gordhan stressed, at that very moment, the principle that all South Africans, including the president, are equal before the law and should pay their taxes? It is also significant that he stressed the principle of taxation on fringe benefits.

SARS spokesperson Adrian Lackay followed up by saying that since 1994, under President Nelson Mandela, it was decided that the president, his cabinet and all elected public officials should be subject to income tax, "like any other South African". Until 1994, presidents and their deputies had been exempt from paying income tax on remuneration.

Three months after Pravin's speech, Zuma reshuffled his cabinet to kickstart a "radical phase of socio-economic transformation". Does that sound familiar? He sent Gordhan packing to the less important ministry of co-operative governance and traditional affairs. Gordhan was replaced as finance minister by his deputy, Nhlanhla Nene, who was generally regarded as more of a "party man" but who soon proved himself a guardian of stern fiscal discipline. He therefore lasted less than two years.

* * *

By early 2014, SARS was still coaxing Zuma to become tax compliant. But his and his lawyer's continued failure to come to the party began to increase the pressure on SARS. This was further compounded by the fact that the opposition political parties had started to do exactly what Ivan Pillay had feared they would do: they laid a complaint at SARS and asked for Zuma to be investigated.

At the beginning of April 2014, Ivan Pillay responded to the Democratic Alliance inquiry about Zuma's liability for Nkandla. He said SARS could not disclose information about a specific taxpayer owing to secrecy provisions in the Tax Administration Act. "However, I can assure you that the matter will be dealt with in the normal course of the duties and functions assigned to SARS for the purpose of the administration of tax laws."

The meeting between Zuma and Pillay was crucial to the events that unfolded next. In one sweeping encounter with Pillay, the president was confronted with the reality that he was a tax delinquent and that if he didn't become compliant, he would face the wrath of the taxman. He knew his son, his family and his nephew, as well as his besties, the Guptas, were all busy digging their own holes and that SARS would probably have buried them as well. At that moment, SARS posed more of a threat to the president than dissent in his own ranks, declining voter support, the public protector's Nkandla investigation or even the reinstatement of the fraud and corruption charges against him.

Some of my sources said that Zuma was seemingly noncommittal during the meeting and offered mostly ambiguous utterances such as "OK, I will look into it", "I was not aware of what you are telling me" and "Are you sure about that?"

Zuma did nothing to douse the whirling flames that encircled SARS and eventually erupted into an inferno. And he didn't just watch it happen; he commandeered Tom Moyane, sent him to SARS, and probably ordered him to stoke those fires.

* * *

Writing this book has almost been like breaking open a pomegranate. A few pips initially spilt out, but as time progressed and I approached more people, the red kernels seemed to tumble from everywhere. This included dirt on the ruling party, because as I neared my deadline, a source asked me if I had ever enquired about the tax affairs of the ANC. Said the source: Speak to Zweli Mkhize, treasurer-general of the ANC and now presidential hopeful. He knows everything. Mkhize was, of course, not going to wash his organisation's muddied linen in the open, but I did confirm the ANC's tax problems through other sources.

In 2011, SARS found the ANC owed them around R22 million in unpaid taxes. This included penalties and interest, which related mainly to PAYE deductions that were not paid over to the tax collector. The ANC didn't keep proper payroll records.

The SARS commissioner Oupa Magashula at first dealt directly with the ANC, with some letters going off to the party demanding immediate payment. The ANC wanted SARS to allow it way more time than what ordinary taxpayers get to settle tax debts. Magashula, Ivan Pillay and Gene Ravele supposedly had meetings with Mkhize and ANC general manager Ignatius Jacobs.

The message from SARS was that the ANC could not ask for preferential treatment. It had to pay up like any other taxpayer. There was apparently a constant exchange between SARS and the ANC, with the matter eventually being assigned to SARS group executive Godfrey Baloyi in 2013. In a compromise brokered by Baloyi, the investment arm of the ANC, Chancellor House, came to the rescue and made a loan to the ANC, which allowed for the taxes to be paid. On the face of it, this would have been the end of the matter.

But, my sources tell me, the loan from Chancellor House would have to be repaid by the ANC. If this was not done, then Chancellor House would itself attract tax implications. In 2014, both the ANC and Chancellor House would have had to make some sort of declaration to SARS explaining the loan and demonstrate how it was being repaid. My ANC source says that some "powerful people" within the ANC were livid with SARS for not conceding to their demands to be treated differently.

It makes a lot of sense why the ANC would not lift a finger while SARS was being swept clean.

* * *

Towards the middle of 2017, South Africans woke up to the thousands upon thousands of leaked e-mails of the Gupta family and their associates. The e-mails, which became known as #GuptaLeaks, provide compelling evidence of how the Gupta family, enjoying close ties with Jacob Zuma, have manoeuvred themselves into a position where they allegedly wield control over state-owned companies and their huge procurement budgets, diverting huge sums into their own pockets and, by extension, the president's family.

You've read much about the e-mails and I'm not even going to attempt to regurgitate them, but what is important for now is to know that by the middle of 2013 SARS was onto the Guptas and investigating them for possible tax evasion. I deal with this investigation in Chapter Eleven.

#GuptaLeaks have shown that the Guptas knew about the investigation not just against themselves, but also into the tax affairs of their cronies. The family had a mole inside the tax collector.

On 15 November 2013 at 17h35, Gupta media boss and family spokesperson Gary Naidoo fired off an e-mail under the headline "Bloemfontein SARS" to Atul Gupta, the middle of the three Gupta brothers and the first to have come to South Africa. The e-mail is clearly part of earlier and later discussions on the topic and seems to originate from someone within SARS based in Bloemfontein.

Said Naidoo: "I was given some info by my investigative contact that SARS was investigating the president." He continued by saying that SARS was investigating the Gupta family and people close to Zuma. The e-mail lists a SARS team: "Johann van Loggenberg, Johannes Muller, Patricia de Lange, Jacqueline Mgade, Sameera Khan – not based in Bloemfontein."

I asked my SARS sources about the misspelling of Van Loggerenberg's name. It is because this was how his name was often reflected in documents. De Lange was the head of the National Projects Unit under him, with Jacqueline Mgade reporting to her. De Lange's surname is actually Langa but her e-mail address incorrectly referred to her as De Lange. Sameera Khan was based at the VIP Taxpayer Unit, which dealt with Zuma's tax affairs, among others.

Naidoo then said his contact gave him a list of people being looked at. These were named as Chief Douglas Zondo from Vryheid, who "apparently had a contract to build part of Nkandla", and his wife, daughter and son, who "are also under investigation and they claim he owes SARS around R48m"; the Guptas; a Mr Parak from the Newcastle area; and a Mr Mohamed from Durban or Pietermaritzburg, "who is apparently close to the KZN ANC structures and to the president". It is true: these people were all at the time under investigation by SARS.

We don't know what the Guptas did after obtaining this knowledge – if anything. Chances are very good that they would have informed at least their poster boy – Duduzane Zuma – about the SARS probe against his father's cronies. Or perhaps they just went directly to Jacob Zuma and complained about SARS, as the gangsters had more than two years earlier.

What these events show is that not only were Van Loggerenberg and his units up against smear campaigns driven by former disgruntled SARS employees like Peega and Mokwena, not only were they being undermined by the Tobacco Task Team and intelligence agencies, not only did they have to contend with gangsters and threats to their lives, homes and families, and not only were they up against people within SARS who had axes to grind or favours to fulfil, but they were clearly also up against the most powerful politicians and politically connected individuals in the country.

By the time Ivan Pillay walked into Jacob Zuma's office, Number One probably knew much, much more than what the acting SARS commissioner suspected.

EIGHT

Tom's tempest

————•————

As storm clouds amassed around SARS, Johann van Loggerenberg battled his own tempest. She came in the form of Pretoria attorney Belinda Walter. She sauntered into his office at the start of September 2013 as the chairperson of the Fair-Trade Independent Tobacco Association (FITA), an organisation supposedly representing smaller and independent tobacco manufacturers.

Known as JvL to friends and foes, Van Loggerenberg has an introverted, almost reclusive personality. He doesn't pose for photographs and his SARS CV, which I asked for in 2014, merely mentioned that he joined SARS in late 1998 and held a law degree from Free State University and a post-graduate certificate in business management from Wits University.

Journalists like me tried in vain for years to befriend him while tax evaders attempted to brown-nose him, to their own detriment. He believed in rules, systems and due process. I came to know a little of him at the time when the storm hit SARS and they gave me an exclusive interview with him.

Van Loggerenberg spent much of his youth as a deep-cover agent for the police's former organised crime intelligence unit. He joined the unit in 1991 at the age of 22. For the next seven years, he cut ties with friends and family while infiltrating crime syndicates. He drove a taxi, became a driver for brothels, traded in second-hand goods and liquor, and even co-owned a nightclub. He manoeuvred his way into the innards of major drug syndicates, some with roots in Brazil and the Netherlands.

This had a massive psychological impact on him. He was lonely, isolated and had to a certain extent lost his youth. It required lots of therapy to adapt to civilian life and he admits in his book *Rogue* that, with the benefit of hindsight, it was too high a price to pay.

When Pravin Gordhan was appointed SARS commissioner in 1999, Van Loggerenberg was his choice to track down organised criminals, money launderers and fraudsters, and extricate taxes from them. The who's who of gangland – Radovan Krejčíř, Lolly Jackson, apartheid assassin Calla Botha, Glenn Agliotti, Cyril Beeka, Barry Tannenbaum, the so-called "Kebble killers" (Mikey Schultz, Faizel Kappie Smith and Nigel McGurk), Colin Stansfield, Jerome "Donkie" Booysen, Mark Lifman, Quinton "Mr Big" Marinus and a host of tobacco smugglers came under his scalpel and emerged much skinnier on the other side. Politicians and business people like Julius Malema, Dave King, Billy Rautenbach and Hennie Delport were also in his sights. Google any of these names and you'd be confronted by a glut of infamy.

Colleagues of Van Loggerenberg said he usually worked twelve hours a day, seven days a week. He had almost no social life, which maybe explains why he fell for Belinda Walter.

The units under him handled around eighty projects at any given time. Those who worked with him tell how he knew the detail of every one of them, grasping the tax scams instinctively, and that he understood the laws and procedures by heart. He hardly lost a court case, and his affidavits and documentation were always impeccably prepared. Many tax offenders he interviewed during investigations would usually cave in, confess and attempt to strike a deal with SARS. He typically recorded all his meetings and phone calls and kept meticulous notes and records.

He wasn't one for small talk, hardly socialised with colleagues, was often irritated when someone got sick or wanted leave, and did silly things like banning the coffee station on his floor because it was an unnecessary expense. Some found him difficult to read and relate to.

His call for perfection and performance created enemies within SARS.

At least two executive committee members couldn't stand him because he was perceived to be Ivan Pillay's blue-eyed boy.

*   *   *

Unbeknown to Van Loggerenberg, Belinda Walter wore a hidden recording device and was a spy. She was on a mission from the State Security Agency (SSA) to infiltrate the tax collector and extract as much information from him as possible.

Two months later, in the last week of October, Walter asked Van Loggerenberg out on a date. He fell head over heels for her. She seems to have been intent on mining him for information for her SSA handlers. Walter became an SSA spy in October 2010 and was registered as Agent 5332 and worked on several intelligence projects.

Early in the relationship, Walter bared herself to Van Loggerenberg as an agent and confessed that she represented the tobacco company Carnilinx. This company was being investigated by SARS for tax evasion and money laundering. He gave her a choice: end the Carnilinx brief and resign as an SSA agent, or walk away from their relationship. Walter resigned from both – or so she claimed.

Walter also confessed that FITA was an intelligence project. Walter claimed to have created and used FITA to infiltrate tobacco companies and shop their secrets to the SSA. By January 2014, Walter conceded to her lover that she also spied for British American Tobacco (BAT), a multinational that in 2014 sold 700 billion cigarettes manufactured in 41 countries. BAT paid Walter for commercially sensitive information about its smaller competitors. She reportedly received over £30,000 in 2013 for her "services".

Walter shopped everyone over time, depending on how the wind blew – her boyfriends, her lovers, her clients, and even her spymasters.

Her relationship with Van Loggerenberg soon turned calamitous. Amid a flurry of upheavals, tantrums and violent commotions, Van Loggerenberg managed to retain much of Walter's cellphone communications and vital e-mails after she asked him to help her to download her phone records. He put the memory stick containing the data in a basket on top of his fridge, "thinking I would look at it later when I had a chance". After the relationship ended, he went through the material on the device. It revealed how Walter had become entangled in a labyrinth of deceit and deception.

Van Loggerenberg wrote in *Rogue*: "What I found was shocking, to say the least. It documents precisely how the interests of informants, state officials who were part of the Tobacco Task Team, as well as private business overlap way beyond what could be considered proper. In some instances, their activities were clearly unlawful."

Walter said in a later affidavit that at the outset of the relationship, Van Loggerenberg "presented himself as my knight in shining armour. He was my exit out of the tangled web and I invested myself into the relationship fully." By the end of the affair, she branded him "mentally ill, unstable, corrupt, a pathological liar and a sociopath likened to a paedophile".

There was another problem that threatened to bring the house down on the Tobacco Task Team, BAT and the SSA. On 23 May 2014, Walter sued BAT in London for £5 million. In her lawyer's legal demand, she indicated that she was also bringing a claim against the SSA because the relationship between them was a sham to steal information from BAT's commercial competitors.

If any of this had to come out in the public domain, the SSA, police crime intelligence, private security firms and BAT would have been exposed for all to see. Just imagine the civil suits that those being spied upon could bring against BAT and the SSA. Walter's cronies persuaded her to withdraw her legal demands and, in return, they offered her a blanket indemnity from prosecution for any crime she may have committed and assistance and support against SARS and Van Loggerenberg. It was a win-win for all. In this way, the Tobacco Task Team's problems with SARS would be solved, their sins would never be revealed, BAT's problems would go away, and so would the SSA's. It was perfect timing for everybody.

She withdrew the demand, and on the same day, just as this "deal" was concluded, Walter sent an e-mail to Van Loggerenberg – copied to several executives – and accused him of unlawfully having shared Zuma's and Malema's tax affairs with her. She said he was corrupt and unfit for office.

At the time, she gave an undertaking to provide her allegations to SARS under oath, and to provide SARS with a complete set of text exchanges between them. When the time came for her to do so, she refused.

I was stunned that Van Loggerenberg, a calculated and measured person, had allowed himself to be bewitched by a charlatan like Walter. What is worse is that she handed his enemies a gun loaded with armour-piercing bullets.

*   *   *

Did Belinda Walter and her SSA handlers set a honeytrap for Van Loggerenberg to wrest information from him about SARS investigations and plant dirt on him?

I asked him at the time what he thought had happened. He wasn't sure, but said that after the initial flirtation, something "very real" happened. The romance was barely a month old when the two embarked on a road journey that took them as far as Zambia in support of charitable causes in which he was involved at the time. They developed mutually strong feelings, which must have conjured in her emotions of betrayal and angst, for the affair was not supposed to happen. After their road-trip, the romance went downhill at the speed of light.

Van Loggerenberg caught her several times going through the messages and e-mails on his phone. By then he should have sent her packing. Instead, he forgave her and attempted to stitch up the relationship.

On 1 February 2014, after a lover's squabble, Walter stormed out in a fury. Intent on revenge, she summoned her former clients, self-confessed tobacco smuggler Adriano Mazzotti and other executives of Carnilinx, to a meeting. Also present was the *Sunday Times* journalist Malcolm Rees, known to both Mazzotti and Walter. She confessed that she was a spy for BAT, the SSA and the Tobacco Task Team, and ratted on her SSA and BAT handlers. She said that Van Loggerenberg was corrupt and supposedly had some sort of untoward relationship with several people.

Walter sought from Carnilinx some financial assurance of her future, in exchange for which she would work with them and assist them if they wished to sue the state and BAT. She later repeated the allegations in front of a senior advocate. Rees left with a pack of documents and an agreement that the *Sunday Times* would publish the story the next week. Details of the meeting and her confession are contained in affidavits made by the Carnilinx directors in support of a High Court application which they later brought against Walter and BAT.

Hours afterwards, Walter had second thoughts about going public. Perhaps she realised she was committing professional suicide by blowing her cover as a spy. Her first step back from the precipice was to kiss and make up with Van Loggerenberg. She sent him an SMS: "*I love you with all my heart. I feel so disgusted and disappointed in myself that not only did I betray you, but the types of things I said to those scumbags. You should hate me.*" And: "*I want to sleep so that all these emotions of extreme guilt, remorse, regret and sadness don't consume me.*"

Walter had to stop the *Sunday Times* from publishing the stories. She cunningly set out to solicit pity and wrote that she had suffered severe "mental and psychological trauma". She withdrew all her allegations against Van Loggerenberg and said her claims about him were based on "rumours in the industry". She apologised for having defamed him.

She sent an e-mail to Rees and retracted what she had said. She told *Sunday Times* editor Phylicia Oppelt that she had lied about certain things. She then advised the paper: "Offers of money had been made by this same company [Carnilinx] for financial benefit in the form of cash, holidays and cocaine to Malcolm Rees on several occasions."

Walter warned that should the *Sunday Times* plan to publish any detail of her relationship, she would apply for an urgent court interdict to stop the newspaper from doing so. "This unfortunately would have the counter-productive effect of forcing me to have to bring into the public domain that which I consider to be intimate and private."

It was not necessary for Walter to bring the interdict – the *Sunday Times* got the drift of her threat and shelved the story.

* * *

Belinda Walter's SSA handlers were probably mortified that Van Loggerenberg possessed her cellphone data and must have reported the quandary to their superiors.

In *Rogue*, Van Loggerenberg refers to an SSA agent, "Toby", who approached him and met him within days after Walter's allegations. My sources helped me to piece together the events that followed and showed me internal memos and photographs that chronicled several meetings between SARS and the SSA.

"Toby" was Yekani Monde Gadini, later unmasked as a member of the SSA's Special Operations Unit and husband of Zuma's legal adviser, Bonisiwe Makhene.

According to a June 2014 High-Risk Investigation Unit report, members had conducted surveillance at the request of SARS officials Gene Ravele and Van Loggerenberg during a meeting with two SSA officials at a restaurant next to the SARS head office in Brooklyn, Pretoria. One was Gadini, the other the head of the domestic branch of the SSA, Simon Ntombela. Gadini wanted copies of Walter's data, he said, because the SSA was concerned about the reputation of the agency. Van Loggerenberg told Gadini that the SSA must formally request the data from SARS, but a request never materialised.

A month later, there was another meeting between Van Loggerenberg and Gadini, which the SARS executive tape-recorded. Gadini made an astonishing revelation when he said that a "new commissioner was being briefed" and would start at SARS "soon enough".

I was intrigued about Gadini's role in the SARS narrative, and a day after seeing the documents, I called Van Loggerenberg again. He was as always courteous but curt. I told him that I knew about these meetings and that it showed State Security's hand in the events. Could we meet?

"It's water under the bridge," he said. "Leave it. Let it be. You've retired, haven't you? So have I. Why are you so interested in this?"

I asked him: "Will Ivan [Pillay] talk? Gene, maybe?"

"Forget it. They won't talk to you, just forget it. Move on. It's over."

I kept on wondering about the continued loyalty that they displayed and asked my sources about it. "Why hasn't Ivan, Pete [Richer], JvL or Gene gone public with this stuff?"

Said the one: "You must understand that Ivan and Pete are old ANC people. They've given their lives to the struggle. They'd never do anything to harm the ANC or the country. No matter the cost. It's just how they are."

"And Van Loggerenberg?"

"He thinks short term, medium term, long term. He'll hold and hold. Not even Gene or Ivan will have what he has. The day they drag him to court and charge him with whatever is the day he will take out his recordings, documents and whatever else he might have collected. He is patient. And he won't want to cause harm to people or the state. He's waiting to see what they do."

This was not the end of Gadini's antics in the matter. Through a former senior Hawks source, I discovered that in July 2014, Gauteng Hawks head Major-General Shadrack Sibiya scrambled the police's elite Technical Operations Management Section (TOMS), which assembled at the Wierda Bridge police station outside Pretoria. A senior SSA official had been kidnapped. Guess who it was? None other than Monde Gadini. Using cellphone technology, Sibiya and his men traced the kidnappers and freed Gadini. His kidnappers were suspected Special Operations Unit members who had snatched Gadini because they thought he had managed to obtain Walter's cellphone data. Sibiya arrested the kidnappers and took Gadini home to freshen up because his captors had roughed him up.

Sibiya brought Gadini and his kidnappers to the Wierda Bridge police station, where a case of kidnapping (CAS583/07/2014) was opened. Present at the police station were police commissioner General Riah Phiyega, the SSA's Simon Ntombela and Zuma's legal adviser, Advocate Bonisiwe Makhene.

Gadini spoke in private with Ntombela, after which he announced that he would not be pressing any charges. The agents were released, and Makhene and Gadini left for their mansion in Pretoria.

Contacts in the SSA told me later that Simon Ntombela was troubled by the shenanigans of his agents and recommended a counter-intelligence project to get to the bottom of the matter. He didn't last long. Two months later, in September 2014, he was dispatched to the Department of International Relations and is now South Africa's ambassador to Poland.

*   *   *

I had known all along that there was no "rogue unit" and that Ivan Pillay, Johann van Loggerenberg and other SARS executives were pursued for ulterior and far more sinister intentions.

Towards the end of July 2014, an SSA contract agent, George Darmanovich – also known as Boris – said to me that Van Loggerenberg was going to be fired. I prompted him and he said: "Just phone him. He's gone. He's done."

After Van Loggerenberg left SARS, he contacted Boris, who was then living in Serbia. Van Loggerenberg said in *Rogue*: "He told me he was the person who had tipped off *City Press* but never explained whether he did so on orders or of his own accord. But he did admit that they were instructed to 'look at us' with, in his words, 'a microscope'. He told me in no uncertain terms that they had been given the official instruction to 'find whatever they could' against us."

Back in 2014, when I phoned Van Loggerenberg after speaking to Darmanovich, he told me to come to Pretoria. I reported to SARS headquarters the next morning for an officially sanctioned briefing with him and spokesperson Adrian Lackay.

The affair between Van Loggerenberg and the double-dealing Belinda Walter was, from a journalistic point of view, sexy as hell but it wasn't the main thrust of the havoc that the relationship had caused. A few days later and after having spoken to more intelligence sources, I was convinced that SSA agents were involved in a stratagem to discredit the top SARS executives.

I discovered a critical piece of the puzzle in the form of an e-mail that Walter had sent to Ivan Pillay and anti-corruption group executive Clifford Collings. By then, Pillay had appointed a panel to investigate Walter's allegations against Van Loggerenberg. Walter said in the e-mail, dated 20 July 2014, that she had concluded a meeting with the SSA's acting head of economic intelligence, Ferdi Fryer at a Pretoria restaurant. "Mr Fryer advised that he was aware of what was going on and needed to see me urgently," she said in the e-mail. Walter had appeared that very same day in front of the panel and Fryer wanted her report and notes. She said he made "innuendos and slights about my safety and my son's safety". It was these threats that prompted her to send the e-mail to SARS. Walter said Fryer stated that he "represents interests within the ANC who would like to see the SARS ruling structure replaced, as well as the minister of finance".

*   *   *

On 10 August 2014, South Africa's two most influential Sunday news-papers – *City Press* and *Sunday Times* – devoted their front pages to the sordid romance and the upheaval at the tax collector. "Sex, SARS and rogue spies," trumpeted *City Press*. In the article I wrote that rogue agents at the Special Operations Unit of the SSA "used state resources to conduct dirty tricks campaigns, smuggle cigarettes and disgrace top civil servants". This unit, I concluded, was intent on removing the SARS top structure and had launched operations to discredit senior civil servants like NPA prosecutor Glynnis Breytenbach and Hawks head Anwa Dramat.

The *Sunday Times* splashed with "Love affair rocks SARS". Their exposé centred on Walter's allegations that her former lover was dishonest and corrupt. The newspaper branded Van Loggerenberg a "former apartheid undercover police agent", without a shred of evidence. They failed to men-tion that Walter was an SSA agent and a self-confessed liar, even though they had known about it for six months. They made no mention of her February 2014 allegations about Van Loggerenberg, which she subsequently admitted were lies. The newspaper was furthermore aware that she was erratic, emotionally unstable and deceitful.

The *Sunday Times* showed no circumspection in dealing with the wobbly Walter. Guess who was the author of the *Sunday Times*'s August story? None other than Malcolm Rees, the journalist who was present at her February "confession".

Walter instructed Rees what to publish in his 10 August "exposé". In an e-mail, sent to him two days before publication, she said his article must include that Van Loggerenberg used illegal interceptions to "groom" her, was promoting "criminal syndicate agendas" and was an apartheid agent. On this same day, Walter also met her handlers at Life Café in Brooklyn, following certain questions that I had put to her for comment.

But the worst was still to come. As I left journalism in October 2014 to pursue my new life as a chef in Riebeek-Kasteel, my exposé about the role of the SSA in the destruction of SARS faded into obscurity. The rest of the media, apart from *Daily Maverick* and the *Mail & Guardian*, preferred the spicier "rogue unit" angle.

I was bitterly disappointed that my former newspaper, *City Press*, didn't pursue the SSA angle. They afforded Walter an opportunity to write a piece about me in *City Press* in early 2015. She said I had caused her "irreparable pain and harm" and that I "appeared to follow a pattern of tyranny" in my reporting about her. She said: "The public is also not aware Pauw continued to harass and intimidate me until I laid a criminal complaint."

This was bullshit, and *City Press* flouted their own press code of fair reporting when they didn't attempt to contact me or give me an opportunity to respond. All the same, it was a drop in the ocean compared to the injustice that Van Loggerenberg and his team members must have suffered. I could imagine how he must have felt when witnessing his labour of a decade being trashed and ridiculed in such a brutal manner.

*   *   *

On 23 September 2014, Thomas Moyane became Zuma's choice for commissioner of SARS, one of the most crucial government positions in the country.

An online document called "They Were Part of Us and We Were Part of Them: The ANC in Mozambique from 1976 to 1990" by Nadja Manghezi gives a fascinating insight into Moyane's earlier life. The author referred to him as Tommy Ndhlela, which was his nom de plume in the ANC. The surname belongs to his mother.

He was born in Soweto in 1953 and was bright and ambitious. After passing matric, he worked as a clerk and got a bursary to study economics at Turfloop University, today the University of Limpopo. When Soweto erupted in June 1976 and the university was closed, he returned to Soweto. The air was thick with tear gas and the smell of burning tyres. He joined the protesting students and was arrested and taken to Jabulani police station. Said an activist: "Tommy was beaten unconscious as they pushed his head against the table. We were beaten up, humiliated. Then we were taken to common law prisoners' cells, not awaiting trialists' cells. The idea was that we were going to be sodomized."

They got bail of R500 each and decided to skip the country. Moyane wanted to go to Mozambique, where his father was born and lived before coming to work on the mines. Moyane said about his time in Mozambique: "Here I was on my own, in a country I knew nothing about. The language was foreign. The money and the manner of dressing was completely alien. They seemed completely, you know, bundu type, rural, backward."

He underwent some military training but was then employed by the Mozambican government to work on a chicken farm. Said Moyane: "Zuma came in a Volkswagen. He came to the farm late in the evening. We started talking. Talking. Talking. Talking. About the struggle."

Zuma arranged for Moyane to join a group of 20 South African students studying at the Eduardo Mondlane University in Maputo. He was the only one who passed and was employed at the Cashew Nut State Secretariat. The rest were sent to Tanzania to become soldiers.

Moyane and his new wife, Zola, lived in a flat on one of the top floors of a Maputo building. It was next to an army installation. ANC comrades in Maputo were not allowed to be armed, but Moyane and his wife had an AK-47 assault rifle, a Makarov pistol and two hand grenades. He heard a noise one night and got up. The intruder ran away.

A night or two later, he heard a noise again. He got up with the AK in his hands. "I had never used a gun in my life except for training purposes. Comrades were killed in their houses in Lesotho, in Maseru, in Botswana, in Angola. And my body became very cold. I was shivering. I felt very cold. As he pushed the door, I opened fire. The first shot went through the forehead. I was just shooting and shooting and shooting. Now the problem was: How do we tell Frelimo who shot this man? Whose gun was it?"

Later that morning, Frelimo top brass arrived. They were concerned because the incident had happened next to army property. Moyane concocted a story that the intruder had arrived with the AK-47 and that he ambushed him with a kitchen knife. The gun fell, he picked it up and pulled the trigger.

When he later became South Africa's prisons commissioner, Moyane was reportedly the highest-paid director-general in the civil service. He was appointed on a five-year contract, but was told in 2013 that he had reached the retirement age of 60 and had to leave.

In August 2017, the Special Investigating Unit (SIU) announced that it will be probing a controversial multimillion-rand prisons fencing tender, awarded during Moyane's term. Among the allegations the SIU is investigating in connection with Moyane are the unlawful and improper conduct of state officials; the unlawful expenditure of public money; and serious maladministration.

*   *   *

Moyane scored serious brownie points with President Zuma when he took part in a four-person panel that investigated the landing of Jet Airways charter flight JAI9900 at Waterkloof Air Force Base in Pretoria in April 2013. The aircraft carried 217 guests who had been flown over from India by the Gupta family to attend the lavish nuptials of Vega Gupta and his bride at Sun City. Almost 200 government officials and 88 cars were used to receive the wedding guests and accompany them to Sun City. Red carpets were rolled out for the arrival of the guests. Jacob Zuma was caught slap-bang in the centre of the controversy because of the abuse of state resources, and he hastily withdrew from attending the wedding reception.

Four top officials – including Moyane – from the justice, crime prevention and security cluster of government departments were appointed to investigate what became known as Guptagate. They heard evidence that the man who had masterminded a clearance certificate for the plane, chief of state protocol Bruce Koloane, claimed he was "under pressure from Number One". He said that the minister of transport was given instructions "by the president to assist the Gupta family".

Zuma was never interrogated but a Presidency official told the panel that Zuma knew nothing about the aeroplane or the landing arrangements. The panel accepted this at face value and confirmed Zuma's blamelessness. The panel pointed at Koloane and a senior Air Force official for dereliction of their duties and found that their actions amounted to a security risk to the country.

Koloane was the fall guy to protect Zuma. The Department of International Relations charged him, he pleaded guilty and was demoted to a liaison officer. But there was no way of keeping a good man down. Just more than a year later, Koloane was appointed as South Africa's ambassador to the Netherlands.

The four-member panel that exonerated Number One were richly awarded with jammy jobs or a promise of easy money. Dennis Dhlomo, then acting director-general of the SSA, also got an ambassadorial post. Dr Clinton Swemmer, then acting coordinator of intelligence, is now political counsellor at South Africa's mission to the United Nations in Geneva, Switzerland. Nonkululeko Sindane has since resigned from the justice ministry and become CEO at UWP Consulting, a black-owned company that thrives on state business. When announcing her appointment in 2016, UWP noted: "Her experience within the public infrastructure sector from where UWP Consulting procures the majority of its work will be invaluable to the company going forward."

Let's face it. Moyane was hand-picked by the president to rein in an institution that, despite being lauded for its efficiency and independence, had become a threat to the hyenas that skulked in the echelons of power.

* * *

Just two weeks after Moyane had taken office, the front page of the *Sunday Times* screamed: "SARS bugged Zuma". This was the first time that the "SARS rogue unit" narrative was introduced to the public. Not even Belinda Walter had ever suggested that there was a "rogue unit" at SARS. The article said that members of SARS's secret rogue unit had broken into Zuma's private residence before he became president and planted listening devices in the house. The story was accompanied by a photograph of Van Loggerenberg, although he wasn't even head of the unit at that time.

This was followed by another front-page exposé, "Taxman's rogue unit ran brothel", claiming that the unit had operated a brothel as a front. It didn't give any detail about the establishment, where it was located, for how long it had existed, or who its clients and employees were.

Week after week, front page after front page, exposé after exposé, the *Sunday Times* presented the narrative of an unlawful and surreptitious "rogue unit" as fact. In more than 35 articles spanning two years, the newspaper falsely claimed that officials of the High-Risk Investigation Unit had committed a host of serious crimes. Van Loggerenberg wrote in *Rogue*: "During this period, numerous reports, documents and leaks – as they were termed – were distributed to the *Sunday Times* from within SARS, by 'former SARS officials' and 'intelligence officials', as one of the journalists involved ultimately acknowledged."

Moyane used the *Sunday Times* "revelations" as a pretext to suspend Pillay, Van Loggerenberg and ultimately a host of other top executives. He said he had lost confidence in the SARS executive committee. He was reported to be "disgusted" that "SARS now ran brothels". Senior managers, investigators, auditors and other senior personnel resigned in droves. The demolition of SARS was in full swing.

Pillay faced ten charges ranging from corruption and dishonesty to contravening the SARS code of conduct, the Tax Administration Act and the Public Finance Management Act. The *Mail & Guardian* reported that Pillay received a letter of demand and a disciplinary charge sheet that alleged that, by establishing the rogue intelligence unit, he had incurred "fruitless and wasteful expenditure" of R106 million.

In May 2016, Moyane went a step further when he opened case number 427/05/2015 at the Brooklyn police station and laid charges against finance minister Pravin Gordhan, Pillay and Van Loggerenberg. His contention was that the "rogue unit" was unlawful and had been engaged in illegal activities. Gordhan, in response, said that the unit had ministerial approval and was legal in every aspect. He declared he was proud of the unit and the way they had executed their duties.

Moyane's big stick to clobber Pillay, Van Loggerenberg, Richer and Ravele was audit firm KPMG, which he appointed in December 2014 to "forensically" investigate the "rogue unit". The scope of the KPMG investigation stretched as far back as 2003. KPMG never interviewed Pillay, Van Loggerenberg or Pete Richer. Moyane claimed they were paid to conduct a "forensic investigation" whereas KPMG's CEO Trevor Hoole contradicted this later by saying that it was only a "documentary review" which did not include interviewing any of those affected.

KPMG ultimately produced a half-baked effort a year later which came with a disclaimer that rendered the report unusable in any "disputes" or "controversies" and prohibited SARS from referring to it in "whole or in part". It wasn't worth the paper it was written on – yet cost the taxpayer R23 million.

Daily Maverick reported that one of the first visits Pravin made after being parachuted back into the ministry of finance in December 2015 was to SARS headquarters in Cape Town, where he ordered Moyane to halt his extensive restructuring of SARS. Moyane ignored him and forged ahead.

Seeking to minimise the collateral damage of Moyane's restructuring, Gordhan delivered an ultimatum to Zuma in February 2016 to fire his SARS commissioner. Zuma, unsurprisingly, chose to let the matter simmer until he fired Gordhan on the stroke of the last midnight of March 2017.

Marianne Thamm commented in *Daily Maverick* that "Moyane's name crops up in the strangest places" and that he is "a key figure linked to some of the most breathtaking events that have occurred under President Jacob Zuma's watch". She describes him as "a quiet kingpin in Zuma's tight band of protectors".

* * *

When I sat in Moscow compiling a list of Jacob Zuma's keepers, I scribbled down the names of three *Sunday Times* journalists, whose reporting, I believe, has helped Zuma's keepers to destroy the finest law enforcement institution in the country. It is a journalistic burden they will carry for a long time.

The *Sunday Times* journalists – Piet Rampedi, Stephan Hofstatter and Mzilikazi wa Afrika – have contributed greatly to ending the careers of dedicated civil servants and ultimately enabled Tom Moyane to break the tax collector.

It took the best part of a year for the *Sunday Times* stories to start falling apart. The press ombudsman ruled against the *Sunday Times* in December 2016 and found that its "rogue unit" stories were unfair and inaccurate.

Rees was the first to resign and silently disappeared from sight. Editor Phylicia Oppelt got the boot and journalist Piet Rampedi quit before the *Sunday Times* could pursue any disciplinary steps against him. Stephan Hofstatter also called it a day and left.

In April 2016, the *Sunday Times* published a full-page article, retracting their "rogue unit" claims. The newspaper, under new editorship, admitted there had been fundamental flaws in its processes. The new *Sunday Times* editor, Bongani Siqoko, told his readers that "today we admit to you that we got some things wrong". He has, to a large extent, restored the credibility of the *Sunday Times*.

Rampedi started a newspaper called the *African Times* (who the hell starts a newspaper these days – unless you have government or Gupta funding!) and has ever since raved like a wounded animal about "white racist monopoly capital". The fact that communications minister Faith Muthambi – a *mampara* of prodigious proportions and a Zuma acolyte – congratulated Rampedi on the launch of the paper says everything. Not long after the first edition, the press ombudsman ordered Rampedi to apologise to Ivan Pillay about yet another invented tirade.

Rampedi also said on Twitter that Van Loggerenberg was a "delusional psychopath" and added that he didn't intend to sue him for defamation because it served no point to go after a madman. He reckoned that Van Loggerenberg was suicidal in 2015 and couldn't have written his book *Rogue*.

Van Loggerenberg described in *Rogue* how he bumped into Hofstatter in June 2016. By then the *Sunday Times* had already apologised for their sloppy reporting. According to Van Loggerenberg: "As most of the 30-plus articles advancing the 'rogue-unit' story featured him as co-author, you could say we kind of 'knew' each other. Out of courtesy, I greeted him, shaking his hand. He asked how I was. I said that it was tough times and that I was taking things day by day. I said that I had heard that the *Sunday Times* was under new management and asked him how he was doing. Hofstatter said he too was taking things day by day. There was no apology. No acknowledgement of error, no mention of any of the articles under his by-line. Nothing. I greeted him and walked away."

The *Sunday Times* was not the only media outlet to feast on the rotten carcass that Moyane threw at the hyenas. By February 2015, rhino-poacher-turned-SARS-whistleblower Michael Peega, Tobacco Task Team member Hennie Niemann and spy Belinda Walter appeared side by side on DSTV's *Carte Blanche*. Peega gave an Oscar-winning performance. With tears in his eyes, presenter Bongani Bingwa said: "Michael is now hoping that his seven-year battle to claw back his integrity is finally over."

Peega whimpered: "I know I have lost time. I cannot buy that back. But I can only, hopefully, start from here and move on."

Belinda Walter was the heroine of the programme. Bingwa asked her: "Why did you do it?"

Walter: "I believed in justice."

* * *

Newly appointed state security minister David Mahlobo instructed the inspector-general of intelligence (IGI), Faith Radebe, to "establish the facts and get to the bottom of allegations made about members of the State Security Agency". This was in response to the *City Press* article fingering the conspiracy by Walter and others at the SSA to discredit the SARS executive.

I had zero confidence in the gutless IGI unearthing anything, but Van Loggerenberg prepared a lengthy submission and appeared before her twice. At the first meeting, he presented her with over thirty instances of possible unlawful or illegal activities that he was aware of and that he believed to be relevant to her investigation. Much of his evidence was meticulously documented and recorded.

He also named over sixty people who should be interviewed or be of interest to the investigation. He presented text messages and e-mails between Walter and her SSA handler in which they described themselves as a "moerse [exceptionally] good team" who could manipulate the SSA, NPA and SARS to do whatever they wanted. He handed her the Agliotti tape recordings which showed how SSA operatives conspired to smuggle cigarettes.

Van Loggerenberg said he detected "reticence" at the IGI. At his second appearance, he said he simply answered questions, but "was asked virtually nothing regarding the 30-plus instances I had raised in the first meeting".

Gorgija Gorg "George" Darmanovich, a South African of Serbian descent, was one of the main contract agents of the SSA's Special Operations Unit. He was the man who tipped me off that Van Loggerenberg was in trouble and who, I believe, was also complicit in the campaigns to disgrace Glynnis Breytenbach and Anwa Dramat.

Darmanovich is a glitzy character who operated from a safe house and drove fast cars with boots full of guns, cash and police dockets. I have shared tables with him and senior police and Hawks officials who ate from his hand and volunteered classified information. He was issued with 11 gun licences in 2011 for assault rifles and sub-machine guns despite an outstanding warrant for his arrest for fraud.

Darmanovich should have been a crucial witness before the IGI, but he was never called. Because his name was blown in the media, he became a liability to the SSA. Although a South African citizen, he left the country and returned to Serbia.

The SSA submitted to the IGI that they knew Darmanovich but that he was nothing but an overzealous and bothersome information peddler with whom they had erratic dealings. The SSA even got some of his scallywag chums – who merrily shared in his booty – to testify that he was nothing but a scammer who had tried to score a quick buck.

I am for a moment going to venture into the muddy world of intelligence. I recently saw a transcript of a recorded meeting of the IGI that took place behind closed doors on 1 September 2014 – two weeks after my exposé in *City Press*. The meeting was attended by Faith Radebe, IGI advocate Jay Govender and several intelligence officials, among them Kobus Meiring of SSA legal services, who was one of the co-signatories of the PAN investigation into Arthur Fraser's PAN project of fraud and corruption.

The headline of the document I saw read: "Investigation: Regarding State Security Special Operations Unit – Alleged Improper Intelligence Activities". The transcript of the meeting provides evidence that the SSA acted in the personal interest of and on behalf of Jacob Zuma. This was in flagrant contravention of the SSA's constitutional obligation to stay out of politics and concern itself with state security.

In January 2012, the head of the Special Operations Unit (SOU), Thulani Dhlomo, instructed the acting manager of the presidential risk management unit, Eric Mtholo, to register what the SSA described as "an information peddler of note" an Agent 5435 in the SOU. The existence of the presidential risk management unit in the SSA has never been revealed, and none of my SSA sources knew about it.

Dhlomo was a powerful man in the agency and boasted about being close to Jacob Zuma. In 2012, he was appointed to his position despite being the subject of a corruption investigation in KwaZulu-Natal. He resigned as head of security of the province's social development department after an internal audit found that he had interfered in tender procedures and awarded dodgy contracts of R45 million. The audit recommended that Dhlomo face criminal charges, but this has never happened.

Agent 5435 is identified as Rian Stander, with whom I've interacted many times in my journalism career. He is a former apartheid policeman, spook, military intelligence operative, information peddler. He used to be close to former Vlakplaas commander Colonel Eugene de Kock, although the apartheid assassin disowned him after his arrest in 1994. Stander was also good friends with another death squad commander, Dirk Coetzee.

The SSA appointed Stander at a salary of R10,000 per month "based on productivity". He had to submit monthly reports that went directly to Dhlomo, but his handler, Eric Mtholo, said that "a lot of information submitted by 5435 could not be verified, especially information concerning the AWB". The AWB is the neo-fascist Afrikaner-Weerstandsbeweging (Afrikaner Resistance Movement). The last remnants of the organisation faded away after the death of its leader, Eugene Terre'Blanche, in 2010 so it is anyone's guess what Stander concocted. He also told his handlers that some of Zuma's close protectors had a plan to poison him. It's always a good strategy for a sleuth to dish up a conspiracy against the head of state. It ensures continued employment.

Dhlomo said in a statement to Meiring: "Stander alleged that he had a lot of information concerning the arms deal and he can obtain evidence in foreign countries that will be proof that the current president was not involved in any wrongdoing."

Dhlomo briefed Mtholo in June 2012 that Stander "has information in five different countries that he must retrieve". Mtholo was instructed to arrange for him and Stander to fly to Europe to retrieve these documents. Dhlomo said he terminated Stander's services after realising that he was an information peddler.

Stander sued Jacob Zuma and the minister of state security in 2013 for R350,000. Meiring explained the claim to Radebe: "The plaintiff would investigate allegations of the arms deal reports by the anti-Jacob Zuma collaborators both domestic and abroad." Mtholo said the trip to the five countries "never materialised".

That is not what Stander says. I spoke to him after seeing the transcript of the IGI meeting. He said the documents he had to retrieve related to German manufacturer Ferrostaal's role in the arms deal saga. The reports, parts of which were later leaked, indicated that several senior ANC members and others benefited from dodgy payments and offset deals directly linked to Ferrostaal's bid to supply South Africa with new submarines.

Stander said he travelled to Europe on behalf of the SSA, sourced the

Top: Jacob Zuma, then ANC deputy president, rallies supporters outside the Johannesburg Supreme Court during his rape trial in 2006. Picture: Gallo Images/*Beeld*/Halden Krog.

Bottom: Schabir Shaik outside court after his leave to appeal in 2005. Picture: Jackie Clausen/*Sunday Times*.

Jacob Zuma's nephew Khulubuse at the Sandton Sun in Johannesburg in 2010. Picture: Daniel Born/*The Times*.

Right: Khulubuse Zuma with Jen-Chih "Robert" Huang at Mpisi, Huang's company, circa 2009. The photo was on Mpisi's website, according to the *Daily News*, until being taken down after the newspaper asked questions in 2012 about a Hawks investigation into a multibillion-rand racket at Durban Harbour allegedly involving Huang.

Bottom: Yusuf Kajee, left, and Edward Zuma, right, in Dubai in 2016.

Jacob Zuma's son Duduzane at *The New Age* newspaper launched by the Guptas in 2010.
Picture: Simphiwe Nkwali/ *Sunday Times*.

Jacob Zuma's son Edward in 2016.
Picture: Thuli Dlamini/ *Sunday Times*.

Ajay and Atul Gupta at *The New Age* offices in Johannesburg in 2011.
Picture: Martin Rhodes /*Business Day*.

Top left: Roy Moodley and his wife, Mumsie, at Jacob Zuma's 70th birthday celebration at the Durban International Convention Centre in 2012. Picture: Jackie Clausen/*Sunday Times.*

Top right: Arthur Fraser in 2008. Jacob Zuma appointed Fraser South Africa's top spy – head of the State Security Agency – in September 2016. Picture: Gallo Images/*City Press*/Khaya Ngwenya.

Middle: Suspended police crime intelligence boss Richard Mdluli in 2014 at Pretoria's Specialised Commercial Crimes Court after charges of fraud and corruption against him were withdrawn. Picture: Peggy Nkomo/*The Times.*

Bottom: Mark Lifman outside the Atlantis Magistrate's Court near Cape Town in 2009. Picture: Shelley Christians/*The Times.*

Top: Glenn Agliotti leaves the Johannesburg Magistrate's Court in 2006 after appearing in connection with the murder of mining tycoon Brett Kebble. Picture: Katherine Muick-Mere/ *Business Day.*

Bottom left: Former Hawks boss Berning Ntlemeza at a press conference in Port Elizabeth in 2016. Picture: Eugene Coetzee/ *The Herald.*

Bottom right: Nkosazana Dlamini-Zuma and Adriano Mazzotti in 2017.

Top: Anwa Dramat and Ivan Pillay during the South African Council of Churches' release of its *Unburdening Panel* report into state capture in May 2017 in Soweto. Picture: Alaister Russell/ *The Times.*

Bottom: Robert McBride, head of the Independent Police Investigative Directorate, in 2016. Picture: Alon Skuy/*The Times.*

Top left: Jeremy Vearey in Vanrhynsdorp in 2016. Picture: Gallo Images/*Die Burger*/Lerato Maduna.

Top right: Johann van Loggerenberg outside the Hawks' headquarters in Pretoria in 2016, when the Hawks summoned Pravin Gordhan, Ivan Pillay and Van Loggerenberg to present themselves for questioning. Picture: Antonio Muchave/*Sowetan*.

Bottom: Nomgcobo Jiba, deputy director of public prosecutions, and National Prosecuting Authority head Shaun Abrahams in 2016 in Pretoria. Picture: Alon Skuy/*The Times*.

Top: SARS Commissioner Tom Moyane and finance minister Malusi Gigaba in Pretoria in 2017. Picture: Gallo Images/*Rapport*/ Deon Raath.

Bottom: President Jacob Zuma at a question-and-answer session – in which he was asked about the Gupta family's influence on cabinet appointments – in the National Assembly in Cape Town in 2016. Picture: Gallo Images/*Beeld*/Nasief Manie.

reports and gave them to Dhlomo. Judge Willie Seriti later ruled that these documents could in any case not be submitted as evidence because Ferrostaal refused to waive its legal privilege over them.

Stander said he reached a settlement with the SSA and that he was paid. How much did they pay you? I wanted to know.

"I can't tell you, but I'm happy," he said. "Why would they have paid me if I didn't go to Europe?"

While discussing the claim of Agent 5435 at the IGI meeting, Faith Radebe, herself a former intelligence official, referred to the Special Operations Unit and said: "I know those guys, I worked with them in special ops. These guys are very dangerous."

I nearly forgot to tell you the result of the IGI's investigation into the SOU. Or can you guess?

Thulani Dhlomo has served his Number One assiduously and in 2017 *News24* announced that he had been nominated as South Africa's new ambassador to Japan.

* * *

The transcription of the inspector-general's meeting also had Mandisa Mokwena on the agenda. She was the former head of economic intelligence at the SSA who became an executive at SARS. She was standing trial in the High Court on more than forty charges of fraud.

During her court case, her advocate revealed that she remained a paid SSA agent throughout her stint at SARS and beyond. He argued that the alleged bribes were not money of ill-gotten gain, but payments from the SSA. This revelation contains an element of desperation. Why didn't she reveal this during her disciplinary hearing, and did she declare the income in her tax returns?

According to a discussion at the IGI's meeting, Mokwena might well have been an SSA agent while working at SARS. The SSA's Kobus Meiring had a meeting with Mokwena's attorney after she wrote a letter to the SSA stating that she was a "deep cover agent" and that "this was sanctioned by an authority even higher than the Minister of State Security".

Meiring asked her attorney: "Are you referring or is she referring to the president?"

"Yes," he said.

Mokwena said she was handled by the head of the SOU, Thulani Dhlomo. Meiring said there was no record that Mokwena was registered as an agent, but added: "When I heard that she's currently, according to her, being handled by Mr Thulani Dhlomo, I thought that can be true."

Mokwena wanted the SSA to come to her rescue in her criminal matter because the "dubious amounts of money that went into her bank account are actually source money that she is receiving from SSA and that's why SSA must now intervene".

Her request seemed bizarre, but it was not. According to the transcription, her husband, Barnard Mokwena, was also an SSA agent. Barnard was the executive president of human capital at the mining giant Lonmin and played a key role during the Marikana strike. He denied he was an agent and at the time promised to disprove the allegations, but ultimately he failed to do so.

Barnard Mokwena was originally charged with his wife and eight other accused in the High Court for fraud. An amount of R600,000 of laundered money was allegedly paid into his bank account. The charge was withdrawn in 2012.

My SARS sources told me that SARS anti-corruption head Clifford Collings reported at the time to the SARS executive that he had a meeting with the SSA and that they requested him to withdraw the charges against Barnard Mokwena because the case could damage the agency. Collings is a former SSA official himself.

Said Meiring: "Her husband [Barnard] was in fact an agent, who has received cash payments from the SSA."

IG Radebe: "What amounts are we talking about, to the husband?"

Meiring: "It was large amounts, but I really can't remember."

What was the role of the SSA in the tragic events at Marikana? Mokwena's harsh stance towards the striking workers was widely condemned after the Marikana massacre in which 34 miners died. He was one of the mine's executive chorus that called for strong police action and refused to negotiate with AMCU-aligned miners.

This is not where it stops. I will once again keep it simple. Barnard and Mandisa Mokwena are also linked to a state security front company, Kazol Enterprises, that was used to set up a new and alternative labour union in Marikana. The other Kazol director was Peter Silenga, another SSA agent who was directly involved in the establishment of the Workers Association Union (WAU). Silenga used to work, like Mandisa, for the SSA. When she went to SARS, he followed her and reported to her. When she resigned, he resigned.

The Kazol people were allegedly told to acquire sensitive information from their rival trade unions, especially on instigators and those perpetuating an illegal strike.

In 2016, Thebe Maswabi, the founding member of WAU, sued President Jacob Zuma, state security minister David Mahlobo and other senior government leaders for R120 million. He alleged in court papers that Zuma had told him to form the new union. He claimed that after government stopped funding him, he ran into serious financial problems.

Maswabi claimed to have had "several meetings" with Zuma, including one in the UK. He said he was initially "well taken care of by Zuma and his people".

Former WAU members provided *City Press* with the cellphone number of a man with "expensive shoes, nice clothes and an expensive car" who allegedly came to help find new union offices. The number was traced to Peter Silenga.

Now, hold onto your chair. Guess who emerged as another player in the formation of WAU? Yekani Monde Gadini, husband of Zuma's legal adviser, Bonisiwe Makhene. A cellphone number listed as one of WAU's contact numbers on the official union registration document belonged to Gadini. As I have said already, he was a powerful man in the agency and boasted about being close to Jacob Zuma.

* * *

The Mokwena couple, Kazol, Silenga, WAU, Gadini and Maswabi: an entangled, mangled and cluttered perplexity of subterfuge, machinations and deception.

There is so much here: a president who allegedly became embroiled in an almost fanciful plot to form a bogus union and pinch support from its bigger competitors; SSA intelligence that probably flowed to an executive at Lonmin and from him to the mining giant's boardroom where sat presidential hopeful Cyril Ramaphosa; failed stratagems that culminated in the bodies of 34 mine workers speckled across the brown and burnt grass veld of the North West platinum belt.

It gets more convoluted: I also came to learn that in 2013 the SARS High-Risk Investigation Unit happened to come across Kazol Enterprises and found that the company was not tax compliant. In hindsight, SARS had stumbled over way too much and had made too many powerful enemies. Having such a controversial front company exposed and its even more contentious agents compromised would have just added to the already volatile mix, ready to explode at any time.

I have no direct evidence to base this on, but by 2014 there must have been enormous resentment at State Security against SARS.

It is when you look at all the different little pieces that one and one becomes two.

NINE

The gentleman gangster and his donkey

————•————

In the shadow of one of the world's natural icons – Table Mountain – lurks a web of sleaze and skulduggery, ruled by nightmarish mobsters and ruffians. Many have relocated from far away to peddle their trade in narcotics, women and bouncers on the shores of Cape Town. Some have settled in idyllic Camps Bay or Clifton while others trade from seaside flats in Sea Point and Three Anchor Bay. Their nicknames often give away their origin: Hoosain "the Moroccan" Ait-Taleb and Yuri "the Russian" Ulianitski. After Yuri died in a hail of bullets, Igor "the New Russian" Russol took his place. They have in turn merged with local gangsters to form one of the most feared criminal gangdoms in the world.

One figure has over the past decade repeatedly emerged from this murky underground domain: Mark Roy Lifman, often referred to as a "businessman-gangster". The clean-shaven and square-jawed Lifman, his coiffed hair neatly parted on the side as he slides in his designer clothes into an array of super-cars, cuts a suave and sophisticated image. He is a far cry from his "business associate", Jerome "Donkie" Booysen (*donkie* is Afrikaans for donkey), head of the Sexy Boys gang on the Cape Flats.

According to the *Mail & Guardian*, Lifman was closely associated with Yuri and joined him at a restaurant hours before the Russian was mowed down. They were co-owners of a strip club in Sea Point. Lifman was also linked to bouncer boss and club owner Cyril Beeka, another mobster who was later assassinated.

After Beeka's death, Lifman filled the void with his own security company and linked up with Ait-Taleb. Their security company had about 350 doormen or bouncers working at 146 clubs throughout the city. That was roughly 60 per cent of the province's nightlife. It is important to remember that bouncers at doors determine what drugs from whom enter the premises.

The *Mail & Guardian* described Lifman as a "shrewd businessman" and quoted Igor Russol as saying that "any business he opens will make money". Underworld sources say that, after owning a taxi company and gambling businesses in Sea Point, Lifman became a property developer, working with gangster Jerome Booysen. He also opened strip clubs in the city.

At the time of writing, full-scale warfare has again taken hold of the streets of Cape Town, this time allegedly between a gang linked to Lifman and that of an East European, Nafiz Modack, who was previously involved in an alleged scam with luxury cars. More reports surfaced, stating that Eastern European men were being brought into Cape Town to assist a planned coup of Lifman and Booysen's turf by Modack. Other reports followed of people shot, two murders and many assaults.

Lifman, linked to corruption, fraud, money laundering, drug trafficking, cigarette smuggling and transnational organised crime, has over the years miraculously escaped prosecution and prison time. In 2009, Lifman was acquitted on charges of indecently assaulting seven boys and attempting to murder their alleged pimp. As so often in the past, it was left to SARS to bring Lifman down. They ultimately presented him with a tax bill of R388 million at the beginning of 2015.

This case should have been settled by now. SARS started investigating Lifman in October 2013 after it appeared that he hadn't paid taxes for years. The investigation, named Project All Out, followed an earlier unsuccessful Project Boy and was headed by a tough and experienced tax detective, Keith Hendrickse, the Western Cape head of the National Projects Unit of SARS. Hendrickse and his team also did the tax investigation that led to the financial ruin of gang boss Quinton "Mr Big" Marinus. He was the gangster who met and complained to Jacob Zuma about SARS some years prior.

National Projects resided under Johann van Loggerenberg, but was entirely separate from the High-Risk Investigation Unit, which the media branded as the "rogue unit". This is important for the purposes of this story because it will illustrate the deceit of Tom Moyane and his henchmen.

The Lifman investigation was massive and expensive. Apart from Hendrickse and his team, SARS appointed attorneys and advocates and the audit firm PricewaterhouseCoopers to penetrate Lifman's entangled financial empire. They investigated 35 close corporations, companies and a trust. According to a SARS document, Lifman was also a loan shark and a debt collector, "particularly within the domain of the illicit and underworld role-players". Lifman used Booysen and his Sexy Boys gangsters to do the collections. Fifty per cent of the collected money was kept as commission.

Lifman also had links with the so-called Johannesburg crowd, led by bouncer and self-confessed Brett Kebble killer Mikey Schultz. He was in turn connected to Czech mobster Radovan Krejčíř and none other than cigarette manufacturer Adriano Mazzotti and Carnilinx.

It is widely known among underground criminals that a fierce competitor of Carnilinx, the tobacco manufacturer Yusuf Kajee (whose fellow director/shareholder was Edward Zuma), owed someone some serious money: twenty million, in fact. This followed the demise of Kajee's earlier venture into tobacco manufacturing, which was in the process of being shut down by SARS. Kajee needed money, and he needed it fast. He borrowed "twenty bar" from a loan shark, but wasn't paying back according to the agreement.

Carnilinx's director Adriano Mazzotti met Lifman and Booysen in early November 2013 at the Mount Nelson Hotel in Cape Town. He was accompanied by Carnilinx's lawyer, Belinda Walter. Little did any of them know that she was a spy for whoever was willing to pay for their secrets. Mazzotti has publicly admitted to this meeting and explained that Lifman had contacted him beforehand about it. He explained that they discussed ways of expanding their cigarette business into the Western Cape.

What I came to learn from insiders in the tobacco industry was that the Carnilinx crowd had a more devilish plan for Kajee up their sleeve. They wanted to choke his business at the same time. They knew of Kajee's debt problem and arranged that Lifman and Booysen "take over" the debt collection. Kajee was suddenly under significant financial pressure from Lifman, Booysen and their bouncer goons to pay his debt. These events appear to have propelled Lifman into the proximity of illicit cigarette traders.

Somehow, attorneys Ian Small-Smith and Belinda Walter seem to have been involved in trying to assist the Carnilinx vendetta against Kajee. In September 2013, the Tobacco Task Team conducted a raid on Kajee's business under the pretext of contraventions of immigration laws. Small-Smith and Walter had inside knowledge of this raid. In text exchanges between them, on the same day of the raid, it is clear that they knew of it, discussed it and exchanged thoughts on getting this to the attention of the media in an apparent attempt to pile up more pressure on Kajee.

Indeed, in September 2013, newspapers carried stories of the raid on Kajee's company in Pietermaritzburg. Kajee retorted by laying criminal charges against members of the Tobacco Task Team who raided him. He accused them of damaging his property, obtaining a search warrant under false pretences and assaulting his workers. Nothing seems to have come of this.

In a 2014 affidavit, SARS acting commissioner Ivan Pillay said of the Lifman case: "SARS officials involved in the case have received several death threats and one official's home was burgled. The home of one of the personnel contracted by SARS to deal with the Lifman inquiry was also burgled and only laptops [were] stolen."

By early 2014, SARS had concluded its full-scale inquiry and audit in terms of section 50 of the Tax Administration Act into Lifman's tax affairs. More than ninety witnesses testified at this tax inquiry. SARS presented Lifman with a tax bill of over R350 million, which had in the meantime risen to R388 million. PricewaterhouseCoopers oversaw the final figures of the audit. This was followed by a year of litigation between SARS and Lifman, which he ultimately lost.

In one of his failed court applications, Lifman described himself as a "maverick businessman" and likened himself to an early Johannesburg

"Randlord", a name given to the entrepreneurs who controlled the gold mining industry in South Africa in its pioneering phase. "I'm like Barney Barnato. I chase the gold, not taking much notice of what is in my path to get there. So I will go off the beaten track to get there . . . Does that make sense to you? I am spontaneous."

At the time, Lifman's financial assets included more than a hundred accounts at four different banks, trendy clothing stores, an extensive property portfolio and at least 14 luxury vehicles. Among his assets was an upmarket brothel, the Embassy. SARS also found a bank account with more than R20 million in cash and 14 luxury vehicles, including three Porsche Cayennes. SARS penalised Lifman for a host of infringements, including tax evasion, failing to submit tax returns, making false disclosures and instructing his tax advisers to miscalculate his tax.

Let us stop for a moment. It is important to remember that after Van Loggerenberg, Pillay and the others left SARS in late 2014 and early 2015, Lifman's tax case was inherited by Tom Moyane and his new appointees. Lifman was ready to be taken down and his taxes collected. The once well-oiled SARS machine would have seen this case through with little resistance.

Millions should already have flowed into state coffers and ultimately resulted in an alleged gangster being financially crippled and possibly facing criminal charges. But hold onto your seat because what followed next is nothing but sabotage of the national fiscus. And once again, somewhere on the horizon, hovers the figure of Jacob Zuma as well as his family.

In April 2015, *City Press* said that Tom Moyane was approached to "go easy" on Lifman as the businessman "is an important man because of his money and influence and his proximity to powerful people". The *City Press* story has not been challenged or contested since its publication and the allegations, said the newspaper, were verified by four different sources.

My sources told me that Lifman is known for his political connections and not shy to flaunt and brag about them. In 2014, he was photographed by the *Sunday Times* at President Jacob Zuma's birthday rally in Athlone, Cape Town, in the company of ANC provincial chairperson Marius Fransman. Lifman wore an ANC T-shirt (imported from China by another Zuma devotee) and had VIP access to the stage, which required clearance by Zuma's bodyguards.

*   *   *

Lifman approached SARS several times with promises to settle his bill and become tax compliant. He always seemed to cancel the meetings at the last moment and has shown complete disdain for the tax service. At one time, he allegedly offered to pay SARS R30 million as a final and full settlement of his tax bill. The tax collector rejected his offer.

Word must have reached the State Security Agency (SSA) that Lifman wanted to settle. On 26 February 2015, the director-general of the SSA, Sonto Kudjoe, wrote to Moyane personally and pleaded with him to reject Lifman's overtures. Kudjoe referred Moyane to an interdepartmental task team that was established in October 2012 to bring down Lifman. The team consisted of members of the SSA, the Hawks, the National Prosecuting Authority (NPA), the police and the Financial Intelligence Centre (FIC). Said Kudjoe: "It has been confirmed that the mentioned individual, Mark Roy Lifman, is involved in criminal activities including transnational organised crime." She said this encompassed intimidation, corruption, cigarette smuggling, drug trafficking, paedophilia and money laundering.

"If the individual settles with the revenue service it is of concern to the SSA that the individual and his syndicate will continue with their illicit activities. Of particular concern to the SSA is the impact that the syndicate has on the social stability of specifically the Western Cape and the possible influence of the syndicate on gang turf wars."

This is an astonishing letter for a number of reasons. The first is that although it is commendable that the state wanted to bring Lifman to book, the exclusion of SARS from the task team is bewildering. Lifman could long ago have been prosecuted on the strength of the SARS investigation against him for at least tax evasion, money laundering and possibly fraud. Why has it not been done? Why didn't this interdepartmental team co-operate with Van Loggerenberg, Hendrickse and the SARS team?

The second concern is that the task team was established in October

2012, and almost five years later, as I am sitting writing this book, Lifman remains untouched and possibly stronger than ever. In fact, in the last few months, as the street war broke out in Cape Town, bodies have begun to pile up in Lifman's vicinity.

As far back as March 2011, assassins on a motorbike shot underworld kingpin Cyril Beeka, just after he had left Donkie Booysen's home. In November 2016, Craig Mathieson, the night manager of Hotel 303, located in Sea Point, which happens to be owned by Lifman, was murdered. Nothing was stolen from the 44-year-old or from the hotel. Just a day or so before this, attorney Noorudien Hassan was killed outside his home in Lansdowne. Hassan had acted in many court cases involving gangs and he represented clients such as alleged gang boss Ralph Stanfield, suspected gun smuggler Irshaad Laher, and Lifman's "business associate" Donkie Booysen. In May 2017, Booysen was shot in the neck and rushed to hospital.

What exactly has this task team been doing all these years? There were several opportunities to get Lifman and his cohorts in the dock. The *Sunday Times* reported in February 2014 that Lifman's Porsche was parked at a house belonging to Booysen's sister and her husband. Both were also known gangsters. Police confiscated three kilograms of tik (an illicit methamphetamine-type concoction) and more than 5,000 Mandrax tablets at the house. Where was the task team? What has happened to this interdepartmental team? Nobody seems to know.

Sonto Kudjoe didn't last long. Five months after writing her letter to SARS, she was gone and replaced by Arthur Fraser. I do not know if the letter had anything to do with her departure, but *Daily Maverick* has reported a link between Lifman and Fraser. The online publication said that Fraser and Lifman were seen entering the headquarters of auditing firm KPMG in Cape Town, two months after Fraser was appointed as Zuma's new spy boss. The publication sent an e-mail to State Security spokesperson Brian Dube, asking whether Fraser's presence at the audit firm was for official business and, if so, what the nature of this was. Dube promised that he would look into the matter, but failed to reply.

In his answer to Kudjoe, Moyane assured her that Lifman "will not receive preferential treatment. He will be expected, like any other taxpayer, to comply with the ambit of the law."

* * *

In a March 2016 memo, SARS's Keith Hendrickse said that Lifman "continues to adversely litigate with SARS", had not paid any of the outstanding taxes or admitted liability, and remained non-compliant "as to the submission of returns, some of which became due even after the last date of the investigation period". Lifman had throughout the process told SARS that he wished to become tax compliant, yet had done little from his side to make this happen. Instead, he launched two urgent court applications and several business rescue applications to avoid sequestration. He lost, and had to pay SARS's legal costs, which he has also failed to do.

Hendrickse said SARS attorneys and counsel had devised a "collection and litigation plan" to collect Lifman's tax debt. He said that the plan recommended the sequestration of Lifman and that these papers would be finalised by March 2016, for issue in the early part of April 2016. Hendrickse added that SARS had appointed independent valuators to provide desktop valuations of fixed property belonging to the Lifman Group. According to the valuations, the property portfolio alone amounted to R92 million. He said there are "good prospects of collecting substantial taxes". "Mr Lifman . . . has a history of flagrant disregard for his tax debts, a history of litigating against SARS without regard of the merits of the matters, not paying costs awards and aborted attempts at settling."

In May 2016, SARS auctioned four of Lifman's luxury cars, among them two Porches, in Cape Town. While interested and potential bidders inspected the cars, Booysen and his lieutenants sauntered in. Within minutes of bidding, Booysen and his cronies bought all four cars – at a tiny fraction of what they were worth. People were hesitant to bid against them.

* * *

In January 2016, Tom Moyane ordered all SARS employees up to level seven to reapply for their jobs. *Daily Maverick* said that "seasoned staff with years of experience and international training and with formidable successes under their belts were flown to Pretoria where they were re-interviewed and assessed by audit, consulting, corporate finance, tax services and risk advisory firm Deloitte". In August of the same year, many learnt their fate. They were gone, along with the National Projects Unit, which investigated Lifman and other notorious tax evaders.

Marianne Thamm commented in *Daily Maverick*: "As National Projects is to be disbanded, says a SARS insider, the type of in-depth national investigation the unit was capable of conducting will no longer occur, leaving a massive gap that organised criminals as well as unscrupulous individuals are bound to exploit." The National Projects Unit had been tasked with investigating underworld figures but, more importantly, it had also probed Zuma family friends and ANC donors.

Seasoned investigators and managers with years of experience were not reappointed and were in some cases forced to accept lower positions. You don't have to be a tax expert to know that this would have resulted in a lack of capacity to conduct sophisticated investigations into tax evaders and criminals.

The rationale for the restructuring, said SARS, was to ensure that the "organisation better meets its mandate to collect all revenue due to the fiscus and to maintain control over all goods entering and leaving the country. We are unable to delve into the details of our enforcement strategies and tactics to prevent any compromise to our investigations."

Why did Moyane disband the SARS investigation units that had once reported to Gene Ravele and Johann van Loggerenberg? Remember that only one, the six-man High-Risk Investigation Unit (HRIU), was branded "rogue" – although no evidence was ever presented to substantiate the allegations that they were implicated in wrongdoing. These units played a crucial role in elevating SARS to world-class status and contributed sig-nificantly to the tax service not just reaching its target every year, but surpassing it. Moyane must know that an investigative capability is a crucial element of any modern and efficient tax collector. Otherwise, why else would he have established, in November 2016, another "rogue unit" aimed at "targeting the illicit economy"?

Tom Moyane had at his disposal a team of dedicated and celebrated investigators, but instead of letting them continue doing their work, he ostracised and shunned them and dismantled their structures. Do you agree that this makes absolutely no sense? Well, you are wrong. It makes complete sense. His intention might well have been not to rejuvenate SARS's ability to get under the skin of organised crime, but to kill those cases that implicated cronies and family members of the president and the ruling party.

Moyane's choice of new chief investigator was acting senior manager Yegan Mundie, a former policeman and long-time, undistinguished SARS official at the anti-corruption unit in Pretoria. On 1 September 2016, Mundie motivated for the approval of a new unit that included features like a safe house, pool cars, infiltrations, interceptions of communications, use of agents, and covert funding through another SARS cost centre. These features all sound uncannily like the fake "rogue unit" stories that Moyane seemed to want the country to believe. This new unit was ultimately approved by the enforcement head of SARS, Hlengani Mathebula, whereafter Mundie was joined by KZN regional head Gobi Makhanya as his new boss.

Forensic investigator Paul O'Sullivan was onto Mundie in a flash. He opened a criminal docket at the Bedfordview police station, pertaining to fraud against Mundie, his wife Diane Mundie, notorious murderer and fraudster Jen-Chih "Robert" Huang and former SARS official Chetty Vengas. Huang is the owner of Mpisi Trading and the subject of one of SARS's biggest tax-evading investigations ever. Vengas, reportedly a former disgraced SARS employee who was implicated in corruption, is one of Huang's directors. You will read much more about Huang in the next chapter.

O'Sullivan said in an affidavit that Mundie was part of a SARS investigation against Huang while Diane Mundie worked for him. From what I could determine, this investigation was being managed by the SARS anti-corruption unit under Clifford Collings, who worked closely with the police on the matter. Mundie used to report to Collings. The forensic investigator also presented evidence that one of Huang's co-directors had allegedly arranged in 2013 for Mundie's damaged BMW 3 Series to be fixed.

News24, quoting four different sources, reported that the new unit was not investigating tax evaders or money launderers, but instead was ostensibly digging for dirt against Pravin Gordhan, Ivan Pillay, Gene Ravele and Johann van Loggerenberg to charge them criminally – for whatever.

Daily Maverick commented: "The irony, for now, is that Moyane appears – officially at least – to have set up a unit exactly like the one he complained to police about in March 2015. This is the same complaint the Hawks and NPA used to go after Gordhan, Moyane's direct and, dare we say, accidental superior in the chain of command."

Following the exposure of Moyane's new unit, Pravin Gordhan demanded an explanation. Moyane wrote to Gordhan: "The SARS officials' mandate is only in as far as it relates to SARS employees involved in alleged criminal activities and tax matters. The team operates in SARS offices and are known in SARS that they are targeting criminal syndicates in SARS."

Moyane did not explain to Gordhan the legislation in terms of which his new unit had been constituted nor what its mandate might be and whether this was approved and by whom. He also did not set out how the new unit differed from the High-Risk Investigation Unit or how it would be funded. He said nothing about the use of "safe houses", "interceptions of communications", "undercover agents" and "traps" either. Moyane was, to put it mildly, as economical with the truth about this new unit as he could possibly have been.

As you will come to see, the mandate of this new unit extended far beyond the "alleged criminal activities" of SARS employees.

* * *

On 10 August 2016, Yegan Mundie wrote a confidential memorandum to enforcement head Hlengani Mathebula. This is an exact quote from the memo: "It is clear that Mr Lifman was targeted by the Rogue Unit and

SARS was used to cripple Mr Lifman's business. SARS is making use of private using Senior Counsel in order to continue to victimize Mr Lifman in a litigation process that will not be finalised soon. There is definitely collusion between the SARS officials and the appointed counsel to delay the matter. Mr Lifman's twelve shops have been closed and some of his assets have been [seized] by SARS, whilst he is still busy objecting to the assessment that was raised against him. Mr Lifman stated that his tax affairs have been published in the media through the Rogue Units." (These were Mundie's exact words.)

Mundie has reportedly met with the National Projects team in Cape Town, which had dealt with the Lifman case all along, and requested all files from them. He must thus know that the "rogue unit" – the HRIU – had nothing to do with Lifman's investigation. Why then did he say so in his memorandum?

In addition, the Lifman audit was overseen by respected audit firm PricewaterhouseCoopers, while Lifman's tax affairs were laid bare in a tax inquiry in which he had top legal representation. This was a court process where evidence was presented and witnesses cross-examined. It had nothing to do with any "rogue unit". Lifman lost his applications in the High Court, which resulted in Hendrickse setting out a plan of action for SARS to collect Lifman's taxes.

Then came Mundie's memorandum. What do you guess happened next? Yes, you are right. Mundie afforded Lifman the gap he so desperately needed.

In November 2016, Lifman lodged an application in the High Court to have his tax audit of R388 million reviewed. He advanced what has become known as the "rogue unit defence", that he was unfairly targeted and victimised. Lifman threatened to interdict SARS from continuing with its efforts to liquidate his companies.

The clincher was when his attorney, Asger Gani, stated in his papers: "Our client [Lifman] has now been formally advised that a review has been authorised and is being conducted of the entire group's tax affairs. Our client has this confirmation in writing. With this in mind, all execution processes and/or legal proceedings must immediately be halted, pending the finalisation of the review."

SARS, through attorney Dirk Pietersen, responded that "neither our offices, nor our client's representatives are aware of any 'authorisation' and/or decision to 'review' the 'tax findings', 'liabilities' and/or assessments relating to Mr Lifman". Pietersen rejected Gani's demands that all legal proceedings be ended.

Asked to confirm whether SARS had indeed agreed to re-audit Lifman, the SARS media office responded by saying: "SARS does not comment on the affairs of a taxpayer."

* * *

When Moyane took office at SARS and allowed the "rogue unit" narrative to play out in the public domain in such spectacular fashion, he obviously never thought about the consequences of his high-stake game plan – of jeopardising a fortune for the fiscus. In December 2014, Ivan Pillay warned Moyane that SARS stood to lose millions if taxpayers in litigation attached value to speculation about the "rogue unit" narrative. Moyane scoffed at Pillay and suspended him.

His dilemma is this: if the SARS leadership wanted to oppose Lifman's latest stratagem, it would have to admit that Moyane's and Mundie's "rogue unit" proclamations were fabricated and manufactured to get rid of Pillay, Richer, Ravele, Van Loggerenberg and the others. Moyane was not going to have any of that.

Shortly after Lifman's court application, *News24* reported that he had received an e-mail from a SARS auditor, Gavin Cairns. The e-mail started with a very congenial "Good day Mark", and then thanked him for a meeting with SARS and said: "As mentioned, I have been tasked to attend to the review of the recent audit SARS conducted on your group companies."

In the e-mail, Cairns told Lifman that a review would be carried out at his offices in January 2017. Cairns cc'd Mundie in his e-mail. *News24* reported that SARS's chief officer for enforcement, Hlengani Mathebula, informed senior colleagues that he had not sanctioned or authorised a review of Lifman's tax bill.

Lifman's court application was set down to be heard in February 2017 in the Western Cape High Court. Unexpectedly, or perhaps not so, the application was removed from the court roll "by consent between the parties". Checkmate. Lifman had seen through the "rogue unit" sham that Pillay had warned Moyane about more than two years previously, and was now capitalising on it.

This has set SARS at war with itself, and it is not difficult to predict the outcome of the mess. It is going to be calamitous for the tax collector, the fiscus and all South Africans because so much is at stake. SARS will probably just let the case slide over time and, when most have forgotten about it, let it die off, or the service will be forced to somehow settle with Lifman. He will likely pay a tiny fraction of what he owes SARS, he will be declared tax compliant, and festivities will commence in gangland down south.

The Lifman case has cost SARS – and ultimately the taxpayer – many millions of rand. Four SARS auditors worked on the case and just the tax inquiry lasted a year, during which time SARS employed the services of an external legal team. The tax collector commissioned Pricewaterhouse-Coopers to oversee the audit at the cost of a fortune. The documents generated during the investigation would fill a small storeroom.

Lifman may have been the first alleged organised criminal or big-time tax evader to benefit from the void left by the disbandment of SARS's investigation units, but he will not be the last. Had the "old" SARS structures been in place, I have no doubt that Lifman would have trudged the path of the likes of Quinton Marinus, Radovan Krejčíř, Lolly Jackson and Glenn Agliotti. He would have been financially ruptured, there would have been evidence of tax evasion and money laundering to put him on trial, and the fiscus would have profited.

To avoid humiliation, Tom Moyane will probably hide behind the confidentiality provisions of the Tax Administration Act and every media enquiry to SARS about Lifman will be met with: "SARS does not comment on the affairs of a taxpayer." I would, however, advise Moyane to sleep with one eye open. Despite many of the public claims by him and his acolytes that morale at SARS is at its highest level ever, the discontent within his own ranks is intense and the disillusionment in SARS is growing by the day.

More documents and information will emerge that will further illuminate how this Zuma crony navigated the once proud tax collector into a quagmire of trash and filth.

TEN

Up in smoke

————•————

I'm afraid things don't get better. On a research trip to Johannesburg in April 2017, I sat down with a SARS official in a swanky Viennese-style café in an elegant shopping centre in Pretoria's north-eastern suburbs. The official was one of the two "deep throats" who had given me the details about Zuma's lamentable tax affairs. I had in the meantime established a safe channel of communication with my SARS sources through encrypted e-mails.

"What is going on with Huang?" I wanted to know. "I have lots about Lifman and the others, but I'm struggling to get anything new on Huang."

The official replied: "Huang is very difficult because the case has always been sensitive. It's handled by the very top. Moyane's people are in charge of it. Nobody knows what's going on because the Centralised Projects Unit that handled it has been disbanded . . . None of the people there have anything to do with the case anymore. The guy who used to run it is now at Law Admin and many of the key people in the case have left SARS."

A week or two later, he/she e-mailed again. "There is some sort of a list. SARS found it the day they raided his company. Someone has told me that it is in Mandarin or Chinese and was translated by SARS. The guy told me it contains the names of important people, government officials and politicians. Next to the names are amounts of money. It can mean one of two things. It is either money that Huang had paid to them. Or it is money that he laundered for them out of the country to foreign bank accounts."

"Get that list!" I told him/her. "It's vital."

"There is no way. People are paranoid. It feels as though everybody is spying on everybody. Our e-mails are constantly being monitored. You can't just pull a file. If you go onto any of the systems, you will leave your details and they will know who accessed it. The guy who told me about the list said those documents were always kept somewhere safe. Only a few people have ever seen them."

I saw both officials a few days later. After we had ordered cappuccinos and exchanged niceties, I wanted to know: "That list you spoke about, the one they found at Huang's place, could you get it?"

"No, I'm sorry. I found out what I could but I won't be able to get a copy. But I did find something else."

"What?"

"Letters and memos," he/she said and pulled out a plastic folder from a dark leather bag. The source handed me a couple of SARS documents and pointed at one. It was a letter written on an Mpisi Group letterhead. The Mpisi Group belongs to Taiwanese-born Jen-Chih "Robert" Huang. The letter was addressed to "Mr J. Makwakwa, Chief Operating Officer" and was dated 15 September 2015. The letter was a record of a meeting that Huang had with SARS at which he proposed a possible settlement of his tax debt, which was more than a billion rand.

Said my source: "It's not so much the content that's important, but the names of the people in the meeting. Look again."

"Makwakwa. And then Baloyi and Lebelo," I said.

"Yip. Godfrey Baloyi was the head of criminal investigations. He left at the end of 2015, so it makes sense that he was there. And Makwakwa too, because after Ivan [Pillay] and the others left SARS, he basically became the boss of almost every unit in SARS. But its Luther Lebelo's name that is the interesting one."

"Why?"

"He's the head of human resources. He's in charge of labour relations. He's got absolutely nothing to do with tax cases, never mind the Huang case."

"What was he doing there?"

"He's Moyane's hit man. At SARS, some call him the 'head of suspensions'.

He is very powerful. It's Tom at the top, then Jonas Makwakwa and then Luther Lebelo. With Jonas now on suspension [more about that later], Luther is the new king. He's clever and moves behind the scenes. I think he's a bigger player than Makwakwa, even if he doesn't know tax. He's also a big shot in the ANC. They are killing that case. Believe me, it's dead."

* * *

Jen-Chih "Robert" Huang calls himself a businessman, an "importer-exporter" and a "clearing and forwarding agent". He also "fixes" business deals from China. He may have imported a few washing machines from the Far East, but his main business is allegedly customs fraud, smuggling and money laundering. He is also a tax evader – and a convicted murderer who has done time in jail.

Taiwanese-born Huang was part of an influx of foreign businessmen from countries such as China, India and Russia who came to South Africa in the early nineties to explore new business opportunities. Little is known about his earlier years in South Africa, but he found himself in the dock in the Bloemfontein High Court in November 1997, charged alongside six accomplices for the murder of Ching-Ho Kao, a Taiwanese businessman. Kao had disappeared from a Chinese restaurant in Rosebank, Johannesburg. His white Mercedes was found abandoned in Pretoria the next day.

The *Mail & Guardian* reported that the trial was conducted under high security conditions because police believed the accused were part of the Chinese triads. Three Taiwanese interpreters, fearing for their lives, withdrew their services before the trial got under way. The state's indictment claimed the motive for the murder was that Kao's family was in debt to Huang.

In his ruling in August 1998, the judge said Huang was one of the "big bosses" and gave evidence that amounted to "infamous lies" and insulted the court's intelligence. Huang was nonetheless sentenced to only an effective 12-year prison term.

Huang reportedly became a reborn Christian in prison and assisted the police in solving crimes in the Chinese community. As a result, he got a significant reduction in his sentence. When he was released in 2003, he established Mpisi Trading 74.

According to Paul O'Sullivan, who has taken a keen interest in Huang, his criminal record has been expunged. It is also peculiar that he continued to stay in South Africa after he was released from prison. Surely he was supposed to be deported back to Taiwan?

Huang has a South African ID number, which indicates that he might have citizenship. His wife, Shou-Fang Huang (also known as Shou-Fang Cho), also has a local ID number. How does a foreigner with a murder conviction who has done prison time get South African citizenship?

Huang built a massive business in South Africa, offering services ranging from forwarding, exporting, importing and warehousing to cellphone tele-communication, machinery and car manufacturing. His modus operandi appears almost a carbon copy of Zuma's close friends, the Gupta family. While the Guptas befriended Zuma's youngest son, Duduzane, Huang cosied up to the president's nephew, Khulubuse Zuma. He was at the time described by Mpisi's website as the "chairman". And just as the Guptas would brag about their access to Zuma, Huang's website (wrongly) exclaimed: "His father is the president of South Africa, Mr Zuma."

Again, just as the Guptas have paraded with Zuma and shared photographs far and wide, Huang's website boasted pictures of Khulubuse Zuma and Huang at the company's headquarters in Bedfordview, Johannesburg. In 2010, the Dongfeng Motor Corporation in China announced a joint venture with Khulubuse Zuma and Huang to distribute its products in South Africa and the rest of the continent. Nothing came of it. After the media jumped on Huang about his presidential connections, he made changes to his website. He was also a member of a business delegation that accompanied Jacob Zuma on a state visit to China in 2010.

In 2012, it was widely reported that the Hawks were probing Huang and Mpisi for a multibillion-rand racket at the Durban harbour. In June of that year, the Hawks in KwaZulu-Natal secured a warrant for Huang's arrest. Investigators from the elite unit also raided his home and business. Huang was at the time in Hong Kong and sidestepped the Hawks by directly

approaching the National Prosecuting Authority (NPA) to make representations as to why he should not be arrested.

The warrant for Huang's arrest came weeks after a former SARS official,
Etienne Kellerman, was arrested on 80 counts of alleged corruption.
Kellerman was suspected of receiving substantial benefits for allegedly
allowing contraband through the harbour. The case against him was later
withdrawn for unknown reasons. The *Daily News* reported that an international syndicate, allegedly with links to Huang, was said to bribe customs
and police officials to allow in container-loads of contraband.

This investigation was the culmination of joint efforts between the
Hawks, the NPA, police crime intelligence and SARS's anti-corruption and
security unit (ACAS), the unit that Yegan Mundie had worked for while his
wife happened to be an employee of Huang.

* * *

In the run-up to the May 2014 national elections, SARS customs officials
pounced on a container entering South Africa. It contained 18,500 ANC
T-shirts, many of them adorned with a portrait of Jacob Zuma. SARS
refused to release the consignment brought into the country by Mpisi
Trading because no import tax had been paid on it.

Zuma's legal adviser, Michael Hulley, who had incidentally worked previously for Huang, was called to assist. The imported T-shirts that were
apparently donated to the ANC were valued at R118 million. With an ailing
textile industry, tax on imported clothing is very high. SARS charged
Mpisi R41 million in import duty.

The ANC was furious at SARS's refusal to release the consignment. A
meeting was reportedly held at ANC headquarters at Luthuli House in
Johannesburg between Ivan Pillay and ANC treasurer-general Zweli Mkhize.
Reports state that Pillay was adamant that the clothing would only be
released once the ANC had settled its tax obligations. The ANC relented
and grudgingly either they or Huang paid the taxes.

Ivan Pillay's refusal to budge illustrated his tenacity and unshakeable
belief in the independence of the tax collector. He was a devout ANC comrade

with impeccable struggle credentials yet was prepared to stand up for the principle that everyone is equal before the law.

Several analysts reckoned that the T-shirt saga, which left the ANC R40 million poorer, contributed to the eventual demise of Pillay and the others at SARS. Respected investigative journalist Sam Sole has written: "Holding up a multimillion-rand consignment of ANC campaign T-shirts before the April elections was one of the factors that fed into the leadership purge of the South African Revenue Service."

It is important to remember that the saga around the ANC T-shirts happened at the same time as SARS was wanting R22 million from the ruling party for not paying their taxes.

Sole said that people close to Zuma in the intelligence sphere told him that SARS must be brought under control because they were "after people".

*   *   *

In June 2014, Judge Aubrey Ledwaba, deputy judge president of the Pretoria High Court, made an order that all assets belonging to Huang and his companies, including cars worth R32 million and property valued at R99 million, be frozen. Among the properties were six houses in the Woodhill Golf Estate in Pretoria, rated as the third-best residential address in South Africa. In granting the preservation order, the court heard that Huang and his companies had 26 accounts at various banks.

The tax inquiry into Huang and the audit of his tax liability formed one of the biggest in SARS history. It took the tax collector almost a year and eight thousand pages of documentation and evidence to present him with an initial tax bill of R541 million. It has since been growing to well over a billion rand – and penalties and taxes have not even been added. *News24* reported in February 2015 that his bill had ballooned to R1.8 billion. The case had cost the taxpayer a fortune. Several auditors and investigators worked on the case and at times SARS employed up to three senior advocates to litigate against Huang and his companies.

SARS Central Projects manager Pieter Engelbrecht said in a court affidavit that Huang used his network of companies "as conduits to evade

Mpisi's tax liability and to export large amounts of money" overseas. They did this by using people who had "virtually no knowledge of the business" as proxies for Huang. The proxies were often asked to sign documents without knowing what they were signing. Large amounts of cash were then shipped out of the country. Engelbrecht said "certain key witnesses . . . were suddenly no longer employed by Mpisi and have either returned to China without any intention of returning, or their whereabouts are allegedly unknown".

One of Huang's employees testified how he destroyed the accounts of one of Huang's companies. "I threw them away in dustbins," he said. When asked why, he responded: "I thought because we're losing money when we closed the company, there's no need to keep the documents." The employee was also shown hundreds of foreign exchange applications, supposedly signed by him, so that Huang's companies could ship cash overseas. The official had signed a single application form in blank and this form was then copied multiple times. As a result, "very large amounts of money left the country".

In April 2013, SARS's Central Projects Unit, which resided under Johann van Loggerenberg, obtained a search warrant and raided Huang's home and his businesses. This must have been when they stumbled upon a list of names including government officials and politicians with amounts of money reflected next to them. It seems that the tax collector couldn't do anything with the list because Huang attempted to have the search warrant declared unlawful. The High Court rejected his application in September 2014 and ruled that the warrant was legal. By then, SARS was under siege. Van Loggerenberg was suspended in November 2014, and Pillay and others followed shortly afterwards. The list was put away in Huang's file, which thereafter undoubtedly fell into the hands of Moyane and his henchmen.

Huang has been adamant throughout that "allegations and suspicions of tax wrongdoing . . . remain vague, speculative, and unsubstantiated". He accused SARS of conducting a witch-hunt against him and his companies – a standard defence for most serial and serious tax offenders.

The High Court appointed a curator to manage Mpisi's financial affairs. In a June 2014 meeting with the curator, Huang said he was willing to learn from his mistakes, which was why "I try my best to do everything by the book". It emerged from the minutes that the curator had told Huang that Mpisi was not banking all its cash, that its accounting system was "problematic" and that the information they were providing to him was untrue. He threatened to have Huang and his accounting officer arrested for contempt of court.

In the June 2014 meeting, the curator noted that "Hulley Incorporated have accepted service on behalf of the First and Second Respondents [Jen-Chih Huang and Shou-Fang Huang]". Hulley Incorporated is the law firm of Jacob Zuma's legal adviser, Michael Hulley.

It is astonishing that Michael Hulley came to represent a tax evader and money launderer who was litigating against the state. It is a priority of SARS to collect as much tax from Huang as legally permitted. Huang, on the other hand – represented by Hulley – seemed willing to do his utmost to frustrate the process and counter SARS wherever he could.

What if Jacob Zuma needed legal advice about the Haung case? Would he ask his lawyer Hulley for his legal opinion? Surely Zuma receives confidential briefings on high-profile and sensitive tax cases, of which Huang would probably have been one. Did Hulley sit in on these briefings and offer his opinion?

*   *   *

In March 2017, just days after Tom Moyane said that the outflow of experienced officials at SARS was a myth, an audit manager with more than two decades of experience packed her bags and left. Lorraine van Esch managed cases involving assessments of several billion rand, among them those of Jen-Chih Huang, Mpisi Trading and a host of linked people and companies.

Not only is Van Esch gone, but so is Godfrey Baloyi, the head of criminal investigations. The unit that investigated Huang, Central Projects, has also been disbanded. Its manager and a key figure in the investigation, Pieter Engelbrecht, was transferred to SARS's law administration division.

The SARS attorney that managed the collection of Huang's tax debts, Elle-Sarah Rossato, left SARS in 2016 and is now an associate director at KPMG. She had a career of 14 years at SARS, and as acting manager of Special Debt Recovery she managed a unit with a debt book of R6 billion.

Besides Pillay, Richer, Ravele, Van Loggerenberg and Baloyi, I have a long list of top SARS officials and managers who left in the wake of Moyane's appointment. Among them were Brian Kgomo, the group executive of internal audit, Elizabeth Khumalo, chief officer of human resources, Vusi Ngquluna, group executive of debt collection, Clifford Collings, group executive of the anti-corruption and security unit, Vusi Ngcobo, SARS representative in China, George Frost, the head of strategic portfolio management, and James Matthews, the head of enterprise quality management.

At around the time that Lorraine van Esch packed her bags, the last remaining Operation Honey Badger man left standing at SARS, Kumaran Moodley, was suspended. Moodley was Tom Moyane's most experienced customs investigator and headed the Tactical Intervention Unit (TIU), one of five investigation units that were once managed by Van Loggerenberg. The TIU had been at the forefront of many of SARS's biggest organised crime investigations and customs busts. Moodley had dealt with Huang's imported ANC T-shirts and was key to the tobacco investigations under the code name Honey Badger, which implicated Zuma and his son Edward.

When asked about his departure, a SARS spokesperson ducked behind the service's HR policies that "prohibited the discussion of internal processes and employee information in the public domain".

When I sat down with my SARS sources, they said that of the Honey Badger cases under Moodley's control, if adjudicated in SARS's favour, the state would have recovered billions of rand in unpaid value-added tax and excise duties. His experience was immeasurable and his institutional memory of the tax evaders he investigated was crucial to the successful conclusion of his cases. Among them were Mark Lifman, Carnilinx, Robert Huang, Yusuf Kajee, Azeem Amodcaram and Edward Zuma.

The timing of Moodley's suspension raises questions. My SARS sources told me that the person behind Moodley's suspension was none other than

Yegan Mundie and his new "rogue unit", and that the suspension was sanctioned by human resources boss and "head of suspensions" Luther Lebelo.

But they also told me something else. The official that headed the SARS anti-corruption and security unit investigation against Huang, Yousuf Denath, had also been suspended. Denath closely cooperated with the police and the NPA in the older investigation that led to a warrant for Huang's arrest. Denath's suspension related to an altercation he allegedly had with Yusuf Kajee some years before. Kajee had "promised" Denath that he would "get him" eventually. It seems he was right, because apparently Kajee lodged a complaint against Denath and the result was his immediate suspension.

Guess who the complaint was lodged with? Yegan Mundie's new "rogue unit".

* * *

SARS issued letters of finding against Huang in 2015, which we know resulted in his meeting with Jonas Makwakwa, Godfrey Baloyi and Luther Lebelo. Baloyi left SARS not long after this meeting. Lebelo, besides being SARS human resources and labour relations group executive, is also sometimes quoted as a SARS spokesperson.

Lebelo is controversial, and not just for dishing out suspension notices. In November 2016, he wrote a letter in *Business Day* in his capacity as head of communications of the Progressive Professionals Forum (PPF), an organisation led by former government spokesperson Mzwanele Manyi. Manyi is an ardent supporter of Zuma and a Gupta praise-singer.

Lebelo wrote that rating agencies "are nothing but organised economic gangs" and must be seen in the context of "fear-mongering colonialism". He also lashed out at the ruling party for caring more about rating agencies' opinions than poor, black South Africans. His comments irked finance minister Pravin Gordhan, who said the letter was ignorant and unwarranted. SARS refused to take steps against Lebelo.

Lebelo seems adept at changing his loyalties as the winds blow. In

December 2013, as chairman of the ANC's Liliesleaf branch in Midrand, he was quoted by *City Press* as being rather critical of the ANC and especially of Zuma on the Nkandla scandal. He apparently said that "anyone who was happy with the state of the ruling party [ANC] needed to see a psychiatrist". Well, clearly his tune changed rather quickly when Zuma's man Moyane arrived at SARS the very next year.

It is not known what Lebelo's contribution was in the meeting with Huang. The latter said through his lawyer that the SARS tax findings were "replete with distortions, half-truths and innuendos" and claimed that the aim of the investigations "was to crucify Mpisi and Mr Huang, notwithstanding that there had been no evidence of any wrongdoing".

A follow-up meeting was held with SARS in October 2015, and in a letter addressed to Makwakwa afterwards, Huang and Mpisi asked the tax collector to lift the preservation order against the company. (A preservation order allows SARS to safeguard a taxpayer's assets to secure the collection of tax.) I don't have Makwakwa's response to the letter, but my SARS sources told me: "The case has gone nowhere. Everyone who knew the details has left. It's hanging in the air. It should have been concluded in 2015 or at the latest in 2016."

"And where does it stand now?"

"The curator is still handling his affairs. This is costing the taxpayer and SARS millions. From what I have heard, there is very little left in Mpisi. By the time it comes to collecting the tax, the business will probably have nothing left to pay."

"So, what is going to happen now?"

"I don't know. Maybe SARS will settle, probably for a fraction of what he owes. They have no choice. He owes over a billion. SARS will be lucky if they get R10 million at this rate."

Long after our last meeting, I received a message from one of my other sources. He/she said: "There is no progress in the Huang case. Only a handful of officials are now assigned to the case. The most experienced auditor amongst them has less than two years' experience."

The other source later sent another message that Huang was going to take SARS to court to challenge the actions against him. No doubt the "rogue unit defence" will once again rear its ugly head. My source said that the capacity and will of SARS to fight such cases has been so diminished, he/she won't be surprised if Huang emerges victorious.

*   *   *

This book was almost going to print when one of my SARS sources phoned me. The person was highly agitated and spoke about the atmosphere of paranoia and fear that has permeated the tax collector. I made notes of the conversation, and this is what my source said:

"Take the Huang case. The main guy in SARS who still understands that case is Pieter Engelbrecht. Almost all the others on the case have left SARS ...

"Well, guess what? Mundie, who runs a real rogue unit in SARS now, is busy with his third investigation into Engelbrecht. This is now after the first investigations couldn't dig up any dirt on him. It is a witch-hunt to take him out at SARS. They perfected their rogue unit ways with Ivan and the others. They manufacture or take bullshit information from an enemy of someone, they act like they believe it, they do some sort of crap inves-tigation, they make findings against the person, the person is suspended, and then they have taken them out of the system and the cases can die a death.

"Watch, soon Engelbrecht will be gone and the Huang case will die, if it is not already dead.

"And you know what's the worst of it? The minute people in SARS know that someone is being targeted by Mundie's rogue unit, they withdraw from that person. That person becomes totally isolated. Suddenly all the people who may have been involved in cases would suddenly claim they know nothing of the case, just in case they are targeted too. And then the details can be covered up. The same is happening to Kumaran and Denath. Watch closely, they're as good as gone. Kajee, Carnilinx, Huang ... the Guptas, Zuma, they have captured SARS. This is how they now run SARS. Mundie's unit on the inside and the criminals on the outside directing it."

*   *   *

I was packing my bags to fly back to Cape Town in April 2017 when one of my SARS sources sent me a message on my phone. It was a "secret conversation" using an app whereby the message destructs itself after it has been read.

"We can meet after work."

"Is it urgent? I'm going back today," I replied. "Can it wait? Back in Johannesburg soon."

"Rather not. We must meet."

We met at Café 41 in Eastwood Village in Pretoria, and with fans twirling lazily from the ceiling and against the background of walls painted in burnt orange to create a Moroccan feel, the source pulled a document from his/her bag and slid it over the table to me.

It was dated 20 March 2016 and was an internal SARS memo that was addressed to "Dear Chief Executives". It was written by Patrick Moeng, executive for investigations, projects and evidence support, and addressed to Jonas Makwakwa, new enforcement head Hlengani Mathebula (the man who approved Moyane's "rogue unit") and Jed Michaletos, the new chief officer for customs and excise. It summarised the contents of a meeting between representatives of independent cigarette manufacturer Carnilinx and the four people I have just mentioned.

I read through the memo and said: "So Adriano Mazzotti and Carnilinx are also getting away with it?

"Yup, it looks like it," the source said. "And we are not sure why."

"I think I know why," I responded.

"Why?"

"It's about Malema. Mazzotti's relationship with Julius Malema."

"What about it?"

"Sit back," I said. "For once I can tell you something."

* * *

SARS and Carnilinx have had a messy relationship ever since the tax service launched an investigation into the tobacco manufacturer in 2012. There were allegations and counter-allegations of spying, counter-intelligence, dirty tricks and discrediting campaigns from both sides.

Back in 2014, mainly under Kumaran Moodley and his unit's control, SARS had wrapped up a part of their tax investigations against Carnilinx and wanted more than R600 million in unpaid taxes from the tobacco manufacturer after seizing over R200 million worth of illicit tobacco. The evidence that Van Loggerenberg and his teams had assembled against Carnilinx was overwhelming.

Carnilinx sought to settle its tax debt with SARS. In March 2014, Adriano Mazzotti approached the tax service on behalf of Carnilinx and said he was prepared to admit that the company had committed fraud and tax evasion and was complicit in other nefarious activities. He signed an affidavit on 6 May 2014 as a "full and frank disclosure to SARS" to obtain a plea bargain from the NPA and a settlement with SARS that would enable Carnilinx to trade lawfully in future.

Mazzotti said in the affidavit that Carnilinx had paid R97.2 million in ordinary taxes since its inception in 2012. He admitted wrongdoing and told how the company "unlawfully and wrongfully" smuggled two tonnes of tobacco every week for 40 weeks to avoid paying excise duty. He stated: "In its drive to promote its business, Carnilinx entered into a host of transactions, some of which were lawful and others corrupt and unlawful." Said Mazzotti: "We request SARS ... to give us a second opportunity to trade lawfully. In trading lawfully, we will not only pay our taxes, but we will employ a large number of people and, in doing so, promote employment opportunities."

In the affidavit, he said that he had attempted to bribe Johann van Loggerenberg and Ivan Pillay through a well-known criminal attorney. He paid the attorney R800,000 in cash to "pay off" the SARS officials. According to Mazzotti, it later turned out that the attorney had no influence over either Van Loggerenberg or Pillay and had pocketed the bribe money.

Mazzotti said he had also handed "gifts" of R500,000 and R780,000 in cash respectively to a prominent senior advocate and an attorney for successfully negotiating with SARS on his behalf. Before the negotiations, Mazzotti admitted that he bribed a junior SARS official for documents to strengthen their hand during the bargaining with the tax collector.

I have documents that show that the advocate was later hauled in front of the Johannesburg Bar to explain why he had accepted a gift on top of his normal fees. He should have declared the "gift", which came in a bag put in the boot of his car, to the Bar.

SARS investigated the lawyers to determine whether they had paid donations tax on their Mazzotti "gifts". SARS then discovered that the attorney who received the bribe money had received other cash payments into his account. When they confronted him with the payments, he admitted that he was an agent for both the State Security Agency (SSA) and the police crime intelligence unit.

Mazzotti also referred in his affidavit to "Political Financing" and said Carnilinx had made a "donation in an amount of R200,000 towards a political party". He was referring to the fee that Julius Malema's Economic Freedom Fighters (EFF) needed to register as a political party to contest the 2014 national elections. Mazzotti and Malema have long been friends, and various publications have described the cigarette man as a generous donor to the firebrand politician.

According to some reports, Mazzotti and Carnilinx had helped Malema to pay his multimillion-rand tax debt. Mazzotti denied this, and was quoted as saying: "I'm being assessed by SARS at the moment and I suspect they are going to hit me hard. I won't be able to afford these payments."

After Mazzotti's affidavit, Carnilinx was down and just about out for the count. All that had to happen was for a final settlement figure to be determined, which would have been several hundred million rand. My one source told me that SARS would most likely have shut the company down. Several SARS sources confirmed to me that SARS was at the time also involved in talks with the NPA to criminally prosecute Carnilinx and its directors for tax fraud, corruption and money laundering.

Before that could happen, Pillay, Ravele and Van Loggerenberg were gone and Moyane shut down the unit that had investigated Mazzotti and Carnilinx. One would nonetheless have trusted the new management to conclude the process and fill the fiscus. Don't hold your breath.

* * *

I want to fast-forward to the March 2016 memorandum from Patrick Moeng to the "Dear Chief Executives". He said the meeting was called because Carnilinx wanted to address them "on the alleged unfair treatment and criminal activities committed by SARS enforcement team whilst they audited the affairs of Carnilinx and related entities".

Like Huang and Lifman, Carnilinx had also seemingly decided to use the "rogue unit defence". The Carnilinx lawyers told SARS that their client was "unfairly treated by virtue of certain SARS officials behaving in a manner which seems to indicate that they are biased".

Carnilinx was investigated by a combination of several SARS units. Moyane's "rogue unit", the High-Risk Investigation Unit, only conducted background work. The investigation was so thoroughly conducted and above board that it ultimately forced Carnilinx to the confession table.

Moeng later noted that the meeting had agreed "that we should accede to the Carnilinx request to appoint a new audit team to investigate the matters presently under investigation by SARS". Moeng further agreed that the team that had been working on the case until then, which would have been mainly Kumaran Moodley's Tactical Intervention Unit, would hand over the entire investigation to a "new team". Said Moeng: "SARS has acceded to their [Carnilinx] demand, and that all Letters of Finding issued against the clients will be withdrawn."

The only assumption one can draw is that Carnilinx and Mazzotti – a self-confessed corrupter, smuggler and tax evader – are off the hook. Years of painstaking examination and probing are going down the drain. Not only is this a tremendous blow to the fiscus and costly to the taxpayer, but the decision by the SARS top executives is on every level – ethically, morally, and juridically – indefensible and reprehensible.

* * *

"You don't understand the importance of the Carnilinx case; the work that has gone into that investigation," said one of the SARS sources. "Everything that was once good about SARS is reflected in this case. The investigation was solid and they were busted with their hands in the cookie jar. It was as clear a case as you would ever get.

"SARS was all over Carnilinx's financial and bank records and combed every transaction for VAT, PAYE, income tax. Big bugs crawled out, because they obviously didn't declare their illegal earnings. They were manufacturing and selling far more cigarettes than what they declared to SARS."

My sources told me that SARS was also busy auditing all the Carnilinx directors and family members as part of the larger project.

"It took years and millions of rand to investigate," said my sources. "SARS spoke to the NPA in May 2014 to charge the Carnilinx directors with tax fraud, money laundering and corruption. They would have pleaded guilty. The case should have been done by 2014."

* * *

The tobacco industry is a cut-throat business in which participants have no qualms about scamming one another, constantly switching sides, ratting on each other and spreading vicious rumours. In short: if I can eliminate a competitor, I might just bag a chunk of his business. There is always money to make: if not as a snitch, then by way of a smear campaign, blackmail or extortion.

Back in 2014, when doing research for the *City Press* stories about Johann van Loggerenberg, Belinda Walter and the SSA, I spoke to a person in the tobacco industry who sent me files of documents, mostly about the misbehaviour of his competitors. The man clearly had a bone to pick with Carnilinx. I told him at one point that I had resigned as a journalist. His e-mails stopped.

I contacted him again during the writing of this book. He again sent me reams of papers, many of them the same as two years ago. I stayed in contact with him, and when he asked me what I am looking for, I said: "Dirt. Whatever you have."

A few months later, he said that he was going to send me "something big". He told me it was a recording made by a Mazzotti associate. Someone recorded a conversation between Mazzotti and a few people, exactly why I am not sure. It may even have been Mazzotti himself. I presume that tobacco smugglers do this all the time (think about the Agliotti-Kajee-De Robillard conversation).

"Download the conversation, listen to it, delete the e-mail and clear the recycle bin," he ordered.

I am not allowed to publish a transcript of the recording and may only use the information contained in it. I was assured that should I have to defend the information in court, the person who provided it to me would convince the owner to come forward and authenticate the recording. The recording is not absolutely clear and sounds as if it was made at a party or in a bar.

A small section of the recording related to Julius Malema. Mazzotti and Malema appear to have been friends for years and the tobacco man even attended Malema's wedding.

One of the voices identified to me by my source was that of Adriano Mazzotti. I have in the meantime confirmed independently that it was in fact his voice. He spoke about his close relationship with Malema and bragged about how close they were.

Just so that you understand the context of the Malema case, I need to give some background. The "old" SARS had pinned a R18 million tax bill on Malema and obtained an order for his provisional sequestration. In May 2014, just days before triple agent Belinda Walter unleashed the storm at SARS, the tax service struck a deal with Malema for the repayment of his taxes. Had this not happened, the firebrand politician would have been sequestrated. Unrehabilitated insolvents cannot take a seat in Parliament.

Just days later, Malema was sworn in as an MP for the newly established opposition party, the Economic Freedom Fighters. He became a thorn in Zuma's side at levels nobody could've imagined. There is no doubt that SARS's settlement with Malema would not have made Jacob Zuma a happy chappy and would certainly have added to Pillay's and the others' woes at SARS when Moyane arrived.

In April 2015, the "new" SARS under Moyane accused Malema of lying about the source of his income and slapped an additional R14 million in penalties on him. SARS said Malema had tried to dodge paying donation tax and had received money from questionable sources. The tax service announced that they were continuing with an application for Malema's final sequestration.

Why did the "new" SARS do it? Simple. If the judge granted the final sequestration order when the case returned to court in June 2015, the president's nemesis would be kicked out of Parliament, saving Zuma and the ANC from the embarrassment of having their debates disrupted and their incompetence exposed so publicly as only the EFF can do.

There is no doubt in my mind that taking down Malema was on Moyane's "to do" list when Zuma appointed him as commissioner of SARS. What else can explain their sudden turn-about and obsession to nail him?

SARS arrived at the High Court with a battery of four advocates. They tried their best to convince Mr Justice Gregory Wright of the need to sequestrate Malema. The judge would have none of it and wanted to know: "What new evidence do you have that will convince me to make the order final?"

SARS had none, and after lunch announced defeat by withdrawing their application and agreeing to pay Malema's legal costs. It was a futile and humiliating exercise that cost the taxpayer hundreds of thousands of rand. There is no doubt in my mind that the "new" SARS didn't bring the application on the grounds of sound tax administration, but rather did so on behalf of their political master. The only parties that had anything to gain from Malema's sequestration would have been Zuma and the ANC.

* * *

This brings me back to the Mazzotti recording. The state seems not to have given up on getting to the president's nemesis and, after SARS's failed court bid, seems to have turned to Mazzotti.

On the recording, Mazzotti bragged that he was close to the State Security Agency and its minister David Mahlobo, and that he and other directors at Carnilinx had been approached for information on Malema. He chuckled how they were playing both sides and how Malema was in on it.

Guess who was the spook that attempted to sweet-talk Mazzotti to part with Juju's secrets? According to Mazzotti, it was none other than Monde Gadini, husband of Jacob Zuma's legal adviser, Bonisiwe Makhene. He is said to have the president's ear through his wife and appears to have possibly played a byzantine role in the demise of Pillay, Richer, Ravele and the others at SARS.

I tried to find out more about Gadini, the spook who has popped up like a spectre during some of the most important events I've chronicled in this book. He emerged as a key player in the protection of Zuma. I went back to my intelligence sources.

Gadini had also once worked for SARS, apparently as a messenger or administrative clerk of sorts. I was told a story about how he had once asked Gene Ravele for a salary increase and a promotion. The story goes that because he didn't have matric, there was nothing that Ravele could do for him, and he was apparently encouraged to further his studies to attain a higher level of education. He apparently resigned from SARS in or around 2005, no longer impressed with Ravele.

My intelligence sources said that he arrived at State Security after his wife was appointed as Zuma's legal adviser. They told me that he was "given some sort of place at the SSA" because of his wife's contacts. Nobody paid much attention to him at the time. He was never around and did very little, reporting to nobody in particular, and nobody knew exactly what he was appointed as. Because he was perceived to be close to Zuma, nobody at the SSA dared to question his movements or what he was up to.

* * *

I was convinced that the SSA's snuggling up to Mazzotti was the main reason for the amicable treatment he received from SARS. But maybe there is another, even more compelling reason. In August 2017, as I was about to send my manuscript to the publishers, I received a message from an old SSA source.

"I'm going to send you three photographs. Sit down when you look at them."

The first photograph showed a black cap with an ANC emblem containing the letters NDZ – Nkosazana Dlamini-Zuma, former wife of Number One and his choice as his successor as ANC president at the next elective conference and as the country's president in 2019.

The second photograph showed the cap from behind and had the words "Radical Economic Transformation" and "www.nkosazana.com".

The third photograph showed a smiling man standing next to Dlamini-Zuma. He has his arm around her. I didn't recognise him and sent an SMS to my source. "Who's with NDZ?"

"Mazzotti."

ELEVEN

Tom's tax bones

————•————

Money laundering, fraud, corruption, attempted bribing of state officials: these allegations have swirled around the state-capturing Gupta family for many years. There were pieces here and there, showing evidence that they were up to no good, but by and large nothing definitive.

In 2017, this changed. With the unleashing of the reams of #Gupta-Leaks e-mails on a weekly basis by several news outlets, continuously spewing hard evidence as proof, it prompted a question on everyone's lips: why has no law enforcement agency reacted to any of these serious allegations? Apart from Zuma, at least one of his wives, his son, a host of ministers, state officials and insiders in state-owned enterprises were caught in the act with the Guptas.

The ongoing reports continue to demonstrate years of the most horrendous and systematic looting, stealing, corruption, money laundering and abuse of our state agencies and state-owned enterprises imaginable. Some losses run into billions of rand. Much of it is taxpayers' money – money that could and should have gone to fund needy tertiary students, build more schools and provide more services to disadvantaged communities; money that could have addressed issues that have been fuelling many of the civil protests in our country in recent years.

Why has no one, not the Hawks with their serious commercial crimes unit or the police's crime intelligence unit, ever investigated the shenanigans of this family? The State Security Agency (SSA) has a unit that specialises in organised crime. What have they been doing all these years? Why have the Guptas and their associates been allowed to amass their ill-gotten fortunes with such impunity for so long? Why, now that evidence of this is out in the open, are our law enforcement agencies still sitting on their backsides?

Four of South Africa's biggest banks closed the accounts of the Gupta family holding company, Oakbay Investments, in 2016. More followed. The Financial Intelligence Centre (FIC) cited 72 suspicious Oakbay transactions, totalling R6.8 billion, which they reported to the authorities.

Standard Bank said they could not be party to alleged financial crimes and cited as reason the Prevention of Organised Crimes Act, the Prevention and Combating of Corrupt Activities Act and the Financial Intelligence Centre Act. KPMG, which was the Guptas' auditor of choice, resigned from them in 2016, citing "risks" as reasons. Sasfin, their sponsor for purposes of stock exchange listing requirements, withdrew from them in 2016. The River Group stepped in as sponsor, but by June 2017 also stepped away. Its decision was based on its "revised assessment of association risk surrounding the company and its shareholders". Any fool who looks at this must know what it implies: *prima facie* evidence of criminal activity, at the very least the laundering of billions of rand.

What would you expect a democratically elected government to do? To instruct their law enforcement agencies to get to the bottom of this? Of course, this is not even debatable. Yet, what happened in this case? Zuma and the cabinet appointed an "inter-ministerial committee" to investigate the actions of the banks in closing the Gupta accounts. Not a word about a possible crime being committed or that the law enforcement agencies should investigate the allegations.

The worst is that Zuma appointed a Gupta lackey by the name of Mosebenzi Zwane to lead the investigation. In September 2015, Zuma plucked Zwane from obscurity as the Free State agriculture MEC and elevated him to the crucial cabinet portfolio of minister of mineral resources. During his time as MEC, irregular payments were allegedly made to a Gupta-linked company for an abortive Free State dairy project in Zwane's home town of Vrede. Money for the farm was allegedly diverted to pay for the multimillion-rand Gupta wedding at Sun City. Three months after his cabinet appointment, Zwane travelled to Switzerland to facilitate a deal for a Gupta-linked company to buy the distressed Optimum Colliery in Mpumalanga.

Zwane, rather predictably, reported to cabinet that the closure of the Gupta accounts was because of "innuendo and potentially reckless media statements" and that Oakbay had "very little recourse to the law". He said cabinet had approved a review of the Financial Intelligence Centre Act and the Prevention and Combating of Corrupt Activities Act, two key pieces of legislation when it comes to fighting financial crimes. Zwane said cabinet had resolved to ask Zuma to establish a judicial commission of inquiry into the banks that closed their accounts with the Gupta family. Cabinet distanced itself from Zwane, and Zuma reportedly told him he wasn't authorised to make his announcement. That was the end of the matter.

* * *

The only law enforcement agency that appears to have been willing to take on the Gupta family was SARS. Or, shall I say, the "old" SARS.

Recently, in early 2017, media reports revealed how a mole within SARS had tipped off the Gupta family already in November 2013 that SARS was busy looking at them, Zuma and some of their associates. From what I could determine from my SARS sources, the Central Projects unit of SARS had commenced investigations into the Guptas towards the middle of 2013 and the High-Risk Investigation Unit (HRIU) was told to assist sometime in April or May 2014.

SARS examined the Guptas' Oakbay empire, as well as their Sahara group of companies. These SARS projects were massive in scope, covering literally hundreds of companies, shareholdings and individuals, and were only at the beginning phases of investigation and audit. One of the issues they probed was how the Guptas – with the help of Zuma's son Duduzane – acquired Shiva uranium mine in the North West Province through their Oakbay company. It was bought from a Canadian company which had all but mothballed it for its lack of productivity.

It's a complicated affair, which is discussed in detail in Pieter-Louis

Myburgh's book *The Republic of Gupta.* I will try to keep it simple. Oakbay took a R250 million loan from the Industrial Development Corporation (IDC) to clinch the deal. The IDC is a state-owned investment enterprise intended to enhance economic growth in our country. The debt to the IDC should have been repaid by April 2013, but by the end of February 2014 only R20 million had been paid and the debt had grown to R399 million. The IDC agreed to restructure the debt with a low interest rate. Before the company listed, the IDC took a 3.6 per cent stake in Oakbay in return for R257 million of the total debt.

Oakbay's interim financials at the end of August 2014 gave the company a net asset value – the total value of its assets minus liabilities – of about R4.6 billion, which translates into an asset value of R5.74 a share. This drops to R4.84 a share if one replaces the mineral asset value in Oakbay's books with the lower value put on them by a "competent person" – a valuator appointed as part of the listing requirements.

Oakbay nonetheless listed at R10 a share, nearly double the underlying asset value. This is significant, as it is this R10 "market" value, minus a 10 per cent discount, at which the IDC got shares in lieu of the R257 million debt.

How did Oakbay achieve the inflated market value? The answer lies in Singapore, the seat of a company called Unlimited Electronic and Computers that paid R10 a share in a private placement shortly before the listing. Unlimited, which acquired 2.3 per cent of Oakbay, is owned by Kamran "Raj" Radiowala, who has been associated with the Guptas since at least 2006. Online company registration data record him as being appointed managing director of an Indian electronics distribution company, SES Technologies, in 2007. SES was co-owned by the Guptas' South African business, Sahara Computers, and its board included Ashu Chawla, one of their closest associates here. The SES chief operating officer for some time was George van der Merwe, who held the same position at Sahara and is now the chief executive of Oakbay.

In other words, Oakbay swapped R257 million of their debt for shares which they valued at R10 each but which were in fact only worth R4.84 each. Doesn't sound right, does it?

Had the IDC held Oakbay to a loan instead, even at a more favourable renegotiated interest rate, the portion of the loan swapped for equity would have been worth about R300 million (as at February 2006), according to a conservative *Mail & Guardian* calculation.

By June 2017, Oakbay delisted from the Johannesburg Stock Exchange, shedding a reported 71 per cent of its value. When the IDC converted interest on its loan to Oakbay into shares, it was done when the shares were valued at R9. Because of the delisting, the shares could no longer be converted into cash, and with the share price at around R5.80, the IDC took a hit of about R90 million.

If you smell blue cheese, clearly so did the "old" SARS. Their investigation focused on several local and foreign bank accounts. There were apparently several suspicious transactions relating to various businesses and bank accounts reported to SARS through its case-reporting system.

There was also the question of an old case in which the tax collector had previously identified R200 million in alleged VAT fraud linked to Sahara Computers, one company that resided under the Guptas' Sahara Group.

I also managed to track down a report by the Reserve Bank's Financial Surveillance Department, prepared by its Compliance and Enforcement Division (CED), which tells how, in 2000, the CED investigated alleged import and VAT contraventions by two Gupta-owned companies, Sahara Computers and Correct Marketing CC. The gist of the allegations was that Sahara used a front to import various electronic goods at undervalued prices. The front company then sold the goods to Sahara Computers at inflated prices as part of a fraudulent scheme to claim VAT refunds.

The matter was reported to the Directorate of Special Operations (the Scorpions) in 2003. No further communications on the alleged contraventions were received from the Scorpions and the matter was never pursued by the NPA. Recently, in 2017, following media enquiries, the NPA announced that they had declined to prosecute the matter back in 2005 but could not give reasons why. They said the records were destroyed.

Some of my sources told me that the Reserve Bank was investigating the Guptas as recently as September 2016. Their Compliance and Enforcement

Division investigated possible forex regulation breaches involving two Gupta-linked companies that did deals with South African parastatals. The Reserve Bank concluded that although no substantial information indicating a contravention of the provisions of exchange control regulations "could at this stage be identified by any member of the Gupta family or any other directly related individuals or entities", it recorded numerous "trans-actions of interest". The Reserve Bank said: "If it were to be found that substantial amounts of money were transferred from the Republic, it is improbable that the Gupta family would have made use of entities in which they have a direct interest. The possibility that funds are exited through more sophisticated methods cannot be excluded." The report also mentioned "recent airport cases where currency was moved abroad, a system similar to the Hawala system bypassing traditional banking systems or using local third parties or intermediaries to transfer funds".

What do we make of all of this? There wasn't a "Gupta smoking gun" at SARS, except the older Sahara case which had been dusted off and brought to life. The case is obviously dead now.

Far more interesting is the Reserve Bank report of September 2016 and the 72 suspicious Oakbay transactions that were reported by the Financial Intelligence Centre (FIC). If the Guptas have been laundering funds out of South Africa, they certainly haven't paid any taxes on that money.

That is, Mr Moyane, why you need an intelligence and investigative capability in your tax service. You should take the FIC reports and the suspicions of the Reserve Bank and cut them to the bone. Every modern-day tax collector in the world has not only intelligence and forensic investigative functions, but also the capacity to scrutinise financial transactions of this magnitude to extract the taxes, excise and duties due to the state. You had this capacity; it had been built up over many years, it had an institutional memory that no money can buy in a day, you held it in the palm of your hand. And then you crushed it. The country and the fiscus lament; Zuma, his cronies and gangland South Africa rejoice.

* * *

Not only have the Guptas and their associates been allowed to loot with impunity, but Tom Moyane rushed to their assistance when they urgently needed a multimillion-rand VAT refund. In his haste to service the president's chums and son, he flouted the tax collector's rules and processes.

City Press reported in June 2017 that the beleaguered family received much-needed relief in the form of a R70 million VAT refund payment to Gupta-owned Oakbay Investments. This caused a huge fallout in SARS that necessitated the intervention of Moyane.

The drama occurred against the backdrop of two important events: the release of the #GuptaLeaks e-mails, which painted the family with a brush of burgling, and the investigation by the tax ombud into an unusually long delay in the payout of tax refunds. The ombud, Judge Bernard Ngoepe, was ordered to investigate after a tsunami of complaints from taxpayers that they were not receiving their refunds. Former finance minister Pravin Gordhan told Parliament that the tax authority had delayed payments of R19.6 billion worth of tax refunds by the end of February 2017. SARS was accused of withholding tax refunds to boost its tax-collecting figures, which its spokesman denied. Its reply to the delay ranged from denial and obfuscation (with complicated explanations) to setting out how refunds needed to be dealt with according to SARS policies and tax laws. Despite the withholding of the refunds, SARS still reported a R30 billion shortfall in its targeted revenue.

One would therefore expect the Oakbay refund to follow SARS policies and tax laws. Not so. My sources set out to me a sequence of events which perhaps shows best the extent to which SARS had been captured in this nest of lies and deceit.

The very week that Oakbay so desperately demanded their R70 million refund from SARS, they insisted that SARS pay the refund into a foreign bank account. VAT refunds can legally only be paid into a taxpayer's South African account, and not into the account of any proxy.

It is unclear which bank account the family is currently using to trade and pay employees from. South Africa's four biggest banks closed their banking facilities in 2016 following "suspicious transactions" that were reported to the Financial Intelligence Centre.

Oakbay insisted: pay it into the foreign bank account. The SARS auditors and legal people involved revolted. This wasn't on. It was against SARS policy and rules and the tax laws. Eventually it was down to an advocate in the SARS law admin division to give a legal opinion. Could SARS pay the refund into a foreign account? The answer was an unequivocal no, given in a detailed legal opinion.

Oakbay didn't give up, said my source. They then demanded that the refund be paid into an attorney's trust account. Once again, the legal opinion said no, this cannot be done either. It would be unlawful. SARS eventually asked an external senior advocate for a similar opinion. The verdict remained the same. SARS could not lawfully pay the refund into a foreign bank account or a lawyer's trust account.

Moyane entered the fray, pulled rank and ordered the release of the refund. The R70 million was paid into the lawyer's trust account that same week. This instruction might well have been unlawful. According to *News24*, SARS officials made the refund "begrudgingly" and it left tax employees feeling despondent and angry. Other taxpayers wait months, some even years, for their refunds to be processed.

The refund proves beyond any doubt that the earlier investigations into the Guptas had ground to a halt. It is policy in SARS to withhold any refunds from taxpayers under investigation or audit, until the inquiries are concluded. Had they been under audit or investigation, the refund wouldn't have been paid out.

When asked for comment, SARS scrambled for the cover of the Tax Administration Act and said they couldn't divulge information about the tax affairs of a taxpayer or trader.

Contrary to SARS policy, two legal opinions and tax legislation, Moyane jumped when the Guptas or Duduzane Zuma ordered him to do so. Why?

My SARS sources said that one of the victims of Moyane's irrational decision was SARS chief financial officer Matsobane Matlwa. At the beginning of August 2017, newspapers reported that he had resigned after receiving a suspension notice. Both parties claimed to have parted amicably, but according to *Daily Maverick*, Matlwa was marched out of SARS's Lehae building in Pretoria under the supervision of security personnel. He left Lehae for the Hilton House offices, also in Pretoria, to fetch some of his belongings and was escorted out of this building too. He was ordered to serve his notice period at home – which is odd.

My SARS sources told me that Matlwa's resignation followed a fallout around the R70 million Gupta payout. He was concerned about SARS paying the refund in the manner it was ultimately done, as any good accountant and chief financial officer would have been. As chief financial officer for SARS, Matlwa, a chartered accountant by profession, would have had to approve the transfer. He apparently recorded his concerns with the auditor-general of South Africa. My sources say that he was then accused of being disloyal to Moyane and of leaking the information to the media.

There is another twist to this sorry saga. It relates to Moyane's relationship with Duduzane Zuma, who is the Guptas' business associate and director of several of their companies. In a radio interview with PowerFM in 2016, Moyane described Jacob Zuma's late wife, Kate Mantsho, as a "family sister". He later said she was not blood-related, but that they grew up together in Soweto. Kate is Duduzane's mother, and according to *Daily Maverick*, Moyane often babysat Zuma's children while they were in exile in Mozambique.

On 24 January 2016, *Daily Dispatch* editor Sbu Ngalwa tweeted: "Just encountered Sars boss Tom Moyane having a seemingly intense discussion with Duduzane Zuma at some obscure coffee shop in Midrand." *Daily Maverick*'s Marianne Thamm said the two either met on SARS matters, which presents Moyane with the dilemma of having met a taxpayer alone and therefore contrary to SARS policy, or it was a social meeting between friends.

Thamm has drawn attention to Chapter 2, Part B, section 7 of the Tax Administration Act 28 of 2011, which states that a SARS commissioner "may not exercise a power or become involved in a matter pertaining to the administration of a tax Act, if the power or matter relates to a taxpayer in respect of which he has or had, in the previous three years, a personal, family, social, business, professional, employment or financial relationship presenting a conflict of interest or other circumstances presenting a conflict of interest". Said Thamm: "Moyane was appointed by President Zuma in September 2014. This means, as SARS commissioner, Moyane may not go near Zuma's tax affairs, nor that of his family's or their business interests. In that sense it would be appropriate then if Moyane stayed well clear of any dealings relating to Duduzane or any of his business associates and left this to an impartial SARS official."

* * *

It was a team from amaBhungane that reported in September 2016 that top SARS official Jonas Makwakwa and his girlfriend, Kelly-Ann Elskie, had been flagged for "suspicious and unusual" cash payments, totalling more than R1.3 million, into a series of bank accounts. The transactions were picked up by the Financial Intelligence Centre (FIC), a state institution to which all business and banks are legally required to report suspicious and unusual financial transactions. The FIC recommended an investigation to determine if the payments to Makwakwa and Elskie were "proceeds of crime arising from corrupt activities" or "acts of money laundering".

The two had made at least 75 suspicious deposits into their accounts. Of those, 48 were cash deposits amounting to R726,400 and made between 2014 and 2015. Part of the evidence is contained in camera footage of the two feeding wads of cash into bank machines.

After the great Moyane purge, Makwakwa had risen to become the second most powerful official at SARS after Moyane. He single-handedly oversaw all the biggest financial investigations and audits in the country. You would expect such a man, in such a position, to be beyond any reproach and an official of the highest integrity. One would also imagine that Makwakwa would have declared this money in his tax returns and paid tax on it. He was also supposed to have reported this additional income in his annual declaration of private interests, as all SARS officials are required to do every year.

To protect the integrity of the service, Moyane should immediately have suspended Makwakwa and removed him from those big cases and audits he oversaw. He should without delay have ordered the anti-corruption unit to commence a full inquiry into Makwakwa and Elskie. Furthermore, anti-corruption laws in our country compel accounting officers like Moyane to report suspected corruption to the law enforcement authorities. If the officer fails to do so, he can face prison time and a huge fine. Isn't that what we as the taxpaying public expect of a responsible civil service director-general?

What did Moyane do? He disclosed the report to Makwakwa, with the result that his number two got his lawyer to write to the Financial Intelligence Centre asking them questions. Moyane then sat on the evidence for four months while Makwakwa went about his normal duties. It was only when the story leaked to the media and the Democratic Alliance asked uncomfortable questions about the matter in Parliament that Moyane acknowledged that he had this evidence all along. He only then suspended Makwakwa and his lady friend, who also worked at SARS.

It doesn't stop there. Instead of ordering the Hawks to get to the bottom of the matter, Moyane appointed a law firm at enormous expense to the taxpayer to probe the matter. When asked, the Hawks said they were not investigating the matter because it was a SARS issue.

The case of Tom Moyane, Jonas Makwakwa and Kelly-Ann Elskie has further eroded Moyane's integrity and caused enormous resentment among the rank and file at SARS. When I spoke to my SARS sources, they were unanimous in their verdict: how come he disbanded the old SARS executive committee, and suspended Pillay, Richer, Van Loggerenberg and the others on the strength of unsourced, biased and false allegations in the Sunday Times, yet had to be forced to act against Makwakwa and his extramarital lover?

Media reports said that Moyane personally walked into the Brooklyn police station to charge a sitting minister and top officials on the basis of rumours and falsehoods, yet in the case of Makwakwa and Elskie – where there was hard evidence – he appointed a law firm to "investigate". And then, they say, he had the audacity to send an internal memo to staff assuring them that SARS had followed "the correct procedures in terms of our policies when it comes to such serious allegations of misconduct. I want to appeal to all of you to remain focussed and keep up the good work you are doing."

Mashudu Jonas Makwakwa has been at the taxman for almost twenty years and became Moyane's confidant after he took office in 2014. He gained a reputation, like HR head Luther Lebelo, of being the commissioner's "hatchet man". Makwakwa often acted as commissioner in Moyane's absence and simultaneously held the titles of chief operating officer for customs and information technology, acting chief officer for digital information systems and technology, and chief officer for business and individual taxes. As such, he was in charge of some of the biggest and most sensitive investigations at SARS, among them that of Jen-Chih Huang and Mark Lifman, to name but a few. The VIP Taxpayer Unit, which dealt with the tax affairs of Zuma and family, and all other politicians and political parties, also resided under him.

Makwakwa became embroiled in a rather messy extramarital love affair at SARS, something almost every staff member at head office knew about. His wife was an official in the enforcement unit and once his subordinate. His new girlfriend was a secretary at the anti-corruption unit and 19 years his junior. They had a child and eventually moved in together.

In 2015, Kelly-Ann Elskie reported for duty at SARS's High Court Litigation Unit as a junior consultant: legal and policy. This unit dealt with the tax authority's most high-profile and sensitive cases, including that of Huang and Lifman. Guess who appointed Elskie in the position? Makwakwa himself.

According to amaBhungane, Elskie stated that she held a BA Law degree from the University of Pretoria, a certificate in corporate forensic investigation, and SARS training in "anti-corruption in the public sector". She also indicated that she intended completing an LLB degree in 2016. However, amaBhungane reported that Elskie's claim to hold a law degree was false. She apparently left the litigation unit after a falling-out with a senior manager. SARS ignored complaints that Makwakwa personally signed off on Elskie's promotion. SARS also failed to investigate grievances that she had lied about her law degree and didn't qualify for the position.

Daily Maverick reported that Makwakwa has since claimed that cash deposits of R785,130, made between 2010 and 2016, were proceeds from a stokvel and taxi business.

The matter has been dragging on for almost a year now. When questioned by the parliamentary oversight committee about the status of the investigation, Moyane said he was in the dark and added that it was a "complex" matter and should be "given more time".

Nobody knows why Moyane appointed law firm Hogan Lovells to investigate such basic allegations against Makwakwa and Elskie. Think about it. He has at his disposal the best forensic investigative and auditing capacity of any state department or law enforcement agency in the country. Every day, SARS investigates the origins of taxpayers' income. Why give this simple task to a law firm? How difficult can this possibly be? The man and his girlfriend received deposits over years in their bank accounts. Isn't this what SARS does when they audit taxpayers?

All Moyane should have done was to call for the tax returns of Makwakwa and Elskie and see whether they declared this income and where it came from. That would have shown whether the money was legitimate or not. And, by the way, doesn't the commissioner now boast a new investigations unit – the one of Yegan Mundie – which he had so coyly described to his finance minister as an instrument intended to investigate corruption within SARS?

In December 2016, the organisation Corruption Watch filed criminal charges against Moyane for failing to report the matter to the Hawks as he was obliged to do under the Prevention and Combating of Corrupt Activities Act and for illegally disclosing the contents of the Financial Intelligence Centre report to Makwakwa and Elskie. Corruption Watch also laid charges against the two. I'm not holding my breath to see the Hawks pursuing them with the same vigour as they seem to have chased Pravin Gordhan, Ivan Pillay, Oupa Magashula and all the others.

SARS spokesperson Sandile Memela said at the end of July that SARS has received the final report, but that the recommendations "are still under consideration".

* * *

When I sat down with my some of my SARS sources for the last time, I was about to finish the section on Moyane and the shenanigans at the tax collector. They had swamped me with information and documentation, and I had warned them beforehand that I simply didn't have space for everything.

We concluded by going down a list we had compiled over the time we had interacted. "Lifman, is he in?"

"Yes, of course. He's very important."

"Huang?"

"The biggest tax evader of them all? He's definitely in."

"The tobacco guys? Azeem? Kajee?"

"In."

"Mazzotti?"

I laughed and told them that I had just discovered that he was one of presidential hopeful Nkosazana Dlamini-Zuma's campaign sponsors.

"Edward Zuma?"

"In."

"Khulubuse Zuma?"

"Sorry, guys. Simply not enough space."

They appeared disappointed and stressed how important the investigations into the president's nephew were and urged me to mention them. So here goes: Khulubuse Zuma and Nelson Mandela's grandson Zondwa Mandela were the chairperson and managing director respectively of Aurora, a company that assumed control of the Grootvlei and Orkney gold mines in 2009 when the previous owners were placed in provisional liquidation.

The company said it would pay R605 million for the two operations and invest a further R350 million. Aurora never came up with the money but took control of the assets under a law that allows purchasers to start mining before the transfer of ownership is complete, to avoid mines lying idle.

The advocate that was appointed by the High Court to lead the inquiry into the affair, Wayne Gibbs, said what followed "has to count as some of the more serious cases of fraud ever perpetrated in the Republic". Grootvlei and Aurora were stripped of assets and laid to waste, leaving thousands of employees destitute and without pay for years. The estimated looting amounted to R1.7 billion. Yet the mines produced about R120 million of gold over the first few months, but there were no accounting records.

Khulubuse Zuma said he wasn't involved in Aurora's day-to-day decision-making and blamed the fiasco on the other directors. The High Court in Pretoria found in 2015 that Zuma, Mandela and the other directors were liable for the destruction of the mines. The judge said Zuma showed "reckless disregard" for his role as Aurora's chairperson in the ensuing chaos. Zuma agreed to pay R23 million in damages to the liquidators.

SARS started investigating Aurora and its directors after they picked up that the company had failed to submit VAT returns. Jacob Zuma's legal adviser, Michael Hulley, was allegedly at some point also a director and fell within the scope of the investigation.

This investigation is dead, said my sources. When Moyane dismantled the investigative units, the case basically stopped along with many of the others.

They continued with their list. "The Guptas?"

"In."

"Fana Hlongwane?"

The name of playboy businessman Fana Hlongwane will always be synonymous with South Africa's infamous multibillion-rand arms deal. He served as the late defence minister Joe Modise's adviser from 1995 to 1998 before moving on to the far more lucrative role of arms deal kingpin.

Hlongwane is an enigmatic character who has avoided scrutiny over the years, despite his name often surfacing at the centre of major controversies. *Business Day* said his companies were alleged to have channelled R200 million in payments from British Aerospace as bribes for the ANC.

Hlongwane featured prominently in Thuli Madonsela's *State of Capture* report. The *Sunday Times* reported that Hlongwane was the "fixer" who took deputy finance minister Mcebisi Jonas to meet the Guptas in 2015 when they offered him the post of finance minister while Nhlanhla Nene was still in office. The paper quoted an ANC insider as saying Hlongwane was a regular visitor at the Gupta compound in Saxonwold, Johannesburg.

Madonsela interviewed Hlongwane, who confirmed that he had known Duduzane for some time and was an "uncle" to him, although he claimed to have no relationship with the president. He said the Guptas were his "casual acquaintances" and that he had no business relations with them.

Despite Hlongwane's high connections, SARS had registered a project and were investigating his companies and his personal tax matters. Hlongwane was presented with a personal tax bill for R3.3 million and paid it in full in July 2012. The tax collector told Hlongwane that two of his companies owed more than R8 million in taxes. He objected and at the end of 2013 he requested more time to gather the required documents and affidavits.

By the time the bomb burst at SARS, Hlongwane's final tax bill was not finalised. He was being investigated by the National Projects Unit, which was later disbanded by Moyane. My sources told me that this case has also never been concluded.

Before we parted ways, I wanted to know: "So what do you think happened to Jacob Zuma's tax case?"

They laughed and said: "Of course it's gone. Where else would it be?"

"Maybe SARS is still waiting for him to submit his tax returns?"

"Maybe. The word is that Zuma may have submitted his tax returns. But there is no way we can check this. Only the VIP unit guys will know for sure. He probably declared just his presidential salary and not much more. The VIP unit would have quietly handled his returns and no questions would have been asked."

In March 2017, Zuma said he was not prepared to divulge whether he declared to SARS the fringe benefits accruing to him because of the upgrades to his Nkandla homestead. Zuma said: "The issue of tax is a confidential matter between the South African Revenue Service and the taxpayer."

SARS cannot legally reveal Zuma's tax affairs, but nothing in law prevents the president from opening his files for public scrutiny. Given the massive public interest in Nkandla and the fact that taxpayers funded the upgrades, surely he should at the very least tell the country whether he has paid his fringe benefit taxes, as we all are expected to do? If not, why should anybody pay any fringe benefit tax to SARS? If our president doesn't have to, how can SARS justify collecting such tax from any other taxpayer?

Said one of my sources: "It is possible that he did declare the Nkandla upgrades in his returns, but then would have attached some sort of an explanation about why he was not liable for tax. SARS would likely just have accepted his explanation, no questions asked, and exempted him from paying any tax."

"And the Royal Security payments?" I asked them

"Those PAYE recons were filed by Royal Security and are on the SARS system. The tax was paid by Royal Security."

"Can they wipe off the records?"

"I can't see how. Why would they? The tax was paid. I suppose it is possible to wipe the records because with technology you can delete or alter anything. But remember that Royal Security made the payments for Zuma through their bank account to SARS. There must be a record of that as well. These payments will also reflect in the SARS account and on Zuma's VIP taxpayer's number."

"So, Zuma got away with it?

"Yes, he did."

I want to line up three rows of people. In the first is Tom Moyane, Luther Lebelo and their cronies at SARS. One could add to this cabal Jacob Zuma, Nkosazana Dlamini-Zuma, Bathabile Dlamini, David Mahlobo, Nomvula Mokonyane, Mosebenzi Zwane and a host of others. These are the proponents of "radical economic transformation" and foes of a scourge they call "white monopoly capital".

In the second row are Ivan Pillay, Johann van Loggerenberg, Gene

Ravele and Pete Richer. I have said enough about them: dedicated civil servants, proponents of Pravin Gordhan's "higher purpose".

In the third stand a group of suave suit-clad men: Trevor Hoole, Steven Louw, Mike Oddy, Herman de Beer and Mickey Bove. They were top executives at auditing firm KPMG, until 15 September 2017.

If you want to point the finger at white monopoly capital, these men represent the worst of their kind. One would think that Moyane would shun Hoole and his crowd, wouldn't you? What on earth would they have in common. One thing: to rid SARS of Gordhan, Pillay and the others at SARS. In doing so, they gutted South Africa's most efficient civil-service institution through falsehoods, slander and deceitfulness.

On 15 September, KPMG withdrew all the findings, recommendations and conclusions in its report on the SARS "rogue unit". KPMG International found after an "exhaustive investigation" that their South African office had no evidence to conclude that there was a "rogue unit" at SARS. CEO Hoole and a number of his executives resigned.

Their report was instrumental in the hounding of Gordhan and used by Moyane to justify why he ousted Pillay, Van Loggerenberg, Richer and Ravele. The report resulted in the disbanding of all the investigative units at SARS. Criminal proceedings were instituted against Gordhan, Pillay and others based on, among others, the KPMG report. Former finance minister Trevor Manuel is still under investigation at the time of writing – yet again based on information derived from the KPMG report. The report has been used as a political whip to lash out at Zuma's opponents. Both former police minister Nathi Nhleko and state security minister David Mahlobo held press conferences based on the KPMG report, entrenching the idea that SARS had a rogue unit and that Gordhan had set it up.

There is, however, one small consolation: KPMG has agreed to pay back the R23 million that it charged Moyane for the report.

* * *

Maybe one day, with Tom Moyane gone and Jonas Makwakwa reaping the fruits of his stokvel, the whole tragic and calamitous chronicle of SARS will fully emerge.

Today we look at the Hawks and say: there was a time when we had an elite law enforcement agency, called the Scorpions, which was feared and revered. There was a time when, with people like Anwa Dramat, Johan Booysen and Shadrack Sibiya, the Hawks showed promise as a worthy replacement. But these people are all gone.

And there was once a National Prosecuting Authority which sent the police commissioner to prison and was eager to take down Jacob Zuma.

We also once had a SARS that didn't just meet its targets, but exceeded them. The tax service once hunted down organised criminals and bled them dry financially.

We will one day dig up the graves where Tom Moyane has entombed the tax bones of the Lifmans, Guptas, Huangs, Mazzottis and Zumas and ask ourselves: how the hell did this happen?

While writing this, I couldn't help thinking of my favourite movie of all time, Martin Scorsese's mobster classic *Goodfellas*. There is a scene in which the novice gangster Henry (Ray Liotta), the jaded Tommy (Joe Pesci) and Jimmy "the Gent" (Robert De Niro) have to dig up Billy Batts's decomposed corpse because the property is about to be developed.

Tommy: "Hey, Henry, Henry, hurry up, will ya? My mother's gonna make some fried peppers and sausage for us."

Jimmy and Tommy laugh while Henry coughs.

Jimmy: "Oh, hey, Henry, Henry! Here's an arm!"

Henry: "Very funny, guys."

Jimmy: "Here's a leg!"

Tommy: "Here's a wing! Hey, what do you like, the leg or the wing, Henry? Or ya still go for the old hearts and lungs?"

Henry: [Vomiting] "Oh, that's so bad!"

TWELVE

The spiders in the centre of the web

———•———

The South Africa's law enforcement community is cloaked by a septic web of deceit, delinquency and depravity. Suspended in its centre are two venomous spiders: Richard Naggie Mdluli and Nomgcobo Jiba. Both are close to the highest political power in the land. These are Zuma keepers so powerful that generals in the police and national directors in the National Prosecuting Authority (NPA) were prepared to lay the institutions to waste to save their skins.

One cannot grasp the flux and upheaval in the police and the NPA without understanding the roles of Mdluli and Jiba. Both were destined to head the police and the NPA, ensuring that Jacob Zuma, his family and his cronies were immune from prosecution. This might well have happened, were it not for the commitment of a handful of dedicated cops, a vigorous civil society and the independence of our courts.

A law graduate from the Walter Sisulu University in Mthatha in the Eastern Cape, Nomgcobo Jiba started her career as a state prosecutor in Peddie in 1988 and was in 2001 appointed as a deputy director of public prosecutions in Pretoria.

I want to quote from an affidavit from one of her underlings, Advocate Vernon Nemaorani, who joined Jiba's group – known as the Warriors – in 2002. He worked with her for five years and left the authority as a deputy director. He said: "Adv Jiba not only became my supervisor, she became a friend, a mentor and a person I relied on. I cannot exhaust the wealth of experience that I gained from Adv Jiba on any piece of paper neither can I say enough about her humanity and humility."

In 2005, Jiba's husband, Booker Nhantsi, also a senior prosecutor at the NPA, was suspended and charged with fraud. When he was an attorney in private practice, he stole R174,000 from the firm's trust account. Some of his partners sent the evidence to NPA prosecutor Gerrie Nel, who was Nhantsi's supervisor. Nel prosecuted him for fraud and he was convicted and sentenced to three years' imprisonment. (Zuma later expunged Nhantsi's criminal record in an "act of mercy".)

During Nhantsi's disciplinary hearing at the NPA, which was chaired by acting NPA head Mokotedi Mpshe, Jiba gave evidence to support her husband. Mpshe dismissed her evidence as unreliable and he suspended Nhantsi. Said Nemaorani: "What followed was a passionate and constant desire to have Advocate Nel pay for the wrong he had committed, and Adv Jiba was not going to stop at anything until it happened." Even if it meant that she had to get Richard Mdluli to do her dirty work.

* * *

Mdluli was an apartheid policeman from Vosloorus on Johannesburg's East Rand and reportedly served in the 1980s in the feared and hated Security Branch.

Mdluli began an affair with Tshidi Buthelezi in 1986 when she was a 16-year-old schoolgirl and he was 28. In 1995, the couple had a son. Another child was later stillborn.

Unbeknown to Mdluli, who had paid R6,000 lobola for Tshidi, she started an affair with Oupa Ramogibe in 1997. She later moved with her new lover to Orange Farm to get away from Mdluli. He allegedly intimidated the Ramogibe family to persuade Oupa to stay away from Tshidi, although the two had in the meantime become married.

Mdluli and his cronies allegedly embarked on a reign of terror to find Ramogibe and get Buthelezi back. Oupa Ramogibe was attacked for the first time in December 1998. After a case was opened, the investigating officer took him to the scene of the attack. The policeman at the scene – one of Mdluli's men – said that he was held up by two men who robbed him of his service pistol. He heard shots being fired and Ramogibe was killed. The men ran away.

The case was investigated by the Germiston murder and robbery unit. The dockets went missing. Almost ten years later, they were found in a safe in the Vosloorus police station. Mdluli was at the time the commander of the station.

Mdluli rose through the ranks and was appointed as Gauteng deputy police commissioner in the 2000s. He oversaw the detectives who investigated the rape charges against Zuma. The trial judge lambasted the police for their shoddy work, and found Zuma not guilty.

It was during his stint as Gauteng deputy police commissioner that Mdluli ingratiated himself with Jiba – the start of a noxious relationship.

*   *   *

Jiba's opportunity to sink her knife into Gerrie Nel emerged during the trial of another top NPA prosecutor, Advocate Cornwell Tshavhungwa. He had allegedly accepted cash in return for sabotaging a major fraud investigation. He was in 2007 convicted in the Pretoria Regional Court on two counts of fraud and perjury and sentenced to an effective six years in jail. (The conviction was later set aside on a technicality.) Nel was criticised by the court for displaying "partisanship towards the case of the accused". Vernon Nemaorani said in his affidavit that after the court's criticism of Nel, Jiba "constantly talked about the fact that they are working and something will happen soon".

A case of fraud, defeating the ends of justice and perjury was opened against Nel. The investigating officers were Richard Mdluli, then deputy provincial commissioner for Gauteng, and Ntebo Jan Mabula, a notorious North West Province organised crime policeman. Mabula later became the head of the Hawks in North West and his name is linked to some of the politically most sensitive cases in South Africa.

Nemaorani said: "She [Jiba] mentioned of meetings that were being held with people from the Presidency, the Department of Justice and members of the SAPS. According to her, meetings were held even at night, in fact late at night. She spoke of a meeting that was also attended by the regional head of KZN, Adv L. [Lawrence] Mrwebi. She said Adv Mrwebi was flown overnight by a police helicopter and was flown back after the meeting. She did not mention the names of other people who attended the meeting but said they are the highest-ranking SAPS members. I had realized that she was completely fixated in having Adv Nel pay for whatever wrong he has done."

On 8 January 2008, 20 heavily armed policemen pounced on Nel, cuffed him in front of his wife and children, and dragged him off to a police station to charge him with fraud, corruption, perjury and defeating the ends of justice. He spent the night in prison and was released on bail the next day. Ten days later, the charges were withdrawn. The prosecutor said there was no evidence of any of the alleged offences in the docket.

Following the Nel fiasco, acting NPA boss Mokotedi Mpshe suspended Jiba for conspiring with Mdluli and Mabula to have Nel arrested. She faced internal charges of unprofessional conduct, dishonesty, fraud and bringing the NPA into disrepute.

Jiba brought an application to the Labour Court to stop her disciplinary hearing. She claimed she was a victim of a conspiracy by NPA management. Mdluli supplied her with an affidavit that the NPA was victimising her as part of a plot to protect Nel. She also petitioned justice minister Jeff Radebe, who undertook to raise the matter with the prosecuting authority's management. The decision to suspend and charge Jiba was reversed and in turn she abandoned her Labour Court application. She was transferred to Pretoria's Specialised Commercial Crimes Court.

After the Supreme Court of Appeal rejected the appointment of Menzi Simelane as the national director of public prosecutions (NDPP) in October 2011, Jacob Zuma was forced to find a replacement. His choice fell inexplicably on Nomgcobo Jiba, whom he appointed as the acting NDPP. Lawrence Mrwebi was chosen to lead the commercial crimes unit, which put him in charge of all major fraud and corruption cases.

Mrwebi had once led the Scorpions in KwaZulu-Natal. When he was appointed as commercial crimes head, the respected former NDPP Vusi Pikoli described his appointment as "astonishing". He said Jiba's elevation to acting prosecutions boss was "baffling".

Jiba and Mrwebi oversaw an institution which was mandated by the Constitution to prosecute without fear, favour or prejudice, in the protection and advancement of democracy. The two would soon flout every one of those principles.

*   *   *

Richard Mdluli was almost secretly appointed in July 2009 as the divisional commissioner of the crime intelligence division. The commissioner of police, advised by senior professional policemen, normally selects the heads of police divisions. Politicians are for obvious reasons supposed to stay out of the process. But police minister Nathi Mthethwa hijacked the process and convened a panel of pro-Zuma ministers, including state security minister Siyabonga Cwele and deputy minister of home affairs Malusi Gigaba, to interview Mdluli. There wasn't a single policeman on the panel.

Shortly afterwards, the *Sowetan* published a story, "Love twist haunts top cop", and told the story of Mdluli's suspected involvement in the murder of Oupa Ramogibe. Mdluli's reaction to the story was to appoint his own pet cop to investigate the allegation: Major-General Mthandazo Berning Ntlemeza, a man you are going to read about a lot in chapters to come. He eventually became the head of the Hawks and caused havoc as he persecuted Zuma's enemies.

Mdluli wrote a letter to the provincial commissioner of the police in Limpopo requesting him to allow his deputy, Ntlemeza, to investigate "alleged irregularities". There must have been a link between the two men then. Why else would Mdluli ask a policeman in Limpopo to investigate alleged crimes committed outside his jurisdiction? And since when does a suspect appoint his own investigator?

After a five-month investigation, Ntlemeza concluded in his top-secret information note: "There was a plot within the Crime Intelligence environment to prevent Mdluli from being appointed as the Head of Crime Intelligence."

Ntlemeza spoke to only one family member of Oupa Ramogibe. He phoned his sister, who he said told him that "no member of the Police was connected with the murder". He said in his report: "She further stated that according to family the matter was already to put on rest but she was shocked when they saw the Sowetan News Paper [*sic*]."

This couldn't be further from the truth, as the family had a burning desire to get behind the truth of Ramogibe's murder and to have Richard Mdluli face the law for his alleged complicity in the act. Ntlemeza's investigation was a whitewash of Mdluli and not worth the paper it was written on.

Mdluli became aware that the Hawks were investigating him. The probe was approved by Hawks head Lieutenant-General Anwa Dramat and conducted by Gauteng provincial commander Major-General Shadrack Sibiya. Both men were later persecuted and hounded for doing their job.

Mdluli knew Zuma's susceptibility to a good conspiracy and in October 2010 he produced a secret intelligence report known as "Ground Coverage". Central to the claims in the 22-page report – riddled with spelling and factual errors – was an alleged meeting of Zuma's opponents in Estcourt, KwaZulu-Natal, supposedly to concoct a plot to unseat him. Among the "plotters" were human settlements minister Tokyo Sexwale, ANC Youth League leader Julius Malema, KwaZulu-Natal premier Zweli Mkhize, ANC treasurer-general Mathews Phosa and police commissioner Bheki Cele.

Tokyo Sexwale responded: "The report is a fabrication . . . it is a fake . . . the rumour has an author and return address and his office is located within the headquarters of our National Police Department – Lt Gen Mdluli, head of Crime Intelligence Division . . . I am informed that we have not seen the last of these dirty tricks."

Mduli had signed the report, but after it was discredited, he claimed his signature was forged. Zuma told Parliament he hadn't seen the report, which is implausible. The president's crime intelligence chief presented him with a report that members of his inner circle were plotting his demise. And he didn't read it?

Mdluli followed "Ground Coverage" with a letter, marked top secret, to Zuma. He repeated that he was a victim of a plot, driven by "the very same members that were involved in negative campaigning at the ANC Conference in Polokwane during 2007. They were in the camp of the Former President and they are now trying to take control of the intelligence environment within the Police by devious tactics." He assured Zuma: "Although I might not have gone outside and actively involved in the struggle, I was active in many other areas. I was, and am still, a loyal ANC member."

Mdluli approached Bheki Cele to stop the investigation against him. Cele refused. This unleashed a ferocious rivalry in the police. Crime intelligence, in charge of all wire-taps, listened to Cele's telephone conversations. Only a judge can give permission for telephone interceptions and only if it is necessary to investigate a serious offence. The *Sunday Times* reported that intelligence officers duped retired judge Joshua Khumalo into signing the order. They submitted a request for certain numbers, but lied about who the numbers belonged to. They claimed that Cele's number belonged to one Thabani Mdlalose of Lamontville in Durban.

Zuma suspended Cele as police chief in October 2011 after he was implicated in a police head office leasing scandal. The first Mdluli enemy was gone.

*　　*　　*

It is indicative of the mess the Hawks find themselves in that 250 of its members in the Western Cape work in squalor in a building in Bellville that has been condemned as unsafe, that is infested with cockroaches and that poses a fire hazard. Somewhere in the innards of that building, on the first or second floor, skulk two Hawks colonels. Both are approaching their mid-fifties and should have been at the pinnacle of their careers. They should have investigated state capture and the recently released Gupta e-mails while overseeing and training upcoming Hawks detectives who can fill their shoes when they finally depart from the service. But they aren't investigating the Gupta e-mails or any other significant cases that I am aware of.

Those who followed the saga of Richard Mdluli will recall the names of Colonel Kobus Roelofse and Lieutenant-Colonel Piet Viljoen, two Hawks of the highest standing. They were among Anwa Dramat's most trusted lieutenants and he dispatched them to Gauteng to work alongside Shadrack Sibiya to investigate murder, kidnapping and assault charges against Mdluli.

Since investigating Mdluli, their careers have never been the same. They were harassed, threatened and ordered by police commissioner Riah Phiyega to stop their probing. Police auditors descended on their offices and spent days shifting through old claims and receipts to find wrongdoing. They were accused of plotting with the organisation Freedom Under Law (FUL) to overthrow the government.

But Viljoen and Roelofse forged ahead, and on 31 March 2011 Mdluli handed himself over to them and was charged with the killing of Oupa Ramogibe, the husband of the woman he was obsessed about. Colonel Nkosana "Killer" Ximba and Lieutenant-Colonel Mthembeni Mthunzi were charged alongside him with kidnapping, assault and murder, and were released on bail.

With Mdluli gone, crime intelligence officers told Roelofse and Viljoen that the crime intelligence head and his cronies had looted the unit's secret service account. The investigation took a new turn when the Hawks team found that Mdluli had used the secret account, worth around R250 million a year, as a piggy bank.

He had established a fake intelligence network, which was a mirror image of the SSA's PAN project created by intelligence chief Arthur Fraser. Mdluli also appointed his family as "principal agents", among them his current wife, her brother and other members of her family, his ex-wife, her daughter and his son, as well as two "girlfriends" in the Eastern Cape. His wife and ex-wife were promoted to colonel within two months.

Fifteen of the 250 posts were awarded to people with criminal records. The principal agents did little intelligence work and went about their usual daily routines. Various safe houses were rented for the exclusive use of Mdluli and his cronies, their families and their girlfriends.

Mdluli greedily helped himself to an array of vehicles: BMWs, a Jeep Cherokee, two E-class Mercedes-Benzes and a Lexus. Another police divisional commissioner got a half-a-million-rand Audi A5 which was meant for covert operations. When the scandal became public, she panicked, gave the keys back and resigned before she could be suspended.

The business class section of South African Airways was at the time packed with crime intelligence officers and their families taking to the skies. Many were on overseas trips.

Even police minister Nathi Mthethwa had benefited. In 2012 the auditor-general found that a wall built around his private home in northern KZN to the tune of R200,000 had been paid for from the secret service fund. He said, however, that the minister wasn't aware of the source of the funding.

Those who tried to stop the looting were victimised, threatened and ostracised. One such person was Colonel Johan Roos, the auditor of the secret fund. He compiled a dossier which detailed, for example, how crime intelligence's chief financial officer Major-General Solly Lazarus allegedly faked hijackings during which R1 million in cash was stolen. Roos had since the middle 2000s reported the cases of fraud and corruption to Bheki Cele and four generals. They did nothing. Instead, Roos was investigated by police counter-intelligence, his house was broken into, he was transferred and his career was destroyed.

* * *

The plundering of taxpayers' money within the police service bordered on the obscene and the salacious, a prime example being a convicted Durban drug dealer and alleged gangster who had all expenses paid plus much more. It was a bit like appointing Al Capone as an FBI special agent.

In 2010, Durban businessman Panganathan "Timmy" Marimuthu hopped onto the stage at a Christian summit in Chicago in the United States to lecture on wealth creation. His lecture was posted on YouTube. The slender, moustached entrepreneur was talking big: how he had blossomed from an apartheid policeman – "I divorced my wife five times and nearly shot her one day because I was a Hindu" – into a billionaire who owned 32 houses. He boasted to his audience that he had in 2009 contributed R15 million to the church.

"I drive a Bentley convertible; my wife drives an Aston Martin convertible. My son, who is 23, drives a Lamborghini Spyder convertible. I have a

Ferrari in the garage that I don't even use. My daughter has a Q7 and a Cayenne Porsche. Two S-class Mercedes . . . an ML63 to make some noise now and then," he boasted.

With the audience in awe, he posed the crucial question: how can we all make it happen? He said the art was to get your foot in the door. He said when Nigeria held elections, he asked God to give him a strategy. He revealed that he met some Nigerian politicians and paid part of their election costs. "So, what did I do? I put my foot in. When the guy came to power, my second foot in. When he takes his office, my whole body is in."

When Marimuthu stood there, he was already a suspect in a host of serious crimes. I have seen a top-secret crime intelligence profile on him that recommended he should be subjected to a full probe by the intelligence agencies. The report said: "He is now apparently boasting that he is getting closer to Zuma. The president should resist any advances of Marimuthu as any relationship that is fostered will invariably cause embarrassment."

Marimuthu was once a policeman but resigned after he was implicated in murder, for which his father was sentenced to death. His sentence was later commuted to life before he was granted a presidential clemency. Marimuthu was also convicted of drug smuggling after he was caught with 4,000 Mandrax tablets and sentenced to five years' imprisonment. The Jali Commission of Inquiry into prisons later heard that he never served a day behind bars because he bribed officials with R100,000. He then started entertaining high-ranking politicians.

One politician whom Marimuthu had on his "books", said the report, was Bheki Cele. He was then KZN MEC for transport and allegedly awarded a host of tenders to Marimuthu to build roads. Marimuthu controlled various companies through his children. These entities allegedly received state contracts worth tens of millions of rand.

According to the report, Marimuthu had expanded his business interests to Mozambique, where he was involved in road construction. "Preliminary investigations reveal that Timmy is paying for pilot training for a person who will fly drugs from Mozambique into South Africa."

For some inexplicable reason, crime intelligence – the very police unit that accused him of corruption and recommended a full-scale investigation – appointed Marimuthu as an agent and paid him R50,000 a month. He got a BMW X5 with blue lights to drive around in. He leased several properties to crime intelligence for which he earned another R250,000 monthly. Marimuthu's wife was appointed as a colonel, his son and daughter as lieutenant-colonels, his brother as a colonel, his niece as a captain, and two of his girlfriends as clerks. None of them had any police experience, and Colonels Roelofse and Viljoen could not find any files for them.

The self-confessed billionaire expected the police to pay even for his dentistry. He submitted a claim of R37,000 for the replacement of his crowns. His daughter, appointed as a lieutenant-colonel, claimed R50,000 for the delivery of her child.

These charlatans might still be still on crime intelligence's books. Who knows? What we do know is that any whiff of an investigation into Timmy Marimuthu's shenanigans died with his appointment as an agent.

* * *

Winter on the Highveld is one of clear skies, smoking chimneys and a brown blanket that has snuffed out summer's green. After negotiating an icy morning and jam-packed highways, I sat down at a restaurant built over the highway between Johannesburg and Pretoria. A few minutes later, I was joined by a crime intelligence officer who glanced around the eatery, leaned forward and wanted to know: "The person behind you, was he here when you walked in or did he sit down afterwards?"

"He was here when I walked in."

Crime intelligence has been in turmoil ever since the appointment of Richard Mdluli in 2009. Eight years later, as I write this book, he's still the commander despite being on suspension for six years. The various police ministers and police commissioners have failed miserably to do their legal duty: institute disciplinary proceedings against him and, if he is found guilty, fire him. Instead, they've allowed the wound he inflicted to fester and become gangrenous. There's enormous resentment among the rank and file, and officers feel unsafe, unwanted and stuck in a hostile environment.

The unit has had a string of acting commanders; none has been able to bring stability. Everyone working there will tell you that Mdluli's spectre is large and omnipresent. His allies are still in place. People are convinced that they meet Mdluli and get instructions from him. One of his disciples is Brigadier Nkosana "Killer" Ximba, who was originally one of Mdluli's co-accused in the murder, kidnapping and assault case against him.

When I sat down with my crime intelligence source, the person surreptitiously placed a flash stick on the table and said to me: "Take it when I leave and have a look at it. There's lots of stuff on that stick." Much of it related to Ximba, said my source.

"Killer is Mdluli's and Zuma's pointman at crime intelligence. He's untouchable and very powerful. Nobody fucks with Killer."

I want to go back to Mdluli's top-secret letter to Zuma in March 2011. Mdluli mentioned Ximba in the letter and said: "Colonel Ximba is an active member of the ANC and during the struggle was a leader of one of the self-defence Units. He was also a bodyguard for Mrs Winnie Mandela and former Minister Steve Tswete [Tshwete]. Colonel Ximba also played an important role in the Polokwane conference and also during the President's trying times with his engagement with the NPA."

When Mdluli wrote this letter, the Polokwane conference was still more than a year in the future. What "important role" was Ximba playing? Identifying enemies? Listening to their phones? Tracking them? During Zuma's "trying times" with the NPA, where was Ximba then? What was he doing?

After Ximba's stint in the self-defence units, he became a community constable on the East Rand before Mdluli appointed him as a fully fledged constable at the Vosloorus police station. He resigned but two years later he wanted to come back. In December 2007, Mdluli asked for Ximba to be reappointed. A few days later, the Kempton Park recruitment centre found that Ximba has a criminal offence for reckless driving, which he had failed to declare. He didn't qualify to be a policeman. When he reported for his medical examination, he was drunk and there was too much alcohol in his blood to evaluate him. When he eventually went for his medical, he couldn't be recommended for enlistment owing to an "abnormality regarding his vision". The police's personnel services said Ximba "has already embarrassed the SAPS" and his re-enlistment "bodes badly for the future".

They were overruled by none other than Lieutenant-General Khomotso Phahlane, then divisional commissioner of personnel services, who later became acting police commissioner. He wrote to the Gauteng provincial commissioner and said: "The application for re-enlistment of the above-mentioned ex-member (N.S. Ximba) has been approved and must be re-enlisted." The *Mail & Guardian* and amaBhungane reported later that Phahlane had links to Mdluli and signed off on a spate of irregular appointments of family members and cronies, including those with criminal records.

On 28 February 2010, Ximba was still a constable. The next day, on 1 March 2010, he was a colonel. All thanks to Mdluli. In April 2012 Ximba was charged with two counts of assault with the intent to do grievous bodily harm and contravention of the Firearms Control Act. One of his alleged victims said in an affidavit that Ximba and his cohorts made him strip naked, dressed him in a plastic bag and tied his limbs together. They then choked him until he passed out. "I could feel I had soiled myself. There was nothing I could do to escape from their barbaric actions. Every time I was suffocated, I would pass out. They continued to kick me with booted feet all over my body."

Deputy director of public prosecutions D.D. Dakana said the case should be handled by a senior prosecutor because this was a "high profile and sensitive matter". The charges were dropped after witnesses refused to testify.

Ximba briefly shot to fame towards the end of 2013 when he arrested Czech fugitive and mobster Radovan Krejčíř. Give Ximba his due: Hawks policemen were sitting on the docket and stalling the case, and there were lots of rumours of backhanders, carrots and sweeteners.

Krejčíř claimed that Ximba and another crime intelligence officer drove around with him for hours while trying to extract a confession from him. Said Krejčíř: "I was blindfolded, cuffed and transported to a remote area. I was made to kneel and tortured through electrocution." The police did nothing about Krejčíř's allegations against Ximba. Instead, he was promoted to the rank of brigadier.

*   *   *

Five months after being charged with murder, Mdluli and a senior crime intelligence officer were arrested for fraud and corruption. The financial head of crime intelligence, Major-General Solly Lazarus, was arrested and charged in a separate case.

Mdluli submitted to Lawrence Mrwebi, the head of the NPA's Specialised Commercial Crimes Unit, that his arrest "is a continuation of the dirty tricks and manoeuvrings relating to the contestation and jostling for the position of Head of Crime Intelligence. The investigators go about intimidating witnesses and telling them what they must say." Mrwebi agreed that the criminal justice system had been abused and in December 2011 he withdrew the fraud charges against Mdluli. He said the charges were brought for an ulterior motive and he could not find evidence that implicated the general in fraud and corruption.

Acting NPA head Nomgcobo Jiba concurred. It would later emerge that she was so hell-bent on shielding Mdluli that she dumped three successive legal teams when they advised her that the decision to drop criminal charges against him was wrong. AmaBhungane reported that Jiba ignored damning criticism from her own lawyers and their explicit warning that she was obliged to play open cards with the court. Instead, she allegedly sought to lie and conceal evidence that might challenge those decisions.

In February 2012, the NPA announced that it was also withdrawing the murder and kidnapping charges against Mdluli and his co-accused and that the matter would be referred to a formal inquest.

It was only the disciplinary charges that still stood between Mdluli and his reinstatement as crime intelligence supremo. Police minister Nathi Mthethwa reportedly ordered the new acting police commissioner, Lieutenant-General Nhlanhla Mkhwanazi, to lift Mdluli's suspension, which he did under protest. Mdluli appeared with Zuma at a Workers' Day celebration in 2012.

In June 2012, Zuma appointed Riah Phiyega as his police commissioner. Phiyega was a businesswoman with no police experience. She was just two months into the job when police shot dead 34 striking mine workers at Marikana in August 2012. She praised the police for a job well done. She also attempted to shield Mdluli by ordering Viljoen and Roelofse to stop their investigation.

Mthethwa was under enormous pressure to do something, especially after it emerged that he was the benefactor of a sturdy wall around his rural KwaZulu-Natal property, courtesy of Richard Mdluli. He announced in Parliament that Mdluli would be transferred to another portfolio in the police. Before that could happen, Judge Ephraim Makgoba granted an interim interdict in the Pretoria High Court barring Mdluli from performing any police functions, pending the resolution of the allegations against him.

Mdluli wrote another letter to Zuma and claimed that five police generals – among them Dramat and Sibiya – were conspiring against him. Referring to the ANC elective conference in Mangaung at the end of 2012, Mdluli further stated: "In the event that I come back to work, I will assist the president to succeed next year."

Not long afterwards, every general fingered by Mdluli was gone or on his way out.

THIRTEEN

Somebody in a neighbourhood full of nobodies

———•———

Sometime in early 2013, I met a chunky Serb with a bull terrier-like appearance at the Randburg Waterfront, Johannesburg's trashy imitation of Cape Town's famed tourist attraction. Constructed like a wrestler and probably as strong as an ox, George Darmanovich, alias Boris, was holding court in a Portuguese restaurant, surrounded by the usual suspects. His closest bro looked like a horse-racing high roller who had fallen on hard times, but apparently he was as lethal as a rabid Jack Russell. The other was also slight with a hang-dog expression but never said a word. He had dark, button-shaped eyes that followed my every move.

In this crowd was a raving Christian who once, while clutching a sack, took me to the toilet of a shabby restaurant somewhere in Germiston on Johannesburg's East Rand to show me its contents. He pulled out a shining new Uzi sub-machine gun and grimaced like a naughty boy.

Darmanovich sometimes phoned me on a Saturday morning and would say: "Listen to this!" In the background, it sounded like the Battle of Stalingrad. He and his crew were on the shooting range, discharging their array of heavy metal. They were armed to the teeth, Darmanovich with a 9mm he loved to flaunt. There was much more shooting stuff in the boot of his BMW.

In the words of Henry Hill in the movie *Goodfellas*, Darmanovich was a "somebody in a neighbourhood full of nobodies". Senior police officers, private investigators and an array of scumbags always dropped in on Darmanovich. Gregarious, raucous and generous, he made sure nobody paid for anything. He carried wads of cash which he referred to as "ops money" or "Inzo's money". Inzo Ismail was then the head of special operations at the State Security Agency (SSA), and everyone said that Darmanovich worked for him. He loved to flaunt a picture of himself and Jacob Zuma that he said was taken when he debriefed the president about a project. The pic looked genuine, but with Darmanovich, who knows?

Among his regulars were a crime intelligence colonel, two Hawks organised crime colonels, a colonel from the Hawks' secretive Crimes Against the State unit and a host of other policemen, spooks and operatives living on that fluid edge where the realm of espionage collides with the real world.

Darmanovich was a minefield of information and regularly shot his mouth off. After meeting him for more than three years, I have little doubt that he was a contract worker for the SSA's Special Operations Unit (SOU). He simply knew too much, he frequently showed off his familiarity with official and secret documents, he had intimate knowledge and contact details of key SOU officials, and someone was paying his entertainment and living expenses. And how else did he manage to get 11 gun licences in a single year for assault rifles and sub-machine guns?

He was the person who warned me in 2014 that SARS executive Johann van Loggerenberg was going to be fired and that the SOU was digging for dirt against him and the SARS top executive. How would Darmanovich have known about the SSA campaign if he didn't work for them?

After I wrote an exposé about the intelligence campaign in *City Press* and mentioned Darmanovich by name, state security minister David Mahlobo ordered the inspector-general of intelligence, Faith Radebe, to investigate. The SSA told her that Darmanovich was an information peddler who attempted to worm himself into the innards of the agency. They got a crime intelligence colonel who frequented his table to testify that he was a debt collector who faked his SSA connections to persuade people to settle their bills. Radebe swallowed the story hook, line and sinker. By then, Darmanovich had already left South Africa for Serbia, from where his father came. He has never returned to South Africa.

It is common practice for intelligence agencies worldwide to use so-called proxies to do their dirty work. A proxy is a person, group or other entity that acts on an agency's behalf. If the proxy is compromised, there's nothing that points directly to the agency. A contract worker should never reveal his/her connection to the agency. This was where Darmanovich failed miserably: he couldn't keep a secret.

I want to return to that 2013 meeting at the Randburg Waterfront. Darmanovich had told me earlier that day that he had a present for me and that I should come to the restaurant. After listening for two or three hours to undercover banter crap, Darmanovich told me to go with him to his car. He flung open the boot, which was full of guns, files and documents. He lifted two thick files from the boot and shoved them in my arms. They were police dockets, which is illegal to possess, although that didn't even cross my mind.

"What's this?" I asked him.

"Go read it," he said. "It sinks Dramat and Breytenbach."

Anwa Dramat was the head of the Hawks and Glynnis Breytenbach the head of the NPA's commercial crimes unit in Pretoria. While Dramat drove the murder and fraud investigations against Richard Mdluli, Breytenbach was intent on charging him. At the time, George was batting for Mdluli and claimed that they regularly spoke. The files he gave me, according to him, were destined to torpedo Dramat and Breytenbach.

Darmanovich and his cronies were engaged in pushing a narrative that both Dramat and Breytenbach were corrupt. He and his crowd loved conspiracy theories and were convinced that Breytenbach was also a Mossad agent.

The file on Dramat related to a police investigation into abalone smuggling in the 2000s. Somewhere in the docket was an affidavit that implicated Dramat in the network. It was made by a discredited gangster. The Scorpions had investigated the allegations and cleared Dramat. The docket was nonsense; the Hawks head was squeaky clean.

The docket that supposedly attested to Breytenbach's dishonesty was a treasure trove – but for all the wrong reasons. At the time, the Competition

Commission was investigating the collusion of major construction companies in some of the country's biggest projects, including the stadiums for the 2010 soccer World Cup. The dockets laid bare the investigation into the collusion. Scared that they might go to prison, a group of executives of one of the companies, Stefanutti Stocks, had approached Breytenbach and admitted their complicity in fixing 60 contracts with other companies. Another of the construction giants, Group Five, had made a similar approach to the Competition Commission.

Breytenbach took affidavits from the executives and gave the managing director of Stefanutti Stocks indemnity from prosecution in return for securing his future cooperation. She then handed the case to the Hawks to investigate fraud and racketeering charges against the others. They decided to wait until the commission had concluded its probe and reached a settlement.

The docket contained all the affidavits and supporting documentation. Darmanovich and his cronies had hoped that I would nail Breytenbach for the indemnity she had dished out to one of the top crooks. She had, however, played everything by the book. It was the cartel in the construction industry that was the lead story, not Breytenbach.

Unperturbed, Darmanovich gave me a few weeks later another document and said it was final proof that Breytenbach was an Israeli spy. It purportedly showed that Breytenbach had met with a former head of Mossad in the Caribbean. The letter, badly written, also made reference to the use of a private jet and R10 million, which had been placed for her in a trust account.

The letter appeared to be a sham and Breytenbach said she'd never seen it. I couldn't publish it and I told Darmanovich it was garbage. The same letter was passed to other journalists, who came to a similar conclusion. Darmanovich lamented the state of journalism when reporters couldn't recognise a scoop even if it was thrown in their laps.

In June 2017, I embarked on a writing holiday to Europe and took a detour to see Darmanovich in the Serbian capital of Belgrade. I wasn't sure what reception I would get, seeing that I had blown his cover when I exposed the role of the Special Operations Unit during the SARS saga.

I needn't have worried. As convivial and hospitable as ever, Darmanovich ferried me to a Serbian restaurant and plied me with šljivovica, a traditional plum brandy, and ordered plates of roasted meat. A popular print in Serbia depicts a moustached peasant drinking šljivovica with the motto "Fuck the Cola, fuck the Pizza, all we need is Šljivovica".

Darmanovich still holds court in restaurants, mostly with South African expats living in the Balkans. His business card identifies him as the president of the Serbian–South African Business Chamber. He claimed to be exporting surveillance equipment to South Africa.

He said the SSA ordered him in 2014 to leave South Africa as a precaution should the inspector-general decide to do a proper investigation. The SSA needn't have worried.

Darmanovich said the SSA still pays him every month and had sent an agent to Belgrade to make sure he's fine and that his mouth is shut – which it will never be.

"Those dockets you gave me in 2013, on Dramat and Breytenbach," I asked him. "Who gave them to you?"

"Richard Mdluli," said Darmanovich. "They came straight from him. He really hated Breytenbach and Dramat. He wanted them out."

* * *

Richard Mdluli had cost Glynnis Breytenbach her career – much as the pursuit of Zuma and his cronies became the downfall of Johann van Loggerenberg, Ivan Pillay and other SARS executives. She was insistent on charging Mdluli while the strategy of Zuma's keepers was clear: prevent the Mdluli case from getting to court because once on the roll it becomes more difficult to get rid of.

In her book, *Rule of Law*, Breytenbach wrote: "Everything I did before Mdluli was building up to Mdluli. When you are faced with a matter like the case against Richard Mdluli, you don't even have to think about it. You have to do it. Not even have to, you are going to. And you understand the consequences for him – and for you. As a prosecutor you learn from the start that you have to be able to act independently. No one else can decide on cases or on courses of action for you. If you want to be any good you have to be independent. You decide on a course of action, and you stick to it. You have to be strong, and it takes a lot of self-confidence. You have to believe you are right."

The National Prosecuting Authority's strategy was probably to ruin Breytenbach financially with drawn-out departmental disciplinary charges. The advantage of keeping it in-house was that, unlike in a court of law, there was no award of legal costs. The NPA thought they could financially gut their adversary.

In April 2012, acting national director of public prosecutions Nomgcobo Jiba suspended Breytenbach pending the outcome of 15 charges in a disciplinary hearing. The NPA alleged that she had failed to act impartially while investigating a mining rights issue and had leaked confidential NPA information to a journalist. She had also allegedly deleted NPA files on her laptop computer.

Breytenbach claimed that the charges were related to her opposition to the decision by her superior, the commercial crimes head Advocate Lawrence Mrwebi, to withdraw fraud and corruption charges against Richard Mdluli. Mrwebi signed off on an internal investigation into Breytenbach after she persisted with the Mdluli investigation.

The NPA underestimated two things. The one was that Breytenbach was like a bull terrier in a dogfight – she had locked her jaws and wasn't going without a noise. The second was her friendship with billionaire businessman Nathan Kirsh, who funded her legal costs and enabled her to obtain the best senior counsel.

In May 2013, Breytenbach was found not guilty on all 15 disciplinary charges. She said afterwards: "I will return to my post . . . to take up the cases that I was dealing with – and I mean *all* the cases that I was dealing with – upon my return to office."

When Breytenbach reported for duty, she was transferred to a different unit. She unsuccessfully applied to the Labour Court to overturn her transfer. She lost and in January 2014 she resigned to become a member of Parliament and the Democratic Alliance's shadow minister of justice.

The NPA was still not backing down. They accused her – on the grounds of the trivial letter that Darmanovich flogged to me and others – of being an agent for the Israeli intelligence agency, Mossad. When interviewed by the head of the NPA's integrity management unit, Prince Mokotedi, she was asked if she was aware that some of the people she had met abroad were "former members of foreign intelligence agencies". He then said: "You are aware, or you must be aware, that if you meet a member of a foreign intelligence agency, [it] must be reported to our State Security Agency."

In February 2016, the NPA charged Breytenbach for defeating the ends of justice by deleting files from her laptop – the same charge for which she was exonerated at her disciplinary hearing. In June 2017, the court threw out this charge, but Breytenbach is still standing trial for contravening the NPA Act.

It is a scenario we have sadly seen too many times under Zuma's rule: an efficient and straight civil servant maligned and expelled on trumped-up charges.

*   *   *

Nomgcobo Jiba was always Zuma's first choice to head the NPA but the Constitution required someone "fit and proper" for the position. Several courts have spoken out on Jiba's and Lawrence Mrwebi's integrity – or lack of it.

In August 2013, Zuma appointed an unknown practising attorney from KwaZulu-Natal, Mxolisi Nxasana, as his national director of public prosecutions. From the moment he took office, Nxasana was at war with Jiba and Mrwebi. At the heart of the dispute was Mdluli, whom they refused to prosecute.

Nxasana appeared to possess a rare quality at the NPA – an independent mind – and his clashes with Jiba very quickly thrust him into Zuma's crosshairs. Number One needed not a prosecutions boss who acted without fear or favour, but a stooge who would keep him and his cohorts safe and free. Nxasana had to go.

Nxasana's hand was strengthened when he asked one of the most esteemed legal minds in the country, retired Constitutional Court judge Zak Yacoob, to investigate the state of the NPA. Jiba and Mrwebi refused to cooperate with Yacoob, and although his inquiry had no legal standing, he said he had found sufficient evidence to warrant the appointment of a judicial commission of inquiry with powers to subpoena witnesses.

Yacoob said of Jiba's and Mrwebi's refusal to charge Mdluli that he had studied the dockets and that there was at the very least a *prima facie* case "on the fraud and corruption as well as the murder and related charges. The fact they were withdrawn . . . are both matters of grave concern."

He said of Mrwebi: "Mr Mrwebi has got a great deal to answer for . . . the courts have accused him, with justification, of not telling the truth, not being fully frank with the court. There is reason to believe he lied under oath and did not respect the court." And of Jiba: "Jiba said in the High Court that she knew nothing about the withdrawal of these cases and the court found it difficult to believe her. We agree . . . we find it quite incredible that she did not know about these cases."

Nxasana launched an internal investigation into Jiba. Senior counsel recommended that she be criminally investigated for perjury and fraud. According to counsel, there was reasonable suspicion that she had lied under oath about the evidence she had assembled against KZN Hawks head Johan Booysen, whom she was intent on prosecuting.

Nxasana later said in an affidavit – which I refer to in a later chapter – that Jiba and Mrwebi undermined his standing with Zuma and did everything to discredit his leadership. Jiba, who resented not becoming national director of prosecutions, apparently told the president that Nxasana was going to reinstate the corruption charges against him.

Nxasana said Zuma accused him in a meeting that he had secretly met Bulelani Ngcuka (Mbeki's prosecutions boss who had charged Zuma with corruption) at a flat in Durban. Zuma told him in Zulu: "I don't want to hear anything about that man. I go crazy."

Issues were raised about Nxasana's security clearance because he had been charged as a teenager in 1985 with murder but had subsequently been acquitted on the ground of self-defence. Nxasana had not disclosed this when applying for the top job, he said, as he had been found not guilty.

This was the ammunition that Zuma needed. Eight months after Nxasana took office, Zuma told him that he was going to appoint a commission of inquiry to determine his fitness for office and intended to suspend him. The minister of justice, Jeff Radebe, asked Nxasana to resign, but he refused.

Nxasana commenced with negotiations around a settlement. He got a R17 million payout and in turn withdrew a court action challenging his suspension and forcing the president to state the reasons for the suspension.

Before Nxasana packed away his settlement, he fired a last salvo at Jiba and Mrwebi and asked the General Council of the Bar to strike both off the roll for their part in the Mdluli affair.

* * *

The decision by Jiba and Mrwebi to withdraw criminal charges against Mdluli was wrong, devious and baseless. In September 2013, Judge John Murphy ruled in a landmark decision in the Pretoria High Court that charges against Mdluli should be reinstated. The case was brought by Freedom Under Law (FUL), the legal watchdog founded by retired Constitutional Court judge Johann Kriegler.

The judge lambasted the NPA officials. Starting with Mrwebi, he said his decision to withdraw the corruption charges was "illegal, irrational, based on irrelevant considerations and material errors of law, and ultimately so unreasonable that no reasonable prosecutor could have taken it". The judge found that Jiba's and Mrwebi's conduct signalled "a troubling lack of appreciation of the constitutional ethos and principles underpinning the offices they held". They did not, he said, demonstrate that they had the capacity to pursue matters without fear or favour.

Everything that could have gone wrong for Jiba and Mrwebi in this case did, and they emerged with their credibility in tatters. Murphy exonerated Glynnis Breytenbach and said the allegations against her were "frankly disingenuous and unconvincing".

Imagine you're the president of the Republic and a judge lambasted your two top prosecutorial officials as irrational and lacking the constitutional character that their offices require? Wouldn't you suspend them? Launch an inquiry? Not in Zuma's gangster state – the state within the state – where filthy hands wash one another.

Jiba and Mrwebi stayed on while the NPA "studied the judgment".

* * *

The president's next move made many scuttle for Google to find out who was Shaun Abrahams, Zuma's surprise choice for national director of public prosecutions. At just 39 years old, Abrahams leapfrogged several steps on the ladder, raising questions whether he had the necessary political gravitas, wisdom and shrewdness for a job that no one before him had managed to survive.

Abrahams was the first NPA head who was appointed from within the organisation and was a senior prosecutor with a good track record. He was, however, at the age of 39 turbo-charged into a critical position that far more experienced lawyers had failed to survive.

Being national director of public prosecutions is an unenviable job. Since 1994, not one prosecutions boss has served out his 10-year term in charge of the NPA. In fact, the average length spent in the top job has been barely two years. Every head has been suspended, fired or else has taken a golden handshake. Nxasana got a R17 million payout with 98 months left on his contract.

For more than a decade, the NPA had been ravaged by infighting and was managed along faction divides and internecine rivalry. The NPA that Abrahams took charge of was ruled by a troika consisting of Jiba, Mrwebi and the head of the authority's integrity unit, Prince Mokotedi.

Despite Jiba's dismal performance as a prosecutorial manager, she was armoured by her closeness to Zuma. The *Huffington Post* recorded that 12 separate judges on four different benches in three high-profile cases have slammed Jiba for her conduct. She was charged with perjury and for lying under oath – she basically fabricated an entire affidavit. She was a softer, sweeter version of Berning Ntlemeza but equally noxious.

New MP Glynnis Breytenbach was the first to ring the warning bells when she said that Abrahams was close to Jiba and we mustn't set our expectation of him too high. She was right. It didn't take him long to show his true colours. He dropped fraud and perjury cases against Jiba, which emanated from her ill-fated attempts to charge Johan Booysen. The judge said that her decisions to prosecute "were arbitrary, offend the principle of legality and, therefore, the rule of law, and were unconstitutional".

Abrahams went a step further and promoted Jiba to head the national prosecution services, effectively making her the number two in the NPA. His decision was short-sighted, ill-fated and smacked of a desperate attempt to appease his master in the Union Buildings.

"Shaun the Sheep" was born.

* * *

Why were Nomgcobo Jiba and Lawrence Mrwebi willing to destroy their careers and reputations in their pursuit of Richard Mdluli's defence? They humiliated themselves, shamed their profession, broke their oaths and irrevocably damaged the NPA and the police. Both behaved like kamikaze loyalists without fear of perishing in the process. They must have been promised substantial reward in their afterlives.

Theories and allegations abound; from an extramarital affair to a child that was born out of wedlock to dirt that Mdluli had on them to phone calls and orders from the west wing of the Union Buildings. None has ever been substantiated, but that both Jiba and Mrwebi acted in an extra-ordinary "unlegal" manner is without a doubt. The host of court judgments against them bear witness to this.

There is no doubt that Jiba has the interest of Jacob Zuma and his cronies – Mdluli and the others – at heart and had no qualms in targeting innocent people and destroying careers to protect them. Her fixation on nailing Gerrie Nel, Glynnis Breytenbach and Johan Booysen bear this out.

The answer might lie in a document on the flash stick that the crime intelligence officer left behind on the table in the restaurant. It is a secret information note, dated 29 May 2012, written by Lieutenant-Colonel Piet Viljoen to Colonel Kobus Roelofse. They were the two Hawks officers whom Anwa Dramat appointed to investigate Richard Mdluli.

Among the documents on the stick is a profile of Viljoen, who joined the police in 1981 at the age of 18. A member of the anti-corruption task team, he was selected by Nelson Mandela in 1997 to be a member of the Presidential Task Team, in which capacity he investigated Mafia boss Vito Palazzolo and testified against him in an Italian court. He commanded a task team from 2000 to 2004 that targeted organised crime. His team nailed scores of gangsters, who received sentences exceeding a thousand years. From 2004 till 2008 he was given the task of combating cash-in-transit robberies. He brought the total number of such incidents down from 56 cases in 2006 to 11 in 2007.

When Viljoen wrote the information note, he was busy probing the abuses of the crime intelligence secret account. He wrote in the note that he had found an instance where the account was used to purchase an air ticket for one N. Jiba.

The crime intelligence secret account is used exclusively to pay agents and informants and their expenses. If an agent must fly from one destination to another and stay in a hotel, it will be paid for by the secret account because his/her identity must be protected. The identity of agents and informants is usually secret, and they are normally identified by their agent number.

On 9 September 2010, N. Jiba flew on South African Airways flight SA563 from Johannesburg to Durban and returned on the same day. The flight was paid for out of the secret account and was approved by the chief financial officer of crime intelligence, Major-General Solly Lazarus.

Viljoen said in his note: "The invoice number 155 allocated to this transaction also refers as payment to SA71, which is an agent number, which means that N. Jiba is a registered agent."

To make sure, Viljoen obtained a warrant which he served on SA Airways, demanding the passenger details of N. Jiba. They gave him the passenger's ID number. This enabled him to conclude: "The identity number belongs to Nomgcobo Jiba . . . who is currently the acting National Director of Public Prosecutions in the country."

I am sure there will be some excuse about why Jiba's air ticket had to be paid from the secret account, but it means only one thing: that she was on crime intelligence business when she boarded flight SA563 at OR Tambo in Johannesburg. Nomgcobo Jiba was not on a mission for the NPA, but for Richard Mdluli. It is incomprehensible, irregular and probably unlawful that secret intelligence money pays for the expenses of a top state prosecutor, who is supposedly independent.

I want to take you back to the affidavit of Jiba's former protégé, Advocate Vernon Nemaorani, in which he told of Jiba's conspiracy to obliterate Gerrie Nel. He mentioned that she had told him that Lawrence Mrwebi attended some of the clandestine meetings to discuss Nel's demise. Viljoen found evidence that at the time, crime intelligence also flew Mrwebi from Durban to Johannesburg and back. His ticket was also paid for from the secret account.

I also found a document that shows that Mrwebi has a criminal record. He was convicted of drunk driving in King William's Town in the Eastern Cape in April 2000. He must have been wasted, because he was sentenced to a fine of R4,000 of which R2,000 was suspended for four years, or imprisonment of eight months of which four months was suspended for four years. His driver's licence was also endorsed. As it wasn't a crime of dishonesty, it would not necessarily have counted against him.

Viljoen stumbled upon the air tickets just before he was taken off the investigation. As I understand, he learnt of the payments almost by chance. What would the two Hawks colonels not have unearthed if they had been afforded more time and support?

I repeatedly tried to contact Viljoen after getting the note. I left messages on his phone, which he didn't respond to. I eventually ventured to Bellville to the sick Hawks building to look for him. I asked reception to call him.

I had first seen Viljoen many years ago when he was a captain and I interviewed him for a television documentary I made about Vito Palazzolo. He had permission to speak to me.

He laughed when he saw me again and said: "Go away! I'm already in shit. You're just going to make it much worse for me!"

He'd obviously grown much older, greyish around his temples and sporting a beard, but with the same boyish expression and inquisitive eyes.

"I can't talk to you," he said. "What do you want?"

When I told him that I had a copy of his information note, he wanted to
know: "How the hell did you get it?"

"You know I can't tell you. But, so it's true?"

He looked at me for a second or two and said: "I will put my life on anything I've put on paper."

FOURTEEN

Gladiators

————•————

The demise of Hawks head Anwa Dramat was inevitable from the time he ordered a murder, kidnapping and assault investigation against Richard Mdluli. The attack on his integrity commenced in October 2011 when, bold and black, a headline in the *Sunday Times* bawled: "Sent to die". Those three words encapsulated the gory details of what was to follow: a group of policemen under the command of Dramat and Gauteng Hawks commander Shadrack Sibiya had conducted illegal "renditions" in cahoots with their Zimbabwean counterparts.

According to the paper, the Hawks arrested four Zimbabweans in Diepsloot in Johannesburg. They were suspected of killing a Zimbabwean chief superintendent in that country before fleeing to South Africa. The four were driven to the Beitbridge border post. Two were dropped off before the border, while the other two were handed to the Zimbabwean police. At least one was killed.

The exposé was written by, among others, Stephan Hofstatter and Mzilikazi wa Afrika, two of the journalists who wrote the SARS "rogue unit" stories. The third author was Rob Rose, for whom I have enormous respect.

A subsequent affidavit made by Hawks Colonel Kobus Roelofse – one of the Mdluli investigators – raised doubts about the credibility of the story. He said a crime intelligence official told him that he overheard Major-General Solly Lazarus, the financial head of crime intelligence, and other officers discussing "the placement of a newspaper article relating to Lieutenant-General Anwa Dramat and Major-General Shadrack Sibiya".

They wanted to get the heat off themselves and cast suspicion on those that posed a threat to them.

The *Sunday Times* reacted angrily to the accusations that their journalists might have been compromised and called it a smear campaign. The newspaper filed requests under the Promotion of Access to Information Act for any evidence in police records of payment made to their journalists. The police said there was none. One of the affidavits on which the newspaper relied was made by a brigadier in crime intelligence who said he had "personally checked all the relevant registers and files where such records would be kept, should it exist, and there are no records or proof of any records". Did the newspaper honestly expect a crime intelligence officer to come forward and spill the beans about the unit's collaborators in the media and expose their dirty tricks in public?

Years of mudslinging, internecine warfare and further erosion of the police and the Hawks followed the *Sunday Times* story. Its consequences have been almost as far-reaching as the SARS "rogue unit" story.

The police minister, Nathi Mthethwa, ordered the police watchdog, the Independent Police Investigative Directorate (IPID), to look into the allegations against Dramat and Sibiya. In October 2012, the case was handed to the head investigator of IPID in Limpopo, Humbulani Innocent Khuba. He was given a docket with 13 statements from crime intelligence policemen and friends and relatives of those deported to Zimbabwe. Khuba later said in an affidavit that the acting executive director of IPID, Koekie Mbeki, had ordered him to work closely with a crime intelligence colonel and share all his information with him. This was highly irregular, but Khuba was instructed to send all his documentation from a private e-mail server to the colonel's private Gmail account. Khuba said he was from the outset under tremendous pressure to produce a report that would enable the National Prosecuting Authority (NPA) to charge Dramat, Sibiya and the other policemen.

One of his crucial witnesses was Lieutenant-Colonel Ndanduleni Madilonga, acting commander of the police station at Beitbridge, who reported that two weeks before the alleged rendition, a convoy of Zimbabwean policemen arrived at the border post. They said they were on their way to Pretoria to see Dramat. One of the policemen claimed that Dramat was assisting them to hunt down Zimbabwean cop-killer suspects in South Africa. Madilonga said he phoned Dramat, who ordered: "Let them come."

Two weeks later, said Madilonga, Hawks Colonel Leslie Maluleke arrived at the border post with two of the suspects and handed them to his Zimbabwean counterparts. He made no mention of Dramat or Sibiya.

* * *

Towards the end of 2013 and the beginning of 2014, two new gladiators entered Zuma's bullring: Berning Ntlemeza and Robert McBride. They were on opposite sides of the ring, and their duel would be fought to the bitter end.

Their worlds couldn't have been further apart. Ntlemeza, a big and brash man with a brooding expression, started his police career in 1982 in the former homeland of Transkei and progressed through the ranks as a detective. In an interview with *City Press*, he said those calling him an apartheid-era policeman should "chill".

In stark contrast stands McBride, a man so despised by white South Africa that bile and outrage bubble to the surface at the mere mention of his name. In their eyes, he's killed innocent women (because they were white), smuggled guns and deviously evaded a charge of drunk driving. In June 1986, as an MK guerrilla and acting upon orders, McBride bombed two bars on Durban's beachfront, killing three white women and injuring 69 people. McBride spent five years on death row until he was pardoned and released on the same day as "Wit Wolf" (White Wolf) Barend Strydom, who had gunned down seven black people and wounded 15 more in Pretoria in 1988.

McBride has been in the news ever since. He was arrested in 1998 for alleged gun-running in Mozambique but eventually released without charge. He said he had done it on behalf of state intelligence; they never denied it. He was then, after a drawn-out court case, exonerated by the High Court of drunk driving.

When Zuma appointed McBride, he probably believed that his choice of head of the police watchdog IPID was a loyal soldier who would ensure that the careers of Anwa Dramat and Shadrack Sibiya were forever encased in an IPID tomb. There was little public faith at the time in his appointment, but within a short while McBride turned into a bad dream for Zuma's chums, demonstrating a staunch belief in justice and independence.

Juxtaposed to McBride is Ntlemeza, the Limpopo detective who exonerated Richard Mdluli and ensured himself a top position in Zuma's army of keepers. He would ultimately rise to become South Africa's top crime-fighter, a position in which he caused havoc and dissent. Ntlemeza is in many ways just a more crude, coarse and unpolished version of Nomgcobo Jiba.

*   *   *

After IPID investigator Innocent Khuba obtained a statement from Colonel Madilonga, he got a call from Ntlemeza, then deputy provincial commissioner in Limpopo, who wanted to see him. Khuba knew Ntlemeza from previous cases he had investigated in Limpopo.

Khuba said in his affidavit that Ntlemeza told him that Madilonga was "his man" and that he was taking care of him. The IPID investigator said he started to doubt Madilonga's version of events.

A month later, Ntlemeza came to Khuba's house to give him a message from Richard Mdluli, whom he had met at the airport. The message was that "I must not be afraid when dealing with rendition because there were people who were looking after me". Ntlemeza also wanted to know when Khuba would submit his report because it was holding back "everything regarding his move to the Hawks". He said his "political principals" wanted him to lead the elite crime-fighting unit.

Khuba declared he was under great pressure to submit his report to an NPA prosecutor, even though his investigation wasn't finished. There were statements missing and the cellphone data analysis was incomplete. Dramat's cellphone records, for example, were not in the report at all. He nonetheless recommended that Dramat, Sibiya and four policemen be charged with kidnapping and defeating the ends of justice.

*   *   *

As Zuma's torturous first term stuttered to a halt in May 2014, taxpayers woke up to the fact that they had spent R250 million on upgrading his Nkandla homestead in KwaZulu-Natal and that an Indian immigrant family was busy capturing the president and the state.

By then, rating agencies had downgraded the country to a notch above junk, the deficit had escalated, unemployment had increased despite repeated promises of job creation, and service delivery protests had engulfed the country because of incompetent local government. The president was under siege, stumbling from scandal to scandal and becoming embroiled in exhaustive and expensive litigation.

In his first five years, Zuma had ripped like a tornado through the state's institutions and wreaked havoc across the land. But the worst was yet to come. In his second term, which has two years left as I write this, the windstorm has been upgraded to tsunami status and Zuma is ravaging the Republic.

But South Africans are resilient people and shine in the face of adversity. A vibrant civil society, a belligerent opposition, a fiercely sovereign judiciary, disillusioned elements within the ruling party and an independent media – fed leaks and information by whistleblowers at the heart of the Zuma campaign – are defying his ultimate quest to capture the vital organs of state.

In a post-election cabinet reshuffle, police minister Nathi Mthethwa was buried in the arts and culture portfolio. As the one stooge crashed, Zuma ushered in the next. Mthethwa was replaced by Nkosinathi Nhleko, who was much the same and would later humiliate himself in his quest to defend Number One. His self-sacrifice didn't help because less than a year later, Zuma canned him. Before that happened, Nhleko played a vital role in ending the careers of Anwa Dramat and Shadrack Sibiya, a step that would ultimately lead to the disembowelling of the Hawks.

*　　*　　*

After Robert McBride had taken control of the police watchdog, an IPID team reviewed the available evidence into the alleged renditions to Zimbabwe and obtained the missing statements and cellphone records. Despite the further investigation, Nathi Nhleko suspended Anwa Dramat two days before Christmas 2014. In a letter to Nhleko after his suspension, Dramat said the minister's decision was "pregnant with ulterior motives". "No doubt you are aware that I have recently called for certain case dockets involving very influential persons to be brought or alternatively centralised under one investigating arm and this has clearly caused massive resentment against me."

Just two weeks later, McBride and IPID cleared both Dramat and Sibiya in a second report, when they found that there was no *prima facie* case against them. The report said there was a case against Colonel Leslie Maluleke and that he should be charged with kidnapping and defeating the ends of justice.

Despite his exoneration, Dramat reached a deal with his superiors and resigned. AmaBhungane reported that Dramat "fears assassination if he goes back to work and has come under immense pressure to resign to defuse a constitutional showdown". The report alleged that Dramat, a former ANC member who was sentenced to 12 years on Robben Island, felt deeply conflicted about his loyalty to the movement.

Since then, further evidence has emerged that shows that crime intelligence was involved in the renditions. In March 2011, the assistant commissioner of the Zimbabwean police, Erasmus Makodza, wrote a letter to the cluster head of crime intelligence in Pretoria, Colonel Themba Ntenteni, to thank him for his men's assistance. Makodza said that soon after murdering the Zimbabwean chief superintendent, the killers fled that country and sought refuge in Diepsloot outside Johannesburg. Makodza mentioned the names of four crime intelligence policemen and said: "We passed on information to the abovementioned officers regarding the two accused persons who reacted swiftly, managed to arrest the two fugitives and recovered a CZ pistol that was taken from the deceased police officer in Zimbabwe."

Makodza's potentially exculpatory letter names neither the Hawks nor Dramat or Sibiya as participants in the rendition. The NPA said to *Daily Maverick* that the crime intelligence policemen apprehended the suspects on behalf of the Hawks and were merely executing a request. Makodza's letter clearly states, however, that the Zimbabwean police "passed on information" to crime intelligence, not the Hawks.

Nhleko maintained that Dramat's suspension was valid and told Parliament's police committee that "had the lives involved been those of white people, the debate and headlines would have been about human rights".

*   *   *

The demise of Dramat made way for the promotion of Berning Ntlemeza as the acting head of the Hawks. One of his first actions was to suspend the Gauteng Hawks head, Shadrack Sibiya, for his role in the renditions. A month later, High Court judge Elias Matojane found that this step was invalid, unconstitutional and unlawful. Matojane didn't mince his words when he declared: "I am of the view that the conduct of the third respondent [Ntlemeza] shows that he is biased and dishonest. To show that the third respondent is biased, lacks integrity and honour, he made false statements under oath."

According to the police website, Ntlemeza holds a law degree and was "studying for an LLB degree". If Ntlemeza had any legal acumen, he didn't show it when he dismissed Matojane's findings as "just the judge's opinion . . . he never put his mind to what he was saying".

Ntlemeza reportedly started a reshuffling of the unit's senior officers. According to *News24*, he removed all heads of "forums" – 12 specialised sub-units within the Hawks that dealt with specific cases such as corruption, tobacco smuggling and organised crime – and replaced them with other officers. He also said in a management meeting that when he was finished with the Hawks, "I will be the whitest man here".

*   *   *

McBride's exoneration of Dramat and Sibiya had put him on a collision course with Nathi Nhleko. The Hawks were digging for dirt on McBride.

The Hawks visited Innocent Khuba to persuade him to make an affidavit about how McBride had "doctored" the rendition report. Khuba said in his affidavit: "The Hawks members have been in my house four times now. I shiver to the core of my spine with fear . . . because members of the Hawks have already made advances. It seems that I am viewed as the only gate to deal with McBride and it kills me with fear."

Nhleko served McBride with a suspension notice in March 2015 for allegedly tampering with evidence and interfering with witnesses to shield Dramat and Sibiya from prosecution. In December 2015, Judge Fayeeza Kathree-Setiloane ruled in the High Court in Pretoria that the laws that had allowed Nhleko to suspend McBride unilaterally were unconstitutional. She described the minister's attitude as "tardy" and ordered him to pay the legal costs of all the parties. The court suspended its order pending the Constitutional Court's ruling on the matter.

Three months later, McBride received an SMS from a policeman at the Hawks' Crimes Against the State unit, saying that he should avail himself "without fail" to be processed. He was charged alongside Innocent Khuba and IPID investigations head Matthews Sesoko with fraud and defeating the ends of justice for the alteration of the report. They appeared in the High Court and were released on bail of R1,500 each. McBride said on Radio702: "There is no crime, there is no misdemeanour. We have been charged for doing our work and the fact that the [police] ministry is unhappy with the outcome of an investigation is the minister's problem. It's not our problem."

In September 2016, the Constitutional Court confirmed the High Court's ruling that McBride's suspension was unlawful and unconstitutional. It also ordered Parliament to "cure the defects in the legislation within 24 months".

One would think it couldn't get worse for the bloodied-nosed Nhleko. It did. Two months later, the NPA released a statement about the prosecution of McBride, Sesoko and Khuba. "The prosecution team, after consultation with witnesses in preparation for trial, established that the state will not be able to prove its case beyond reasonable doubt, hence the withdrawal of the charges."

Nathi Nhleko has not just proved himself to be hopeless, but is a legal delinquent. By the end of 2016, he had reportedly spent R17.2 million of taxpayers' money on the legal hounding of Anwa Dramat, Shadrack Sibiya, Robert McBride and Johan Booysen – without much success. He reminds me of a chubby little boy with an expression of purity caught standing on the edge of a stretch of burnt veld. He holds in his hands a packet of matches.

* * *

Riah Phiyega will rot in the dustbin of history as probably our worst post-1994 police commissioner. The Farlam Commission of Inquiry into the Marikana massacre made findings of dishonesty against her. In addition, she failed to institute a disciplinary hearing against Mdluli, despite a court ruling instructing her to do so. She did everything she could to protect him. When he finally took to the dock in 2015, the court struck the fraud case against him from the roll after the state asked for yet another postponement. Prosecutors said they needed more time to declassify documents required for their case against Mdluli. They told *Eyewitness News* that they believed police management, including Phiyega, had purposely frustrated the investigation into Mdluli to shield him from prosecution.

In November 2015, Nhleko reported to Parliament on the findings of a ministerial task group he had set up to investigate 16 complaints against Phiyega. In a damning indictment of incompetence, the task group said she should be prosecuted for misconduct, perjury, fraud and a host of other misdemeanours. Zuma was forced to suspend her. He appointed a board of inquiry, which found that she was unfit to hold office and should be fired. Zuma inexplicably didn't fire her, and Phiyega chilled at home until her five-year contract expired in June 2017. Parliament heard in the same month that after her suspension, the taxpayer had to fork out R3.2 million for her salary, allowances and pension contributions.

Richard Mdluli has been on suspension for more than six years pending a disciplinary hearing. Police minister Fikile Mbalula said in Parliament in June 2017 that Mdluli had collected R8.3 million since his suspension in

May 2011. Despite sitting at home, Mdluli had also been paid a bonus of R413,957.

Mluli is close to retirement age. I predict that he will retire long before the disciplinary process is concluded – with full pension benefits, an unblemished record and probably a monetary nod of appreciation.

* * *

With the men in blue having hit rock bottom, Zuma's choice for an acting successor did nothing to restore faith in the top echelons of the police. Zuma plucked Lieutenant-General Khomotso Phahlane from obscurity at police forensics and elevated him to the position of acting commissioner in October 2015.

The ink of Zuma's signature on his appointment letter was still wet when there were allegations that Phahlane had been working on his own, smaller version of Nkandla. It was forensic investigator Paul O'Sullivan who first blew the lid on the acting commissioner's R8 million gated mansion on a private estate and asked: how could he afford such luxury on a policeman's salary, seeing too that his wife was also a policeman?

"Phahlane, I want to ask you where the money came from to build this mansion in Sable Hills Waterfront Estate. I've got a copy of the title deeds, and bond details. As I see it, you had spare cash of between R3m and R5m. Did you win the lottery?" O'Sullivan said in the e-mail which he widely distributed.

It then emerged that within three years Phahlane had bought a number of luxury cars – including a Mercedes, Range Rover, Land Rover, a Volkswagen Amarok and a three-litre 4x4 – to the value of R4.3 million. A company that had a multimillion-rand tender to supply chemical and forensic supplies to the SAPS sourced a R80,000 electronic sound system on the policeman's behalf. Contractors who worked on his house were allegedly paid in cash which was transported in black bags.

A police spokesperson responded that the allegations were factually inaccurate and were nothing but an attempt to defame and humiliate Phahlane. IPID's new head, Robert McBride, was onto Phahlane like a flash, igniting a war of attrition that rages to this day.

As Phahlane fought for his career, his minister came under the glare of public scrutiny, humbling himself to salvage Jacob Zuma. The *Mail & Guardian* counted: in the first hour of his presentation in Parliament, Nhleko wiped his face 31 times and incessantly sipped water, presumably to hide his anxiety. If he was an accused in a court of law, he was facing time.

Nhleko was dealt a tricky hand. After public protector Madonsela's scathing report on the Nkandla upgrades, Zuma appointed Nhleko to determine how much money he must repay for his non-security upgrades at Nkandla that he said he wasn't going to pay for. Nhleko's mission was to ensure that everything that government money paid for at Nkandla was security-related. His finding had to show that Zuma owed zero. That would safeguard his job.

In a 23-page report riddled with grammatical and factual errors, Nhleko declared that Madonsela found "no public funds was [*sic*] used to build the president's house(s)". In a statement the next day, Madonsela rapped him on his knuckles. "This," her office said, "could not be further from the truth."

In Nhleko's report, the amphitheatre became a "retention wall" and the swimming pool the country's most maligned fire-pool. To prove his point, Nhleko commissioned a video of fire-fighters pumping water from the pool, accompanied by a gut-wrenching Italian opera aria. The cattle kraal, he said, was a cultural necessity.

As journalists watched in astonishment while Nhleko bumbled himself into infamy, he once again dabbed his face and said that more money should be spent on the upgrade because there was outstanding security-related work that must be completed.

*   *   *

Berning Ntlemeza's lack of sense and logic was exposed when he appeared before several parliamentary committees. He asked the police portfolio committee for more money and added that to pounce swiftly on the enemy, he needed a jet or a helicopter. ANC MP Leonard Ramatlakane reminded Ntlemeza that without "something on paper" there was little the committee could do to help.

When the Democratic Alliance (DA) asked him about the perceived "independence" of the unit and their recent "hit squad-like" methods, he used an unfortunate choice of words when he said: "We are hitting, and hitting, and hitting and hitting."

It didn't show in the performance of the Hawks. In a written reply to a parliamentary question, the Hawks responded that at the end of 2015 there had been a 60 per cent decline in arrests and an even greater drop in conviction rates. The DA pointed out that during the 2010/11 financial year, there were 14,793 arrests and 7,037 convictions. But four years later, there had been only 5,847 arrests and 1,176 convictions.

Ntlemeza's performance in front of Parliament's standing committee on public accounts (Scopa) is reminiscent of Nathi Nhleko's antics when he twisted Jacob Zuma's swimming pool at Nkandla into a tragi-comic fire-pool. He appeared as the chairperson of the government's Anti-Corruption Task Team (ACTT), which had come to account to Parliament for the first time. The ACTT was established in 2010 to "fast-track" investigations and prosecutions for corruption in the public and private sectors. All the law enforcement agencies sit on the ACTT.

Daily Maverick reported that since its inception, the ACTT has uncovered irregular expenditure of R25 billion per year, which adds up to R150 billion over six years. Its success rate is the recovery of only R10 billion and the arrest and conviction of 399 government officials since 2014.

Ntlemeza told Parliament that the team had dealt with 189 cases, 68 of which had been finalised, with 77 still under investigation. ANC MP Vincent Smith challenged this and said: "Can I refer to page 11 of the presentation, Lieutenant-General. You say that the total number of persons convicted is 128, but three pages later the total number of government officials convicted since 2014 to date is 399. Please explain that to me."

At some point, the Hawks boss relented, saying: "I am lacking . . . we are now swimming."

FIFTEEN

Top Hawk down

———•———

Johan Booysen is the archetypal lawman: stern, unflinching, with a back-bone as straight as an arrow and impaling hazel-coloured eyes. For forty years, the man sitting in front of me has fought robbery, homicide, mas-sacres, gangsterism, taxi violence, rape, corruption and fraud in one of the most volatile provinces in one of the most violent countries in the world.

We met on the last day of February 2017 at a coffee shop in Morning-side in Johannesburg. An early morning shower had made way for a clear and blue sky and an earthy scent permeated the air. Minutes after we sat down, he said: "Today is my last day in the police."

I had read his book, *Blood on Their Hands: General Johan Booysen Reveals His Truth*, and recall that he left school after failing Standard 9 (today Grade 11) and joined the railways as a clerk. The son of a boilermaker who was retrenched and one of eight children (they shared one toothbrush), he went back to school to complete matric but his girlfriend fell pregnant. He married her and joined the police in 1977. He later finished schooling through correspondence studies.

"And how do you feel about your retirement?"

"A little sad. I will always be a policeman. But I'm happy to put the mess of the last five years behind me. It was exhausting," he said.

"Is the top brass not giving you a farewell party?"

"You must be joking. Some of them hate me."

After he launched his book, written by astute journalist Jessica Pitchford, someone asked him about his biggest achievement in the police. He said it was his ability to have adapted to change and become part of the post-apartheid police service. He entered the new South Africa as the acting commander of the Durban murder and robbery unit; he left as the head of the Hawks in KwaZulu-Natal and with the rank of major-general.

A journalist once remarked that policemen don't come like Johan Booysen any longer. It's true. He's like the unshaven caballero in black – preferably played by Clint Eastwood – who saunters into the bar, his feet slightly apart, a grass sprig between his teeth and his hands poised above two Colts on his hips. The piano stops playing. The barman, a bottle of bourbon in his hands, freezes. The bargirls purse their lips, the sheriff's cigar slips from his mouth, and baddies edge their hands towards their holsters. This is a grave mistake. Those with itchy fingers have .45 slugs in their chest.

The story of Johan Wessel Booysen is an example of how the government's law enforcement agencies have been disembowelled to guard the politically connected cronies of our rulers. The president's keepers drove Booysen from his office, leaked a docket to discredit him and laid trumped-up charges against him.

Said Mandy Wiener in *Daily Maverick*: "Johan Booysen has that aura about him. That one that has sadly become ubiquitous in South Africa – of a government employee who has been sent to hell and back, worn down by years of attempts to erode their resolve but has nevertheless remained committed, fiercely determined and stoically principled."

Like the SARS "rogue unit" saga, the story of Booysen is convoluted; the cast is vast, the agendas numerous, there's a new twist every week, and the legal principles are complex. You need a book in which to untangle and unravel the state of disarray.

Over the past five years, Booysen has fought the gremlin in his saga – Nomgcobo Jiba – tooth and nail. While others like Anwa Dramat and Shadrack Sibiya have backed off to start new lives, Booysen has spent every inch of his energy to engage his adversary and her benefactors. He said in his book: "Complacency will allow people like her [Jiba] and Richard Mdluli to capture vital state institutions to advance their own financial and other interests. That's why I won't back off. Many people turn silent when faced by injustice, but it's apathy that creates a breeding ground for the evil monsters that will in the end devour us all."

Much of what I have to tell you is in *Blood on Their Hands*, but Booysen's story is vital to the narrative of this book. It started in April 2010 when police investigators found an alleged criminal enterprise within police supply chain management in KwaZulu-Natal, which included businessman Thoshan Panday. Suave, fabulously rich and connected, Panday is a trader in precious metals and diamonds.

Panday was also used as a broker for police supplies, accommodation and travel. He had allegedly conspired with Colonel Navin Madhoe, a procurement officer, to defraud the police by inflating a R60 million contract to supply temporary accommodation for police members in KwaZulu-Natal during the 2010 World Cup.

Panday had several policemen on his payroll and allegedly paid for a lavish birthday party for the KZN provincial commissioner, Lieutenant-General Mmamonnye Ngobeni. He also paid for a birthday party for her husband, Major-General Lucas Ngobeni. A case of corruption was opened against her in 2011.

Ngobeni ordered Booysen to stop investigating Panday. Instead, he obtained a warrant and raided Panday's home, where he found incriminating documents. Panday allegedly attempted to bribe Booysen with R2 million through Colonel Madhoe. It started with a meeting in the plush Elangeni Hotel in Durban where Madhoe confronted Booysen with images of dead bodies on his computer. Booysen recognised the images as crime scenes, some of which he had attended. Madhoe allegedly told the Hawks commander that in return for the pictures, he must alter the report on the Panday investigation to ensure that the case was thrown out in court.

Booysen played along and told Madhoe that "everything came at a price". How much? Madhoe allegedly wanted to know. Booysen said he would send him a figure and Madhoe must add three zeros.

Booysen went to Pretoria to brief Anwa Dramat. He showed Dramat a message from Madhoe: "Good morning Gen. wot happened no sms. when u back. (2)"

Dramat and Booysen assumed the (2) meant R20,000. On his return to Durban, Booysen met Madhoe at a shopping centre. The latter allegedly told him that "TP" – this was how he referred to Panday – had managed to get together "one bar", and that another would be forthcoming. The (2) had meant R2 million.

The money exchange took place in the parking garage of police headquarters in Durban. In the boot of Madhoe's car was a suitcase stacked with R100 and R50 notes – totalling R1.4 million. As Colonel Madhoe handed over the money, the Hawks pounced.

Panday was arrested at the airport in September 2011 on his return from a trip to the Democratic Republic of Congo. He was charged with fraud and corruption and was in custody for two weeks before being released on R100,000 bail. He said in an affidavit: "This arrest, I believe, happened because of my refusal to implicate the KZN Provincial Commissioner."

Enter Richard Mdluli. Booysen said Mdluli drove from Gauteng to KZN to speak with Hawks Colonel Vasan Subramoney, whom Booysen had appointed to investigate Panday. Mdluli told Subramoney his life was in grave danger. He should transfer to Johannesburg as a matter of urgency and continue working on the Panday investigation from there.

Subramoney later testified that he had been lured away from Durban by Mdluli and dumped in an office on Johannesburg's East Rand. There, his attempts to continue the Panday investigation had been thwarted. He said his life had become a living hell; he was never allocated any work and had lost all sense of self-worth, attempting suicide more than once.

Zuma's son Edward made an appointment to see Booysen. He said he had invested R900,000 in one of Panday's businesses and wasn't getting his dividends because Booysen had frozen R15 million in police payments. He wanted Booysen to release the money, which the policeman said he couldn't do.

* * *

In December 2011, the *Sunday Times* plastered on their front page a photograph of gun-toting and drinking policemen allegedly celebrating the killing of five robbery suspects near Camperdown in KZN in January 2009. The headline said it all: "Shoot to kill: Inside a South African police death squad".

The exposé evoked images of the apartheid-era police death squad at Vlakplaas – and Johan Booysen was branded, almost like Eugene de Kock or Dirk Coetzee, as the "ultimate commander" of this modern-day bunch of killer policemen. According to the newspaper: "The Cato Manor organised crime unit in Durban has allegedly committed scores of assassinations, some in retaliation for suspected cop killings and others related to ongoing taxi wars."

Two of the three journalists who wrote the story, Stephan Hofstatter and Mzilikazi wa Afrika, were also the authors of the SARS "rogue unit" revelations and the rendition story that targeted Anwa Dramat and Shadrack Sibiya.

The news report raised serious questions about the legality of the many shootouts that the Cato Manor serious and violent crime unit – which was one of the Hawks clusters that fell under Booysen – had with known gangsters, robbers, heisters and killers. The unit had an incredibly high "kill rate" and therefore the questions were legitimate, although there were allegations that the scandal was deliberately exposed and planted by police sources to create a pretext for action against Booysen.

Booysen said the images that the *Sunday Times* published were the same as those that Madhoe showed him at the Elangeni Hotel and tried to bribe him with. In the newspaper, Madhoe was portrayed as a hero who had tried to blow the whistle on the alleged atrocities.

Nomgcobo Jiba authorised murder and racketeering charges against Booysen and the Cato Manor policemen. In June 2012, 18 cops appeared in court on 14 counts of murder, as well as on charges of housebreaking, possession of unlawful firearms, theft, assault, and malicious damage to property. In August of the same year, Booysen was charged with racketeering. The gist of the state's case was that he had managed a team of police officers who had, over a three-year period, murdered 28 people; broken into their homes to kill them; planted unlicensed firearms to create the impression that they'd been armed; and stolen items of value and cash from the deceased and their families. Then they'd either claimed SAPS awards or been paid by rival taxi groups.

Racketeering is a relatively new charge in our jurisprudence. It is a "super charge" that enables the state to convict anyone who is party to a corrupt enterprise. It has been designed to neutralise crime syndicates and carries a fine of a billion rand or life imprisonment.

Following their appearance in court, Booysen and some of the Cato Manor policemen sat for several weeks to study and investigate the evidence against them. They identified 379 pages of mistakes and irregularities. In the 23 dockets of 500 pages, including attachments, Booysen featured only twice and was mentioned by only three of the 290 witnesses, who confirmed his presence at crime scenes – after the action. Nor was there damning evidence against the Cato Manor policemen. "Either Jiba had been duped by the prosecutors and the investigators, or she had failed to apply her mind. The only explanation that I can conceive of is that the investigation into Thoshan Panday was sufficiently sensitive to cause me to tread on 'connected' toes," said Booysen.

Durban High Court judge Trevor Gorven agreed in 2014 when he declared Jiba's decision to prosecute Booysen unconstitutional and invalid. He said the charges didn't meet the barest of minimum requirements. The judge said about Jiba: "I can conceive of no test for rationality, however relaxed, which could be satisfied by her explanation. The impugned decisions were arbitrary, offend the principle of legality and, therefore, the rule of law, and were unconstitutional."

* * *

Booysen and his team had assembled devastating evidence against the connected Thoshan Panday and his alleged police accomplice, Navin Madhoe. Panday's fingerprints were on documents given by Madhoe to Booysen that would have exonerated him; there was spycam footage of the money being handed over, an event which was witnessed by two Hawks officers; and there were cellphone intercepts that implicated both accused. Yet, in October 2014, KZN prosecutions boss Moipone Noko – a known protégé of Jiba – said there was insufficient evidence against Madhoe and Panday and dropped the charges against them. Noko had sat on the docket for two years and it seemed she hadn't even read the statements. She thought, for example, that the suspended Cato Manor unit had conducted the Panday–Madhoe investigation and said the "objectivity" of the detectives in the case was "questionable".

During the investigation, the police legally intercepted telephone calls by Madhoe and Panday. It was the telephone intercepts, said amaBhungane's Sam Sole, that prompted the withdrawal of the charges. The conversations were replete with Panday's boasts about his relationship with the Zuma family and, specifically, his claim to have paid towards "houses at Nkandla" and to have contributed "one bar or two bar" – one or two million rand – to the Jacob Zuma Foundation. This is partly confirmed by an affidavit by KZN crime intelligence veteran Colonel Brian Padayachee, who was tasked with investigating alleged death threats that Panday had made against police investigators. He said: "The intercepts also revealed very sensitive information implicating high profile individuals who has [sic] and or had a general corrupt relationship with Mr Panday. Payments for favours were also evident." Padayachee also wrote a memo to police commissioner Riah Phiyega in which he said he would reveal the contents directly and personally to her only "as it is not related to the current investigation and it is highly sensitive and controversial".

AmaBhungane reported that instead of support, Padayachee received a notice of intention to suspend him, based on allegations made by Panday that his communications were illegally intercepted and were used to try to pressure him to become a witness against the provincial commissioner.

*   *   *

Booysen had waited almost two years for his police disciplinary hearing, chaired by the esteemed senior advocate Nazeer Cassim. The police arrived with two senior advocates. The hearing cost the police R1.7 million.

The original investigating officer, Colonel Vasan Subramoney, testified that KZN provincial commissioner Ngobeni "orchestrated" his removal from KZN by getting Richard Mdluli to put the fear of God in him. He said Ngobeni and Madhoe were in a corrupt relationship with Panday, resulting in large sums of police money being unaccounted for.

Ngobeni refused to testify, prompting Cassim to say he would have expected her to appear before him to deal with the "serious and damning allegations" that "suggest corruption at the highest level".

Cassim rejected the charges against Booysen and ruled: "It would be unjust not to forthwith reinstate Booysen . . . so that he can do what he is best suited to do, that is to fight crime."

* * *

It was just before three in the afternoon of 16 August 2015, and standing next to a Toyota parked outside the Gautrain station in Sandton was Johan Booysen. In the car sat his son Eben. The general was visiting Gauteng three days before his interview for the position of national head of the Directorate for Priority Crime Investigation (DPCI), otherwise known as the Hawks. This position is occupied by South Africa's premier crime-fighter, in charge of the unit dealing with organised and serious crime. The position had been vacated by the respected Anwa Dramat and was occupied on a temporary basis by the disastrous Major-General Berning Ntlemeza. The minister had to appoint a full-time Hawks head and the job was advertised. It required a policeman with extensive crime-fighting experience, an unblemished record and a person of the highest integrity. It should have excluded Ntlemeza, who was branded by a judge as a liar.

There were four generals on the shortlist, of whom Booysen was one. He received a notice on 13 August 2015 that he must report six days later to the police minister's office in Cape Town for an interview. The shortlist was secret and not in the public domain.

Two days earlier, Ntlemeza had sent Booysen a "notice of contemplated suspension" for fraud. He had allegedly supplied false case numbers to obtain a financial award. I suspect that Ntlemeza was at his devious best and concocted the charge to make sure that Booysen didn't get the top Hawks job, despite being the most experienced candidate with an impressive track record.

Earlier in the afternoon of 16 August, Booysen had received a phone call and was told to wait at the Gautrain station in Sandton. Father and son didn't have to wait long. A black Rolls Royce slithered up to the station and parked behind them. The window of the Rolls rolled down. In the driver's seat sat Duduzane Zuma, the president's youngest son.

He waved at Booysen to get into the passenger's seat, and Booysen in turn told his son to follow them. "Where are you taking me?" Booysen wanted to know.

"I want to introduce you to someone," said Duduzane.

As the two made small talk, they cruised down Jan Smuts Avenue and turned at the Johannesburg Zoo. Booysen recognised the military museum. Minutes later, Zuma steered the Rolls into Saxonwold Drive and stopped in front of number seven. Gates opened to South Africa's most written-about residence: several storeys of luxury and opulence on six thousand square metres of paved land. The likes of Jacob Zuma, Malusi Gigaba, Brian Molefe, Nkosazana Dlamini-Zuma, Des van Rooyen and many other presidential cronies have stepped through the large doors into the marbled foyer with the spiral staircase.

Eben Booysen parked his Toyota behind the Rolls and joined Booysen. He wanted to know: "Dad, are we where I think we are?"

* * *

In the winter of 2017, I again sat down with Johan Booysen, now employed as the head of investigations at Fidelity Security Group. He said he was doing basically the same as before – combating attacks on cash-in-transit vans and staff – but he was now wanted and respected. "We have to deal with the mess that Ntlemeza and his cronies have left behind," said Booysen, referring to crime statistics that show that cash-in-transit heists and ATM bombings increased by 30 per cent between 2015 and 2017. "We are going to harvest their fruit for years to come. I believe I could have made a difference, had I been allowed."

I waited for Booysen to finish his *penne arrabiata* (extra chilli on the side) before I said: "Johan, I want to ask you about a meeting you had on 16 August 2015."

He looked up from his plate, grasped his wine glass, took a sip of sauvignon blanc and said: "What about that day? I had many meetings."

"That was the day you visited the Guptas. It was three days before your interview for Hawks head."

He looked for a moment as though he had taken a blade in his back, his eyes stabbing into mine. I'm sure that stare has convinced many a criminal that it was in their own interests to confess. "How do you know about it?"

"You made an affidavit about the visit and gave it to General Matakata [the acting Hawks head]. You did it after you left the police."

"And how did you get hold of it?"

"Someone in the Hawks gave me some stuff. It was among it."

"*Bliksems!*" he growled. "Nothing is safe any longer."

Booysen has never spoken about his visit to the Guptas, and has probably not even told his biographer, Jessica Pitchford. And if he has, he has sworn her to silence.

"Excuse me for a moment," Booysen said and walked away. He spoke with someone for a few minutes.

"I've spoken to my attorney. I said to him I'm going to play open cards with you. What do you want to know?"

*   *   *

Duduzane Zuma must be the envy of his older brother Edward. While Edward scavenges at the door of tobacco smugglers to scrape together a living, Duduzane has cast his destiny with the mega-wealthy Gupta family. Edward couldn't pay for his own wedding and neither would anyone else; the Guptas settled the bill for Duduzane and Shanice's lavish nuptials in April 2015.

The Guptas needed someone close to the president to serve as a vital channel and conduit to influence his official decision-making. Their man was Duduzane, who became truly kept and captured.

The release of thousands of personal e-mails from the Gupta family and their associates – known as #GuptaLeaks – has exposed Duduzane Zuma as the key middleman for the Guptas to ensure that their choice of ministers, parastatal CEOs and top officials were appointed to divert lucrative contracts to some of their companies.

The Guptas early on appointed Duduzane as a director of Sahara Computers but he has since then been elevated to directorships of key Gupta companies. They took care of his every need, from paying for a Mauritian getaway for him and his girlfriend to setting him up with a R18 million Dubai apartment in the world's tallest skyscraper, the iconic Burj Khalifa. He flew first class, was chauffeured by limousine and stayed in five-star hotels, among them the Oberoi in Dubai and the Hotel National in Moscow. The Guptas took care of some R180,000 in arrears on municipal charges that he had built up on his Saxonwold abode, around the corner from the Gupta compound. In March 2015, he drew R300,000 per month in director's fees, more than any other director, including the Gupta brothers.

Atul Gupta questioned the veracity of the emails in a BBC interview in August 2017, but they show that on the night of 1 February 2014, when Zuma lost control of his Porsche and slammed into the back of a minibus taxi, killing Phumzile Dube, the first person he telephoned was the youngest Gupta brother, Rajesh "Tony" Gupta. When the young Zuma allegedly impregnated another woman, the family's lawyer provided advice on the terms of a R3.5 million maintenance settlement for the child and mother.

This was the man that on 19 August 2014 called Johan Booysen and said he wanted to introduce him to someone.

Booysen initially met Duduzane Zuma through a police colleague. The young man had invested money in a scheme that appeared fraudulent and laid a charge. He saw Duduzane several times after this. Booysen had also met Jacob Zuma on several occasions. He has been to Nkandla a few times and was the investigating officer when one of Zuma's wives was raped in 1998. Zuma mentioned the incident in 2014 as a justification for the security upgrades at Nkandla. Booysen returned to Nkandla several times after that, and once met the president in Durban to discuss taxi violence.

"When you got into the Rolls, did you know where you were going?" I asked Booysen.

"I had no idea," he said. "I didn't say a word. I wanted to see what was going to happen."

"And when did you realise where you were going?"

"When we got to the Zoo, we turned. I saw the military museum. We were in Saxonwold."

They were taken into the house, where they were asked to hand their phones to a member of the house staff. They were then ushered into a lounge and introduced to Rajesh Gupta, known as Tony. He is at 45 the youngest of the brothers and, according to the #GuptaLeaks, he enjoys a close relationship with Duduzane Zuma.

The #GuptaLeaks e-mails suggest that Tony holds some unpleasant racial attitudes, having called security guards "monkeys" and having asked Sun City to confirm that all butlers used at his niece's wedding would be white.

Booysen said they drank tea and discussed the education of their children. Gupta said to Eben Booysen that if he had any business ventures that he needed to get off the ground, he should talk to the family. This is an old ploy of the Guptas: to dish out benevolence and generosity to the children of those they wish to capture. This extends far beyond Duduzane Zuma. Take the case of Free State premier Ace Magashule, an avid Gupta acolyte. The Gupta leaks and amaBhungane have revealed how Magashule's provincial government handed the family control of a dairy farm project in the Free State town of Vrede. The Guptas sucked some R84 million of the farm project to a company of theirs in the United Arab Emirates.

In much the same way that Duduzane Zuma was captured, the e-mails suggest that Magashule's sons were similarly primed to become Gupta intermediaries. Tshepiso Magashule started working for the Guptas as a consultant in November 2010, the year after Duduzane was brought into the Gupta fold. Tshepiso was getting R90,000 a month. Both he and Maga-shule's other son, Thato, were treated to an eight-day stay at the super-luxurious Oberoi Hotel in Dubai, paid for by Gupta company Sahara.

When Eben declined Tony Gupta's generosity, the latter turned to Johan Booysen and said: "And so, we hear that you might soon become the new head of the Hawks?"

Booysen said he was shocked and taken aback that Gupta was privy to information outside the public domain. He said he didn't want to engage the businessman and merely answered: "We will have to see where it goes."

Gupta said: "If you do get elected, there will be a dinner in Durban."

Booysen said that this was the extent of their discussion about the Hawks job and they left shortly afterwards in his son's Toyota. He didn't make any promises or create any expectations.

"What do you think Tony Gupta tried to achieve?"

"The only thing I can think is that he tried to create the impression that should I get elected, it was because of his or their input and doing. They could then expect a quid pro quo in one form or another. There would have been a Gupta dinner, probably also with the other brothers. Who knows what then? An offer of a directorship for my son?"

"How did he know you were on the shortlist?"

"I have no idea. He also knew I was in Johannesburg on that day. Who knows, maybe he had also met some of the other candidates as well."

"Do you think the Guptas tried to capture you?"

"Without a doubt."

"Why have you never told anyone?"

"I couldn't. My boss was Ntlemeza, and we had a terrible relationship. He tried to charge me and wanted me out. I didn't trust him. The day after he left the police, I made an affidavit and gave it to his acting successor, Yolisa Matakata, whom I know and whom I trust."

* * *

Berning Ntlemeza is the perfect and model policeman. There are no areas for development or improvement. He is so skilled at functioning at a high level that he doesn't need to undergo the required competency test. So please, let us appoint him as the national head of the Hawks.

This was what police minister Nathi Nhleko told Jacob Zuma and his

34 cabinet colleagues in September 2015 when he recommended the appointment of Ntlemeza for the top Hawks position. He didn't tell them about the High Court's finding of dishonesty (don't these people follow the news?) and reportedly no one asked. Cabinet approved the appointment.

Ntlemeza was not on the original shortlist and Booysen said he had told the provincial Hawks head at a conference in Polokwane that he was not going to apply for the job. When the four policemen reported for their interviews on 19 August, Ntlemeza was not among them.

The interviews with Booysen and the others were probably a sham as Nhleko had always planned to have Ntlemeza appointed. According to reports in *City Press* and *Daily Maverick*, Nhleko went to extraordinary lengths to appoint him and promote him to the rank of lieutenant-general.

The candidates were interviewed by Nhleko, justice minister Michael Masutha, state security minister David Mahlobo and the deputy minister of police, Maggie Sotyu. Major-General Yolisa Matakata acted as secretary of the panel. According to *City Press* and *Daily Maverick*, the panel recommended that Ntlemeza be appointed without undergoing the required competency test, on a seven-year contract – despite being close to retirement age – and at a generous remuneration of R1.6 million a year.

In a subsequent memorandum to cabinet, Nhleko asked his colleagues to endorse the appointment. Nhleko said that the panel identified no areas for Ntlemeza's development and that he displayed an in-depth knowledge of the area of work, and a high level of proficiency to function at this level.

The appointment of Ntlemeza was bizarre and made no sense. Why settle on a shamed loon to head the Hawks . . . or is this perhaps precisely why he was appointed?

* * *

Back to the "notice of contemplated suspension" that Ntlemeza sent to Booysen on the eve of his interview with the ministerial panel. One of the first things Ntlemeza did as Hawks head was to fly to Durban to personally suspend Booysen. He wanted to do it in style. When he arrived at police headquarters in Durban, provincial commissioner Mmamonnye Ngobeni led him and heavily-armed members of the Tactical Response Team to Booysen's office – only to find it locked.

In November 2015, the High Court once again shamed Ntlemeza when they found that there wasn't a "shred of evidence" to support the fraud case against Booysen, and that the Hawks boss had relied on "opinion, unsubstantiated by facts".

Ntlemeza applied for leave to appeal. It was refused. Then Ntlemeza petitioned the Supreme Court of Appeal (SCA), which meant that Booysen remained suspended. A month before the matter was to be heard in the SCA, Ntlemeza withdrew the petition to the SCA but not before he had appointed a new Hawks head in KwaZulu-Natal.

Zuma's creatures were intent on keeping Booysen away from his office. On 16 February 2016, two years after the NPA had withdrawn charges of racketeering against him, Shaun Abrahams signed authority for him to be recharged. It was the same charges, the same evidence, the same indictment.

The Cato Manor policemen are still fighting the original charges, but Abrahams signed an authority for them as well. In the process, he charged a man who had in the meantime died. They have appeared three times in the regional court and 15 times in the High Court, just for the case to be remanded yet again.

Booysen has yet again launched an application to have the charges against him declared unlawful. He said the case against him rests on the evidence of two deceased witnesses whose statements are in any case hearsay twice removed. The photographs and videos contain no evidence of the commission of crimes. One of the videos is of a policeman shot during a robbery. How is that relevant? One of the statements on which the state relies is still unsigned, five years on.

Booysen lashed out at Abrahams and said he was wasting time, money and judicial resources; he has ulterior purposes and is amateurish; his actions are procedurally irrational and unconstitutional; and his arguments haphazard, desultory and confused. He concluded: "The NDPP is invited to explain on oath whether he acted irrationally or dishonestly."

Booysen also filed a notice of intention to sue Jiba and the NPA for malicious prosecution. But in the end, he knew: "It didn't matter what the courts ruled – it seemed the NPA would just carry on and on until I was out of their way. No matter how many times I beat them in court, they would continue litigating until I disappeared off their radar."

After forty years, Johan Booysen's police career was over. He also had to accept that Thoshan Panday, Navin Madhoe and Mmamonnye Ngobeni would probably never face justice.

It was time to move on.

SIXTEEN

Jeremy of the Elsies and the woman of trouble

———•———

In 2014 and 2015, the Salt River morgue in Cape Town reported a marked increase in murdered victims that had died of gunshot wounds. The morgue, which services the gang-infested Cape Flats, reported that gun-shot victims dumped on their stainless-steel pathology slabs increased from 290 in 2010 to 695 in 2015. Several were children gunned down in crossfire.

Cape Town is a two-world metropolis. The one basks in the glory of Table Mountain which towers over pristine beaches, sublime eateries and colonial architecture; the other half is deadly and ruled by gangs of toxic young men, armed to the teeth and with an aura of invincibility courtesy of white pipes and crystal meth.

Around 17,000 people are murdered in South Africa every year. The country's murder rate is about 30 people per 100,000, which is among the world's highest. In Cape Town however, it is much higher, at 55. The Cape Flats is notoriously difficult to police because ordinary citizens refuse to come forward out of fear of gang reprisals. Gangsters commit murders in broad daylight without fear of eyewitnesses facing them from the witness stand.

Enter Major-General Jeremy Vearey, the Western Cape's most avid anti-gang crusader. In 2012, Vearey and his men detected an influx of weapons into the Western Cape, which fuelled the death toll. One of those who took a bullet was six-year-old Leeyana van Wyk, who was playing with friends outside her home in Hanover Park. A stray slug slammed into her head.

Police forensics determined that the gun that maimed Leeyana was involved in at least 14 other incidents. One was in May 2013 at a school in Athlone. As matric pupil Glenrico Martin climbed out of a taxi, one of his co-pupils, 18-year-old Wilston Stoffels, shot him in the head. He died on the scene in full view of his fellow pupils. Stoffels entered into a plea agreement and was sentenced to 24 years' imprisonment. He alleged that his victim was a member of a rival gang and that he was ordered to perform a revenge killing.

The gun that Stoffels used was sent for ballistic and forensic analysis. Not only did the experts discover that the same gun was used to shoot Leeyana van Wyk, but they found that the serial number was removed in a peculiar manner. Gangsters often scratch out serial numbers, but in this case it was removed in a neat and professional way, probably by a gunsmith.

Vearey and his men started sifting through literally thousands of ballistic shooting reports. The policemen discovered that as far back as at least 2010 guns that had been altered by the same gunsmith had been used by gangsters on the Cape Flats. Many of the victims were children.

"We are onto something big," Vearey told his men. "This is not your ordinary gangster selling a gun or two or a criminal who steals a pistol in a housebreaking and sells it to gangs. There is a supply line into the Cape Flats. We have to get that supplier."

Vearey, now in his mid-fifties, is a passionate man and has always struck me as a bundle of inexhaustible energy. Despite his boyish features, his eyes are fierce and intense and his hands never rest.

Vearey registered Operation Impi in August 2013 to find the guns and the supplier. He and his men eventually retrieved 22 guns that had had their serial numbers removed in this identical manner. The guns came fully loaded, with two magazines, and had been adapted to be almost untraceable.

Police ballistic experts struck gold when they examined serial and laboratory numbers on different components of the guns. Nineteen of the guns had previously belonged to the police while three were privately owned. A corrupt cop or cops were clearly in on the action.

* * *

You may be justifiably asking by now what a corrupt cop's arsenal on the Cape Flats and gang-busting Jeremy Vearey have in common with President Jacob Zuma and his pack of scheming, plotting and conniving Rottweilers.

Under Zuma, the police have declined into a bunch of fractured, bungling and hopeless law enforcers who are fast losing the war against crime. It is amid this mayhem that crooked cops blossom because they can conduct their criminal enterprises without fear of detection. Quality and dedicated cops like Jeremy Vearey are thinly spread in the service and one would assume that top command would cherish him. This is unfortunately not the case. But the situation is much worse than that. What I am going to demonstrate now is that Zuma's keepers will stop at absolutely nothing to shield their master – even if it means the lives of children.

I decided to write this chapter to illustrate the devastating impact which the legal and political protection of the president has had on the lives of ordinary people. Read what follows, and you will agree with me: they simply don't care.

* * *

Jeremy Vearey, calling himself "Jeremy of the Elsies", has chronicled his childhood extensively on Facebook and is about to publish his memoirs about growing up in crime-infested Elsies River on the Cape Flats. His first contact with gang violence was as a young boy when he witnessed gangsters executing someone lying on the ground. They chopped him up with machetes.

Much of his childhood memories are happy. "When I was about 14 years old an uncle gave me an aluminium frame racing bicycle, soon after it fell off a truck in Elsies River. It always fascinated me how many things fell so easily off trucks. Trucks did load-shedding long before Eskom and shed the most amazing things while driving through Elsies River. Back then, falling things ranged from fridges, lounge suites and even cars, to boxes of Crockett and Jones shoes, frozen chickens and Nevada trousers. Trucks with things are like cargo ships sailing in rough seas – sometimes they must get rid of excess weight to remain afloat."

After school, he went to the University of the Western Cape and qualified as a teacher. He became embroiled in struggle politics and joined the ANC's underground structures in the Western Cape. He became a member of an MK cell that was instructed to plant bombs across the region. Among the cell members were the celebrated MK soldier Ashley Forbes, Anwa Dramat, who later became the head of the Hawks, and Peter Jacobs, later the head of crime intelligence in the Western Cape. They planted a limpet mine against an electric pylon in Goodwood, bombed a railway line near Heide-veld, attacked the homes of three policemen, and set off a symbolic limpet mine explosion near the entrance to the official residence of the state president. Vearey stashed some of the limpets and grenades for the unit.

Vearey was in his classroom at the West End Primary School in Mitchells Plain when the security police walked in and took him away. By then, most of the cell members had been apprehended and held under section 29 of the Internal Security Act. The accused were held in solitary confinement, had no access to a lawyer, family or doctor, and were badly tortured by one of the security police's most notorious enforcers: Captain Jeff Benzien. A burly beast with popped eyes and claw-like hands, he gained infamy at the Truth and Reconciliation Commission when he demonstrated his torture methods to the commissioners.

The accused, by then known as "the Fighting Fifteen", refused to plead in court but admitted their complicity in the attacks. They were sentenced to between two and fifteen years' imprisonment. Vearey, then 25, got seven years' imprisonment.

Upon his release from Robben Island prison in 1990, Vearey was appointed bodyguard for ANC leader Nelson Mandela. He called him "Tata" and said that he was unconditionally prepared to take a bullet for him. He tells how he accompanied Mandela to the Bahamas in December 1993. The elder statesman, suffering from swollen ankles and high blood pressure, had to take a rest. Mandela's trip was supposedly secret and nobody knew about it, but he wanted to attend a festival on the island. When Mandela, Vearey and the other bodyguards arrived at the festival, they discovered that the theme for the event was Nelson Mandela. Hundreds of people wore

Mandela masks, rum flew freely and a whiff of dagga permeated the air. Tata spontaneously joined the party, was swallowed up by the crowd and went missing! Vearey couldn't spot him among the masses and it took some time to locate a weaving and bobbing Mandela. "I'm having a really good time," he said.

Vearey joined the police and spent several years at crime intelligence before he was appointed in 2000 as the commander of the so-called Slasher task team. Top command gave him 30 men and 1,500 unsolved murder and attempted murder dockets to investigate. Initially, the unit had spectacular success: 237 suspects were arrested in 236 previously unsolved cases.

A few years later, Western Cape premier Ebrahim Rasool requested that Vearey be appointed to arguably one of the worst posts in the police: that of station commander of Mitchells Plain police. The statistics were staggering. The area under its jurisdiction housed more than a million people – with only one police station at the time. There were only 240 cops and a mere 70 vehicles to patrol the area.

While Nyanga is South Africa's murder capital, Mitchells Plain claims the highest number of drug-related crimes. It also has the highest incidence of indecent assault, common assault, and robberies and burglaries at residential premises in the Cape.

One of Vearey's biggest accomplishments was his participation in the team of policemen and prosecutors that brought to justice one of Cape gangland's most infamous sons: George "Geweld" (Violence) Thomas. In 2015 the boss of the 28's gang was, after a four-year court battle, convicted of seven murders and a host of other crimes and sentenced to seven life sentences and 170 years' imprisonment. He had personally pulled the trigger in three of the cases while he orchestrated the other four from an isolated prison cell. Sixteen of Thomas's gang members were also convicted. Six of his cohorts would also serve life sentences for their crimes. The rest of his co-accused were handed sentences of between 12 and 25 years.

* * *

By the time Jeremy Vearey embarked on Operation Impi to sniff out the corrupt cops who were plying Capeland gangsters with guns, he was the deputy provincial commissioner for detective services in the Western Cape. Gangsters armed with guns with similar alterations on them were increasingly killing innocent bystanders on the Cape Flats. In 2014, 13-year-old Imeraan Pretorius, one-year-old Fatima Samuels, three-year-old Kashiem Ceres, 15-year-old Gavin Witbooi, 16-year-old Ryan Petersen, six-year-old Lihle Mgwayi, 12-year-old Jucinta Matros and one-year-old Iegshaan van Staden were all gunned down.

The team found similar guns in gang-infested areas in Gauteng. Some of the weapons were also smuggled to KwaZulu-Natal where they were used in taxi violence. The supplier had a country-wide distribution network.

The head of crime intelligence in the Western Cape, Major-General Peter Jacobs, joined Vearey at the head of the investigation. The two have a long history, dating back to the armed struggle against apartheid. The team knew by then that the thefts of the weapons had taken place at around the same time that the firearms were scheduled for destruction.

They narrowed their investigations down to Colonel Christiaan Lodewyk Prinsloo, the policeman controlling the Gauteng firearms register, who was widely regarded as one of the country's firearms "gurus". He was the custodian of an armoury where firearms were stored before they were destroyed. A lifestyle audit of Prinsloo revealed that he hadn't touched his police salary for two years but lived comfortably, well enough to spend holidays overseas, buy cars and pay for his children's university fees. The crime intelligence policemen surveyed Prinsloo's weapons store in Germiston on Johannesburg's East Rand. They detected him taking heavy boxes home.

Before long, the cops discovered two vital cogs in his criminal enterprise: Cape Town businessman Irshaad Laher, who was the middleman and who sold Prinsloo's guns to the Cape gangsters, and Vereeniging weapons dealer and gun collector Alan Raves. Prinsloo allegedly supplied Raves with heritage guns which citizens had handed to the police for destruction. They saw Raves walking into the police armoury on a Sunday and leaving again with what looked like weapons. The syndicate also issued fraudulent sport firearms licences to known gang leaders, who used them to purchase large quantities of ammunition to augment the gang arsenal. A sport licence allows the holder to buy unlimited amounts of ammunition.

On 16 January 2015, police raided Prinsloo's home, where they found illegal guns, ammunition and R120,000 in cash. Under interrogation, he confessed to his role in gun smuggling and a host of other crimes.

Prinsloo reached a plea agreement with the state. In return for a lesser sentence, he agreed to cooperate to trace the other missing weapons and testify against his accomplices. He had sold arms and ammunition to the value of R9 million to gangsters, who paid around R4,500 for each gun.

In June 2016, the 55-year-old Prinsloo was sentenced to 46 years' imprisonment – as some sentences run concurrently, this amounted to an effective 18 years – for his crimes. Prinsloo admitted that he had supplied about 2,000 weapons to his Cape Town middleman, Irshaad "Hunter" Laher, who in turn sold them to gangsters.

According to a police ballistic audit handed in during Prinsloo's sentencing, 900 of his guns had been recovered and were linked to 2,784 violent crimes in the Western Cape, including 1,066 murders, 1,403 attempted murders and 315 other crimes. That means that 1,100 guns were then still in gangster hands. The tally of victims killed or injured will have risen significantly by the time you read this book, unless police made an extraordinary effort to recover Prinsloo's guns.

When police raided the premises of Prinsloo's alleged Gauteng accomplice, Alan Raves, they found weapons of war: several light machine guns, a host of assault rifles, semi-automatic rifles, sub-machine guns and fully automatic pistols. The cops confiscated 507 firearms from Raves, but because the search warrant was illegal, they had to return the guns. They later reapplied for a search and seizure warrant and confiscated 109 guns from Raves. More than 30 of the guns originated from Prinsloo's police store and had allegedly been altered.

Prinsloo said in his affidavit that he became aware that Raves had rightwing connections. "I formed the view that Raves might be selling unlicensed semi-automatic rifles to the right wing so I ceased being involved in any transactions."

Raves faces a host of charges. He said in his bail application that he was a father of two and a respected businessman in the community. He was released on R20,000 bail and his case is currently before the High Court.

Prinsloo's accomplice "down south", Cape Town businessman Irshaad Laher, has been charged with racketeering, corruption, possession of prohibited firearms and money laundering. He is out on R100,000 bail and his case has also been transferred to the High Court for trial.

Laher owned two Spur franchises and was also part-owner of a Nando's. The Asset Forfeiture Unit (AFU) obtained a court order to freeze R9 million of his assets, including his Rondebosch home, vehicles and interests he had in the restaurants. Laher said in an affidavit before court that Prinsloo was merely "an acquaintance", that they had a mutual interest in firearms and went hunting together.

As Prinsloo was led down the steps of the Bellville regional court to commence his 18-year sentence, Vearey told his men that the battle had just begun. On the Flats were still more than a thousand of Prinsloo's guns, killing and maiming one- and two-year-olds and turning the lives of ordinary, law-abiding citizens into a living hell.

In September 2015, Vearey and Jacobs proposed in an information note to police commissioner Riah Phiyega that Operation Impi should be extended for another three years to trace the other Prinsloo weapons and to overhaul the Central Firearms Registry (CFR). Vearey said: "These acts of organised criminality have fundamentally compromised the systems integrity of our CFR. Indications are that recurring corruption is now institutional. It is apparent that the CFR and their personnel are central to the perpetuation of serious criminality and resultant organised crime."

But Phiyega had problems of her own and never approved the extension of Operation Impi. Three weeks after receiving Vearey's note, she was suspended pending a commission of inquiry into her fitness to hold office. She was replaced as acting national commissioner by Lieutenant-General Khomotso Phahlane. He never approved the extension of Operation Impi either. Neither did anyone in the police top command congratulate the Operation Impi team for the conviction of Prinsloo and the arrests of his accomplices.

Is it because of the embarrassment that top cops were aiding and abetting the crime wave on the Cape Flats? Or because of the possibility of litigation against the police? The Operation Impi policemen doggedly followed the track of Prinsloo's weapons for years and this case is testimony of their honour, tenacity and devotion to law and order. They are the faceless heroes of our police force – unlike those who clog the headlines by chasing our minister of finance on behalf of their political master in the Union Buildings.

As Marianne Thamm said in *Daily Maverick*: "If this were part of a comedy routine, it would be too soon to point out that the only positive spin on this tragic and obscene story is that South Africans no longer needed to fear home invasions by criminals in search of guns and weapons. Police were supplying them directly."

*   *   *

On an autumn day in May 2016, a larger-than-life woman strutted into the Durbanville police station and said she was looking for General Jeremy Vearey. She wanted to make an affidavit and he had to take it down. Her name was Mabel Petronella "Vytjie" Mentor.

Mentor hails from the Northern Cape, where she was a Department of Education official and local ANC councillor before she was sworn in as a member of Parliament in 2002. Two years later, Mentor was elected as ANC caucus chief and chaired Parliament's public enterprises committee. She was also the chair of the rules committee.

A few months before walking into the charge office, Mentor had shot to prominence during the political storm around the claim of deputy minister of finance Mcebisi Jonas that the Gupta family had offered to make him a rich man in return for his becoming the minister of finance. The offer allegedly happened around the time that Zuma fired his finance minister Nhlanhla Nene in December 2015. According to reports – which were later confirmed by the public protector's *State of Capture* report – Jonas was told that the job was his if he wanted it, but would come with conditions: he must push for the approval of the nuclear procurement programme and get rid of certain top Treasury officials.

Mcebisi declined, which led Zuma to appoint an ANC backbencher, Des van Rooyen, as minister. His reign lasted only four days, during which time the rand plummeted and the government pension fund lost R95 billion in the first two days. Zuma was forced to parachute Pravin Gordhan back into this crucial portfolio.

A Democratic Alliance politician wrote on Facebook that "deputy minister Jonas is the second person (after the then minister of sport, Fikile Mbalula) who was approached by the Guptas for a job as minister instead of by President Zuma. It is now clear that Zuma abdicated his job of appointing ministers to the Guptas."

Mentor was on holiday in Thailand but responded by posting: "But they hap [sic] previously asked me to become Minister of Public Enterprises when Barbara Hogan got the chop, provided that I would drop the SAA flight-route to India and give to them [sic]. I refused and so I was never made a Minister. The President was in another room when they offered me this in Saxonwold."

Her post caused a storm. Zuma predictably declared he had no recollection of Mentor. She responded by saying she had chaired the ANC national parliamentary caucus when Zuma was deputy president. "He is the one who introduced me to the ANC Caucus then as a new Chair of Caucus. I had a bi-monthly with him in his Tuynhuis Offices then. He knew me right from when he arrived from exile."

I am not sure why Mentor asked for Vearey when she walked into the Durbanville police station, as there is no relationship between them. Her request was probably based on his reputation as being fearless and uncompromising. When the Durbanville police phoned Vearey, he sent one of his detectives – a captain – to debrief Mentor. He instructed him not to immediately take down her confession, but to first listen to her and report back to him.

The next morning, Vearey and the captain met and thrashed out Mentor's testimony. Vearey is by all accounts a politically sussed person and must have known the implications and ramifications of her evidence. This was, he said, "a woman of trouble". He sent the captain back to Mentor to assist her to write the affidavit.

Mentor said she had travelled from Cape Town to Johannesburg on a South African Airways flight, believing she was going to meet with President Zuma. Instead, she was taken to the Gupta residence in Saxonwold, where the job offer was made and where she was told that she could become the public enterprises minister within a week if she helped to influence the SAA cancellation of the India route. Mentor declined the offer and said that President Zuma emerged minutes later from another entrance. She stated he was not in the least upset she had declined. He apparently said to her in Zulu something like 'It's OK, *ntombazane* [girl] . . . take care of yourself".

Mentor commented: "I am of the conclusion that the Gupta family, the son of the president [Duduzane Zuma], and some ministers I have named in this statement – as well as the president, to a certain extent – all have [a] corrupt relationship that gives unfair advantage to the Gupta family and their associates at the expense of the state, using state resources and agencies all the way for their own benefit."

After Vearey had studied the affidavit, he discussed it with intelligence chief Peter Jacobs, who agreed that the allegations contained a *prima facie* case of criminality. The two conducted a preliminary investigation to verify some aspects – such as dates and places – of Mentor's affidavit and found that she might be telling the truth.

Vearey registered an inquiry that included allegations that the Guptas had attempted to bribe Mentor. Jacobs lodged the affidavit for safekeeping in the crime intelligence vault. Vearey then briefed his old ANC comrade and recently appointed deputy national police commissioner, Lieutenant-General Gary Kruser, about the affidavit. Kruser in turn notified Phahlane, who ordered that Vearey seal the affidavit and hand it to Western Cape Hawks head, Major-General Nombuso Khoza. She in turn hopped on a plane to Johannesburg and hand-delivered the envelope to Hawks boss Berning Ntlemeza. Vearey was instructed to stop any further investigation into the matter.

News of Mentor's affidavit and its content was leaked to a Sunday newspaper and Vearey was named as the cop who took down the statement – which was not entirely true. This reportedly angered police management, who probably regarded Vearey as being embroiled in factional politics.

*   *   *

Just after Christiaan Prinsloo pleaded guilty to trafficking guns to gangsters but days before his sentencing, Vearey was instructed to attend a workshop for top police commanders in Paarl near Cape Town. He didn't suspect anything was wrong. In fact, Vearey and Peter Jacobs were the flavour of the month in police circles in the Western Cape.

During a break, the head of police human resources, Lieutenant-General Bonang Ngwenya, approached Vearey and told him that he had been transferred to cluster commander of Cape Town police stations. She didn't provide any reason for the decision. Peter Jacobs was demoted to a similar position in Wynberg. Said Vearey: "It came as a shock to me. I had no indication whatsoever that there was any dissatisfaction on the part of SAPS [the South African Police Service] with my performance. I was demoted in the sense that I moved backwards from provincial management to cluster level where I would have limited jurisdiction, powers and responsibilities." When he asked for reasons, Ngwenya said to Vearey: "The acting national commissioner will explain the reasons and rationale in the plenary sessions."

Khomotso Phahlane didn't raise the matter either at the workshop or afterwards. Nobody in the police has ever explained the rationale behind the transfers to either Vearey or Jacobs.

Both policemen have taken their employer to the Labour Court. Vearey said in his papers that the decision "was made for an ulterior motive and in bad faith. SAPS acted contrary to their constitutional mandate. No reasons were given and I was not afforded an opportunity to make representations objecting to the transfer."

Police regulations stipulate strict checks and balances in the selection and appointment of police officers. Written records of all proceedings in the selection process must be kept safe for three years. The police chief is empowered to make appointments without advertising, but only in "exceptional circumstances". These circumstances must be recorded in writing.

To test the rationality of the decision to redeploy them, Vearey and Jacobs requested minutes of meetings or deliberations by top command in the time leading up to the transfers. In a mysterious twist, the provincial head of legal services said that he had "diligently" searched for the requested record but without success. "I discovered that when the decisions under review were made on 13 June 2016, there were no documents or minutes before the decision-makers at the time," he stated.

Police top command stared down the barrel in the Labour Court case and could not provide a shred of evidence to justify their decision. The taxpayer was yet again burdened with the cost of counsel to concoct a defence from the indefensible.

*   *   *

Vearey said in his Labour Court papers that more murders will take place with the Prinsloo firearms, and they must be recovered before more people die. He continued: "Instead we have been transferred and Operation Impi has been decimated on the orders of SAPS management. Second applicant [Jacobs] and I were close to making arrests when we were transferred and disbanded."

The Hawks had taken over the investigations of the missing firearms but Vearey said they lacked the knowledge or expertise to make significant progress. "Their investigation ignores the comprehensive use of [the] Prevention of Organised Crime Act to defeat criminal gang activity. They lack interpretative skill and expert insight into gangs. They have no acquired knowledge of the investigation. SAPS now lack the capacity to understand the networks, whom we discovered and investigated, and to take the matter further. Furthermore, we have never been debriefed. There has never been an operational hand-over. The whole operation has simply been allowed to grind to a halt."

The top brass wouldn't even allow the cops that were left at Operation Impi to continue their investigations. One of the leading investigators, Lieutenant-Colonel Clive Ontong, said in an affidavit that he had to fly to Johannesburg in September 2016 to place a witness in witness protection in the Raves case. A colonel in the provincial finance office told him that Operation Impi "was not renewed and he would not make funds available".

The director of public prosecutions in the Western Cape, Advocate Rodney de Kock, has also pleaded with police top brass to extend Operation Impi. He said it was "imperative" that at least Ontong remain the lead investigator and that he receive a dedicated team to assist him. He said the prosecution urgently needed Ontong to assist them to prepare for the trials of Laher and Raves.

Another Operation Impi investigator, Belhar detective Captain Ken Sampson, said in his affidavit: "Our successes turned into distress and uncertainty when Vearey and Jacobs were transferred. We were told that we will be sent back to our police stations although the investigations were not finalised. There are still many investigations pending."

Vearey ended his submission on a chilling note when he remarked that the police were "consciously increasing their potential liability for unlawful and negligent death and injury of members of the public caused by the stolen firearms. This is neither in the interests of the service nor the fiscus. The decision to transfer us endangers the public."

*   *   *

My take on the demotion of Vearey is twofold. Firstly, his handling of Vytjie Mentor's affidavit was the final straw that broke the camel's back. How could he register a potential bribery case on the police system that implicated the president's friends?

Vearey has always been candid and outspoken, and his handling of Mentor's case illustrated his fierce independence and dedication to the call of duty. It also makes him dangerous because, as a general, he doesn't need permission to investigate any case. His potential to cause political damage is far too big. The same goes for Peter Jacobs.

Did Zuma personally play any role in Vearey's demotion? I don't know. Zuma lives in his own dreamscape and seems oblivious of the country corroding and decaying at his feet. It wasn't necessary for Phahlane or Ntlemeza to consult Zuma about Vearey. If you employ rabid dogs at the head of your pack, you don't have to order them to attack. You simply let them loose.

There might have been another perverse incentive to dump Vearey in the cluster. In September 2016, Vearey, Jacobs and two police generals briefed Major-General Philip Jacobs, head of the police's legal division, about Operation Impi. A policeman of forty years' experience, Jacobs also interviewed gun-runner Christiaan Prinsloo.

Jacobs wrote a presentation, "Back to basics: Towards a safer tomorrow", in which he argued that because of a Constitutional Court judgment, the police are probably liable for the consequences of Prinsloo's gun-running syndicate. He said the commissioner of police is the registrar of firearms and must have foreseen that the theft of weapons could lead to murder. "The scope of the possible litigation is enormous, should the deceased have been breadwinners and were either killed or injured leading to future medical costs, pain as well in income." Jacobs concluded that the SAPS were duty-bound to ensure that all Prinsloo's weapons are retrieved.

Can it be that police top command are hesitant to retrieve the remaining Prinsloo weapons to sidestep civil litigation? Remember what Vearey and his team had done: they had painstakingly linked every one of the 900 guns they had retrieved to a victim, creating the potential for massive lawsuits against the commissioner and the minister.

It was not beyond the likes of Khomotso Phahlane and Berning Ntlemeza to attempt to slam a lid on the investigation to prevent the names of more victims coming to the fore. Their decision to transfer Vearey and Jacobs and kill Operation Impi otherwise made no sense.

And it doesn't seem as though the new acting police commissioner, Lieutenant-General Lesetja Mothiba, holds much promise either. *News24* reported that at a parliamentary police portfolio meeting, he admitted that "many of the actions of Project Impi were in disarray". He said he was aware that members were being transferred out of the project, but he did not know why. Police spoke about a new Hawks task team leading the investigation into the missing guns. By the time I submitted my manuscript in September 2017, there was still no sign of the task force.

*   *   *

In August 2017, Judge Hilary Rabkin-Naicker ruled in the Labour Court that the demotion of both Jeremy Vearey and Peter Jacobs should be set aside. She said both must be moved back to their old positions.

Following the court's decision, Vearey said: "This is not just a victory for us, but also for the ordinary constable in the police. I have gone through a lot of strain and stress. And to come off this victorious is quite a significant thing. I can breathe now."

One would have expected Vearey and Jacobs to pick up the remnants of Operation Impi, reassemble their team of gun sniffers and search the Cape Flats for the remainder of the police guns. Not so. Days after the judgment, police management announced that they were taking the judgment, as far as it related to Vearey, on appeal. They said Vearey was only in an acting position and would continue to serve in his demoted position as cluster commander until the legal process has been finalised. They gave Jacobs 21 days to make representations about his transfer.

Vearey said to the *Cape Times*: "This is a sign of high-handedness. If they think they will intimidate us, they are mistaken. Jacobs and I have been tortured [by the apartheid security police], we've been to Robben Island. We are not scared of them, we are going teach them what 'no retreat, no surrender' means."

After yet another child was killed with a stray bullet on the Flats in July 2016, Jeremy Vearey wrote on his Facebook page: "A gun was reborn in the murder of a child on the Cape Flats yesterday. It had been reincarnated several times before in the deaths of nameless others. But this rebirth was different. This gun was supposed to be dead. It was supposed to have been, in what in police parlance is called, 'destructed'. It is this resurrection of the 'destructed', that reincarnated into deaths and injuries of those we now know whose lives were destroyed by its hand. If you listen carefully with your conscience, you will hear its birthing breath in the last gurgle of its victim's dying breath. You might even catch it in the forever wailing wind of screams of the maimed."

SEVENTEEN

Killer, KGB and a guy in a crumpled suit

——•——

On 15 February 2017, selected crime intelligence officers assembled to meet the division's new head of security and counter-intelligence. This is a prized and crucial position; the holder is the guardian and protector of the integrity of the state. Counter-intelligence agents must gather information to protect the Republic against espionage, other intelligence activities, sabotage, terrorist activities, uprisings and assassinations. The State Security Agency (SSA) has a similar unit, and their functions overlap, although the spooks at "the Farm" are also supposed to sniff out external threats.

As I write this, the state's integrity is in peril. Our state institutions have been hijacked for the benefit of the elite few. The public protector's *State of Capture* report and the thousands of leaked Gupta e-mails have painted a sordid picture of the extent to which the state, the government, the ANC and the president have been infiltrated and turned into enablers of the violation of our sovereignty. This has impoverished the nation, crippled key state institutions and jeopardised our security.

This is nothing but treason, a breach of the allegiance that every citizen owes to his or her country. It becomes more serious when committed by those entrusted by the Constitution, and by law, to prevent this and prosecute those guilty of committing it. As with any crime, wrongful intent is a crucial element of treason.

A former director-general in the Presidency, Cunningham Ngcukana, said the Gupta e-mails provide proof of intent on the part of Zuma, who showed dereliction of duty in his appointment of cabinet ministers. By creating a shadow state, Zuma has intentionally ignored the established procedures and protocols of appointing cabinet ministers and board members of state-owned enterprises (SOEs). Ngcukana concluded that Zuma is the "ultimate traitor" for having subverted the police, the Hawks, the National Prosecuting Authority (NPA) and the intelligence agencies.

Predictably, a full-scare intelligence and propaganda war has been unleashed in the run-up to the ANC elective conference. Crime intelligence is perched at the centre of these hostilities.

City Press reported in August 2017 that police minister Fikile Mbalula was embroiled in a war against rogue police spies who threatened his life, as well as the lives of his family. The newspaper was in possession of a report of a top-secret undercover crime intelligence operation called Project Wonder. The report detailed illegal cellphone taps on five ministers, and plans to plant evidence against Mbalula to get him fired, and to use "young women" to "trap" him and his senior staff.

I was also sent a copy of the Project Wonder report, plus an additional report that named a "parallel intelligence structure" led by Richard Mdluli, Khomotso Phahlane, Berning Ntlemeza, Dumezweni Zimu, Mthembeni Mthunzi, Morris Tshabalala and several others. The report refers to Mbalula as "FAM", who was to be "dislodged" by linking him to the 2015 murder of a tender mogul who allegedly paid the minister R1 million. It said a suspect in prison had been interviewed to "frame" Mbalula.

According to the report, IPID boss Robert McBride was also a target. On the same Sunday that *City Press* exposed Project Wonder, newspaper reports alleged that McBride had assaulted his daughter. This followed reports a week earlier that Cyril Ramaphosa had beaten his wife.

Project Wonder appeared to be a classic disinformation exercise: elements of the truth – to give it a semblance of credence – layered with loads of half-truths and falsehoods. The report was also utterly confusing, and it was difficult to determine if the intel document was sympathetic towards Mbalula or plotting his demise.

Huffington Post said these kinds of reports – as dodgy and as far-fetched as they may seem – have had the desired impact of disruption and destruction. The one just before Project Wonder was called "Check Mate" and wasn't much more than a series of WhatsApp messages about finance minister Pravin Gordhan's plans to undermine the government. It was enough to give Zuma an excuse to fire him.

By the time you read this book, a few more will have been sent packing.

We more than ever need credible counter-intelligence to combat these scourges and protect the state against further capture. Let us look then at our country's security and counter-intelligence chief.

The incumbent who was introduced to the February 2017 gathering of crime intelligence officers was an unimposing and reserved man, dressed in a crumpled suit. He was presented as Major-General Zimu from Kwa-Zulu-Natal. There are only a handful of generals in the division, most of them men and women with vast experience in the force.

What Zimu said next stunned his audience. I have never been a policeman before, he admitted, and don't know much about policing. He mentioned that he owned a liquor store near Pietermaritzburg. He said he was once an adviser to police minister Nathi Mthethwa and had served briefly on the Police Secretariat, a body within the ministry that provides civilian oversight over the police. Other than that, he has no crime-fighting or intelligence expertise.

Zimu then disappeared, never to be seen again by any of the senior officers. When I was first told about his appointment, I asked my crime intelligence sources to go back and find out more about this stealthy character and what he's up to in the division.

His name doesn't appear on the police personnel register, they told me, because he has been appointed at the special agent project, which is funded by the crime intelligence secret account. Why is the head of counter-intelligence funded by the secret account? And who is this man?

We have no idea, they said. But we will try to find out.

* * *

The crime intelligence division is in a shambles, lacks decisive leadership and is plagued by infighting, maladministration and division. There is still tension between the Mdluli acolytes and those who turned against him and gave him up. Officially, Mdluli remains the commander of the unit, although he has been on suspension for six years. Many of his men, I am told, are still in place.

The division has had a string of acting commanders since Mdluli's suspension in March 2011. The cowardly failure of police commissioners to bring disciplinary charges against Mdluli has ravaged the unit, and it will continue to limp along until decisive leadership brings stability. I have spoken to three senior crime intelligence officers – people with vast experience – and they sketch a picture of a rudderless and dysfunctional division of deflated and demoralised policemen.

As I wrote this, the division's latest acting commissioner was Major-General Pat Mokushane, appointed in June 2017. He had hardly taken over the reins when the storm clouds gathered as *City Press* revealed that he had failed his security clearance, a prerequisite for the job. Mokushane has a criminal record after being found guilty in 2002 for violating the National Road Traffic Act. A newspaper said he was once arrested for being in possession of stolen goods. He owns three businesses, although they are being de-registered. In 2010, when he was unable to meet the repayments for the vehicles he had bought for his transport business, he allegedly hid them from the sheriff in the basement of crime intelligence headquarters. The newspaper said he also used his former secretaries to manipulate the unit's secret account for his personal gain. He has denied this.

My sources tell me that several other generals in crime intelligence, among them the head of covert intelligence collection, don't have a top-secret security clearance or else it has expired. Neither does the Western Cape head of crime intelligence, Major-General Mzwandile Tiyo. It gets worse: when he was appointed following the transfer of his predecessor, Peter Jacobs, he allegedly had no matric certificate, faced a pending driving under the influence probe and was unfit to possess a firearm.

Apparently, the division has lost a host of expertise, such as lie detector technicians, to the private sector, and the backlog for security clearances is months, if not years, in arrears.

City Press has described Mokushane as a known ally of Richard Mdluli and said his appointment was discussed at a high-level meeting between the acting police commissioner, Lieutenant-General Lesetja Mothiba, and representatives of the Umkhonto we Sizwe Military Veterans' Association (MKMVA). The story, which was never denied, is bizarre. Why were the veterans in any manner consulted or engaged about the appointment? The veterans' association is a fervent supporter of Jacob Zuma and has said it will guard the ANC from "hostile forces" such as the Communist Party and Cosatu, both of which have called for Zuma to step down. In turn, Zuma has called for the MKMVA to unite and close ranks against "antagonistic forces". Mokushane has been described as an ANC veteran "in good standing" and reportedly attended the MKMVA elective conference in July 2017.

It is completely out of order for an acting police commissioner to discuss policing matters and strategic appointments with members of the MKMVA. They have no role in the appointment of police officers or in their intelligence activities.

City Press said there was a discussion during the meeting that crime intelligence must gather covert intelligence to assist the ANC in the build-up to the elective conference scheduled to take place in December 2017. They should gather information on individuals and organisations that were anti-Zuma and place them under surveillance. These included journalists, opposition party members, civic organisations "fighting the state" and individuals who were vocal against the president.

Mokushane said he would not participate in such plans, but he spelt more bad news for the division at a time when there is little faith in the police's ability to curb crime. The core function of the division, with an annual budget of R4.7 billion, is to gather information especially on organised syndicates to prevent them from committing crime.

According to the crime statistics for April–December 2016, aggravated robbery – the so-called trio crimes of car hijacking, house robberies and robberies at non-residential premises – has increased by more than eight per cent.

As I wrote this chapter, on 1 August 2017, I incidentally spoke to former general Johan Booysen, now employed by the Fidelity Security Group. He said in the preceding 24 hours there had been eight cash-in-transit heists involving Fidelity vehicles. In three of the attacks, the robbers used explosives to blow open the cash vans. The raiders were brazen, confident and seemingly without fear of the police.

These crimes should be preventable through good intelligence, but this is simply not forthcoming. One of the main objectives of crime intelligence is combating drug trafficking and targeting drug syndicates.

"Crime intelligence simply don't have the skills any longer," said one of my sources. "Because of the Mdluli mess, some highly skilled and experienced policemen were removed, as they posed a threat to him. Others have left. We've never recovered."

* * *

Major-General Dumezweni Anthony Zimu is our chief of security and counter-intelligence. He was already appointed in August 2016, introduced to a select group in February 2017 and was never seen again at headquarters in Erasmuskloof, Pretoria.

A Google search reveals almost nothing of Zimu, except that he is mentioned in the 2015/16 Police Secretariat annual report as the chief director of partnerships – whatever that might be.

In 2013, a person with his names was allocated a liquor licence for the Mpilwenhle liquor store near Pietermaritzburg, where he lives. Mrs Zima got a licence for a tavern.

Zimu was never cited on the police ministry website as an adviser, but his name is mentioned in a report of public protector Thuli Madonsela. In 2010, she investigated officials in the police ministry for flouting travel regulations. Police minister Nathi Mthethwa and some officials had stayed in five-star hotels over Christmas, New Year and Valentine's Day and spent R700,000 on their accommodation. Madonsela was scathing about "ministerial special adviser" Dumezweni Zimu and the minister's chief of staff for staying with Mthethwa while they weren't entitled to do so and for "raiding" the minister's minibar while he was in Parliament.

Zimu is an MK veteran and this might have been a reason why he was appointed. His name appears in three documents that chronicle the ANC's armed resistance against the apartheid regime. Zimu was studying at Wits University when in 1988 he suspended his studies and returned to KZN to join the struggle. He received military training and eventually organised and commanded an MK unit that was made up mostly of old school friends. Towards the end of 1989, MK commander Siphiwe Nyanda instructed Zimu to identify cadres who could be trained for Operation Vula (discussed in Chapter Four).

After the unbanning of the ANC in 1990 and with the onset of civil strife between Inkatha and the ANC, Zimu's unit operated throughout the Natal Midlands, and although two members were arrested and imprisoned, they didn't talk and the unit stayed intact.

"Does Zimu know Zuma?" I wanted to know from my sources.

"It's possible, but we're not sure," they said.

"So why has he been appointed?"

"You must connect the dots. Zuma . . . the veterans . . . Zimu . . . Zuma's enemies . . . the ANC conference . . ."

They told me that Zimu and about 15 policemen operate from a safe house in Irene, an upmarket suburb south-east of Pretoria. They have all been appointed in the special agent programme, which is funded directly by the secret account.

Richard Mdluli abused the special agent project to appoint scores of cronies and family members as agents, while the secret account funded his luxury cars and exotic holidays. The secret account has in the meantime ballooned from R250 million annually in Mdluli's time to around R550 million at present. Financial controls, my sources told me, are as negligible as ever and the account continues to be milked by registering non-existent informants and agents and submitting false invoices.

My sources also told me that Zimu's unit has been showered with an array of luxury cars – among them BMW 340i's and Audi A3's. One of the projects crime intelligence registered was the "Fees Must Fall" campaign which spread across South African universities in 2016. Crime intelligence recruited students as agents and agreed to pay them cash and their fees, accommodation, cellphones and other expenses in return for infiltrating student organisations that advocated free higher education. By the first half of 2017, the money for the project was gone. They couldn't pay the newly recruited agents' class fees or any of their living costs. The project has ground to a halt.

My sources gave much of the blame for the shambles that is crime intelligence to the quality of people who have wormed their way into the unit. Many of the friends, girlfriends and family members that Mdluli and his cronies appointed are still employed.

One would have thought that after the fiasco of appointing someone like convicted drug dealer Timmy Marimuthu as an agent, new vetting measures would have been introduced to prevent the police's most secretive unit from being captured by shady characters.

What my sources told me next belongs on planet cuckoo-land.

*   *   *

More than five years after Richard Mdluli's arrest for murder, assault, kidnapping and a host of other crimes, his trial sputtered to life in the Johannesburg High Court. After the NPA had withdrawn the charges in February 2012 against Mdluli and his co-accused, the murder of Oupa Ramogibe was referred for a formal inquest.

The inquest found that there wasn't enough evidence to finger Mdluli or his cohorts, but made no verdict about the kidnapping, assault and intimidation charges. They stood, and after the Murphy judgment in September 2013, the case was put on the roll. The charges against crime policeman Colonel Nkosana "Killer" Ximba were withdrawn, leaving Mdluli and his former henchman, Lieutenant-Colonel Mthembeni Mthunzi, to face the music. The state added defeating the ends of justice to the charge sheet.

While the court heard evidence of shoddy police work and of a brutal campaign by Mdluli and his cohorts to get his girlfriend back from the man who had "stolen" her, Mdluli rejected the evidence of his accusers and said they had been coached to implicate him. "They were tasked to dig for any dirt against me," he said during his testimony in his own defence.

The court case is expected to proceed well into 2018, but what is significant is that after the state had concluded its case, Mdluli and Mthunzi applied for a discharge because they were of the view that the state had failed to present sufficient evidence upon which a reasonable court might convict the accused. Judge Rata Mokgoatlheng rejected the application and ruled that Mdluli and Mthunzi have a case to answer. He did, however, drop the intimidation charge against them.

The police careers of both Richard Mdluli and Mthembeni Mthunzi must be over. Both are approaching 60. While Richard Mdluli is still employed and earning his full salary, Mthunzi bought his discharge in 2016. Even if they are found not guilty, there cannot be a way back for them.

This was my conviction until my sources told me: "You will not believe who has been appointed at crime intelligence: Mthembeni Mthunzi. He is now a principal agent, apparently with the rank of brigadier."

"When?"

"He took his discharge, walked out of the police and straight into crime intelligence. We heard he's working with Zimu."

At first, I didn't believe them. I sent my sources back to check. They did, and reported that Mthunzi has been appointed in the special agent project. His appointment doesn't reflect on the personnel register.

"Who appointed him?"

"We heard he was personally appointed by [acting police commissioner] Phahlane."

"Why was he appointed?"

"We're not sure. But if you thought Mdluli was over and gone, this is your proof."

"How did he get a security clearance?"

"He didn't."

I thought it couldn't get worse. A few moments later, it did when they told me: "KGB is also back."

* * *

Between 1998 and 2002, 237 members of the ANC's self-defence units (set up by the ANC to protect communities during the violence in the run-up to the 1994 elections) were enlisted in the police. The project, referred to as Thathazonke – "everyone is welcome" – was the brainchild of Gauteng deputy police commissioner Lieutenant-General Afrika Khumalo. None of the new recruits were vetted, which meant a host of criminals found their way into the police. One of them was Morris Tshabalala, who joined the police in 2002 with the rank of constable.

Had Tshabalala been vetted, police would have discovered that he was a convicted criminal and a fugitive. He was found guilty in 1996 of armed robbery in Mamelodi, Pretoria and sentenced to 10 years' imprisonment. The court ordered he be declared unfit to possess a firearm. He spent only two weeks behind bars before lodging an appeal and was released on bail. He abandoned the appeal, and a warrant for his arrest was issued in 1998 but never enforced and was reportedly removed from the police computer.

Tshabalala joined Thathazonke and became a member of the "Smanga unit" in Soweto, a group of feared crime intelligence policemen under the command of Colonel Smangaliso Simelane, aka Smanga. They drove flashy cars, including one with an illegal personalised number plate that read "Satan". More than ten cases, including murder, have been opened against Simelane. None have got anywhere.

Tshabalala was promoted from constable to captain in six months, acquired the alias of "Captain KGB" and got a top-secret security clearance. He was involved in numerous high-level intelligence operations, including risk assessments of President Jacob Zuma.

In June 2013, Tshabalala was arrested and accused of orchestrating a cash-in-transit heist in Sasolburg in the Free State, when gunmen stole R3 million from a Protea Coin cash van. *The Times* reported then that he was being investigated for his alleged role in seven additional heists in which more than R30 million was stolen.

The 1998 warrant was produced at Tshabalala's appearance in the Sasolburg magistrate's court, and he had to go back to prison to do the rest of his sentence. He was incarcerated in a single cell in a maximum-security prison.

The state's case against Tshabalala and his co-accused in the Sasolburg case fell apart, despite several witnesses being placed in witness protection. The news site *Harare24* reported in September 2013 that two crucial witnesses in the case, both Zimbabwean, were assassinated within days of each other. Both men were reportedly shot in the head and then stripped naked. The Hawks confirmed the murders.

Tshabalala inexplicably served only a third of his ten-year sentence before walking out of the Groenpunt prison and back to crime intelligence.

"The next moment, we saw Captain KGB at headquarters," said one of my sources. "It was as though he'd never left."

"And how was he appointed?"

"One of the generals took him to Phahlane and told the acting commissioner that KGB has picked up vital information about planned heists and robberies. The next moment, he was back. He drives a flashy A3 and is as untouchable as ever."

City Press reported that a senior crime intelligence official compiled a confidential dossier about Tshabalala's appointment and sent it to Parliament's police portfolio committee. According to the dossier, crime intelligence paid Tshabalala his salary in full while he was in jail. The dossier alleged that Tshabalala was among a band of robbers that pounced at OR Tambo International Airport earlier in 2017 and got away with R200 million, which was about to be loaded onto a cargo plane. According to information in the dossier, his cellphone records placed him on the scene and he allegedly spent the entire night in the home of one of the suspects prior to the robbery. In late March, seven suspects, including a police officer, were arrested for their alleged involvement in the heist and were granted bail of between R50,000 and R100,000 by the Kempton Park magistrate's court. The investigation continues.

My sources told me that Tshabalala's commanders said afterwards that he had infiltrated the heist gang and was in no way directly involved in the robbery. They claimed that because he became caught up in the planning of the heist and had to stay with the robbers, they were unable to issue him with a section 252A notice. This notice grants policemen immunity from prosecution when they conduct an undercover operation that might implicate them in criminal activity. It will, for example, be issued to a cop to buy drugs to nail a peddler.

"You can't give someone a 252 after a crime has been committed," said my sources. "It's ridiculous. If KGB was on official duty, they should have applied for a section 252A at the outset of the undercover operation. Prosecutors are hesitant to issue one in cases of robbery because so much can go wrong."

Whatever the case, it doesn't matter. It shows how those elected and appointed to safeguard us have yet again betrayed our trust.

When Tshabalala was arrested in 2013, police commissioner Riah Phiyega said it was "extremely serious" and ordered the Hawks to get to the bottom of the matter. The Hawks promised the nation feedback on the outcome of their probe. Nothing happened. Phiyega was far too busy protecting Richard Mdluli, nailing Anwa Dramat and covering her dirty tracks at Marikana.

Top policemen are trying to cover for KGB once again. What does he have? Wads of dough that originated from a Protea Coin cash van in Sasolburg in 2013? Or dockets on his superior's dirty tricks?

* * *

The divisions in crime intelligence have degenerated into a bitter feud with acting divisional commissioner Mokushane in one corner and counterintelligence chief Zimu in the other. This emerged when police top command made representations to Parliament's police portfolio committee in August 2017. It was Zimu who pulled the plug on Mokushane's lack of security clearance and reported him to acting police commissioner Lieutenant-General Lesetja Mothiba.

In June 2017, Mothiba told the committee that the vetting and polygraph process for Mokushane had been completed and that his certificate was forthcoming. In August, he confessed to the committee that the process had not been completed and that a certificate had been fraudulently issued. *News24* reported that Zimu said in a letter to Mothiba that a senior crime intelligence officer, Brigadier Leonora Bamuza-Phetlhe, had ordered the printing of Mokushane's clearance certificate while there were still outstanding issues. He recommended that she be criminally charged or internally disciplined and that the inspector-general of intelligence investigate her. Zimu's letter also referred to R50,000 transferred to Bamuza-Phetlhe's bank account – in contravention of Treasury stipulations – when she was tasked with organising refreshments for a three-day police conference.

News24 said that after Zimu's letter, Bamuza-Phetlhe registered a grievance, got a protection order and opened a case against Zimu for allegedly threatening her life. She also wrote a letter to Mothiba, saying that Zimu had threatened her life in an abusive phone call. "His actions have left me numb, confused and in danger . . . I feel scared for my life and these threats have already instilled a sense of uneasiness and thus distract me from performing my duties effectively and efficiently."

Mothiba told the members of the police portfolio committee that Mokushane had issued Zima with an "invalid" suspension letter. ANC MP Livhuhani Mabija said Mothiba was "untrustworthy" and added: "I would like to know when are you firing Mr Mokushane and when are you resigning yourself because you are unfit to lead the SAPS because you are very untrustworthy."

By the time I had finished writing this chapter, Pat Mokushane was also toast. In August 2017, Mothiba fired him and replaced him with a former bodyguard of Jacob Zuma, Major-General King Bhoyi Ngcobo. Regarded as one of Zuma's most trusted allies, Ngcobo came with his own baggage. According to *City Press*, there are questions about the validity of his matric certificate.

* * *

When Brigadier Nkosana "Killer" Ximba and teams of crime intelligence agents left for the ANC's elective conference in Mangaung in December

2012, he allegedly took more than R2 million in cash with him. The *Mail & Guardian* said Ximba was the "main go-to guy"; the "getting-it-done guy" in Mangaung. Ximba, one of the "untouchables" at crime intelligence, is a close associate of Richard Mdluli – who promoted him from constable to colonel within a day – and is well acquainted with Jacob Zuma.

"There is to this day a dispute about the reconciliation of the Mangaung expenses," said my sources. "Nobody is sure where the money went."

"Where do you think it went?"

"Buying votes for the right side and spying on Zuma's enemies."

The ANC's elective conference scheduled for December 2017 is not just bigger than Mangaung in terms of numbers, but much more is at stake. The potential for corruption in the run-up to and during the ANC's five-yearly national conference is vast. The ANC's electoral process is distorted by money, patronage, factionalism, vote-rigging and, quite often, violence.

Presidential hopeful Cyril Ramaphosa warned in April 2017 that money was already being exchanged to secure votes at the conference. "The problem is money. Money has come in between us, and today there is patronage, there is money being passed around, in bags, paper bags and brown envelopes."

ANC veteran Frank Chikane said he believed that funds laundered during the state capture project would be used to steal the 2019 general elections. "Some of the billions of rands have been siphoned from this country and are laundered back and used as part of a war chest to make sure that the corrupt remain in power."

My sources told me that the planning for the deployment of crime intelligence policemen and agents at the December 2017 conference is already under way and that the contingent will be far, far bigger than in 2012.

They might all be there: Brigadier Ximba, principal agent Mthunzi, General Zimu and, who knows, Captain Morris Tshabalala. They will have bags of cash.

The problem with the recent history of crime intelligence is this: there is little honour, no moral compass, a complete lack of integrity. And that is why South Africans should be very, very concerned.

EIGHTEEN

The one who laughs while grinding his enemies

————•————

The table is set; Zuma's keepers have taken their seats. It is time for the great disentangling; the final face-off between the good and the bad in the ANC.

Since 2009, the president's keepers have been shifted into place to launch their final offensive in defence of Jacob Zuma. Behind them lurks a militia tactically lodged in the Hawks, crime intelligence and the State Security Agency (SSA).

Zuma's parallel state – the state within the state – with its felonious and complicit bands of cronies, thieves, derelicts, brutes, conspirators, fraudsters, insurrectionists, vagrants and gypsies are setting sail for the ANC's 54th elective conference in December 2017 and, beyond that, for the 2019 general election. They are propelled, says Marianne Thamm, by an "ill-wind of grand corruption, plundering and no consequence". After living for several months on the edge of this spectral realm where Zuma's keepers skulk and plot, I think South Africans should guard against the very real possibility that they will attempt to rig, steal and influence both the ANC's national conference and the general election.

To prevail and to enrich himself, Zuma has been prepared to defy the Constitution, risk the economy, jeopardise social grants, allow his cronies to plunder and capture the state, and look on while the law enforcement agencies implode.

So why would he not unleash his pack of Rottweilers to ensure his continued liberty and prosperity – by getting his former wife, Nkosazana Dlamini-Zuma, elected as ANC president at the coming national conference? If he can, furthermore, elevate her to the presidency in 2019, this will probably guarantee his eternal liberty and affluence. But an ANC election victory in 2019 is no sure thing, and Zuma might have to pull a few more strings to ensure that the election boxes are stuffed with ANC-marked ballot papers.

If Dlamini-Zuma's closest rival, deputy president Cyril Ramaphosa, is elected ANC president, South Africa's political landscape will change dramatically and Zuma will face a real possibility of going to prison, alongside some of his cronies. It is therefore imperative for Zuma that the law enforcement agencies continue to be paralysed by incompetence and cronyism and the Treasury and parastatals are stripped of proficient leadership to bare them for the final act of pillage.

Says Richard Poplak: "His handlers have built an enormous blockhouse for him, and he almost never strays from its air-locked confines. We only encounter him at the occasional press conference, where we are never allowed to ask follow-up questions, or in Parliament, where he trundles through the proceedings. Think about this for a second: a sophisticated, populous, middle-income nation with a large international profile has no fucking idea what the president thinks, if he thinks anything at all. How did we come to be led by a shadow?"

One would think that Zuma would be out on his feet and almost down for the count. How many times over the past year or two have you seen this headline: "Is this the beginning of the end for Zuma?"

Zuma may have the appearance of a scuzzy ghost, but the war against his wretched, calamitous, inept and divisive rule is far from over. Those who thought that Zuma was down and out have underestimated him. Beware: his middle name is not for nothing *Gedleyihlekisa*. It means "the one who laughs while grinding his enemies".

* * *

In the war of attrition that is raging in our country, the president's militia has suffered terrible losses since the start of 2016. Jacob Zuma himself has been slated by the courts, scorned by growing numbers in his own party and maligned by civil society. His downhill curve picked up speed in December 2015 when he fired finance minister Nhlanhla Nene and replaced him with an obscure ANC backbencher, Des van Rooyen. For once, the ANC top leadership rallied against Zuma and forced him to bring back the respected Pravin Gordhan as finance minister.

In March 2016 the Constitutional Court ruled that the president had violated the Constitution in challenging and ignoring the binding remedial action of the public protector, Thuli Madonsela, in relation to the improvements to his Nkandla compound. This forced Zuma, who had just weeks before scoffed and giggled in Parliament at the effort of opposition parties to get him to repay some of the costs, to reimburse the state to the tune of R8 million and offer the nation a half-hearted apology.

The very next month, a full bench of the High Court in Pretoria over-turned the decision of the National Prosecuting Authority (NPA) to drop the 783 corruption charges against Zuma. Deputy judge president Aubrey Ledwaba said that NPA boss Mokotedi Mpshe's decision to withdraw the charges was "irrational" and that he had ignored the importance of his oath of office, which demanded of him to act independently and without fear or favour. The court ruled that the charges against Zuma be reinstated.

Shaun Abrahams has lodged an appeal to delay the reinstatement of the charges. But when their bucket finally runs empty, it will be up to the national director of public prosecutions to charge Jacob Zuma, appoint a team of prosecutors and provide them with every means to fight and conduct the case of their lives. Can Abrahams be trusted to do this?

* * *

In September 2016, two of Zuma's most trusted keepers – his kamikaze pilots who fearlessly dive-bombed his enemies – were shot to smithereens by two Pretoria High Court judges. After they had inflicted so much devastation on South Africa's criminal justice system, it was the day of reckoning for Nomgcobo Jiba and Lawrence Mrwebi.

Their indefatigable attempt to preserve Richard Mdluli came back to haunt them when judges Francis Legodi and Wendy Hughes concurred that both had lied, were dishonest, and had brought the National Prosecuting Authority (NPA) and the legal profession into disrepute. They were unfit to be advocates and were struck from the roll, which means that they can never practise as advocates again. The judgment related to charges that NPA head Mxolisi Nxasana had instituted against them at the General Council of the Bar. The judges said they couldn't believe that the two "would stoop so low for the protection and defence" of the crime intelligence policeman. They remarked that Jiba and Mrwebi should have "stood firm and vigorous on the ground by persisting to prosecute [Mdluli] on fraud and corruption charges. This kind of behaviour diminishes the image of the country and its institutions, which are meant to be impartial and independent."

Section 9 of the National Prosecuting Act states that a person in Jiba's and Mrwebi's post must be "a fit and proper person, with due regard to his or her experience, conscientiousness and integrity, to be entrusted with the responsibilities of the office concerned".

Zuma was forced to suspend two of his most avid keepers while they took the judgment on appeal. This left Abrahams to carry Number One's flag, which he did with disastrous consequences, thereby earning himself the *Sunday Times* accolade of "Great Mampara of the Year".

* * *

Pravin Gordhan, the holder of the state purse and a proponent of tight fiscal discipline, was a prize scalp. It was up to Zuma's keepers Shaun Abrahams and Berning Ntlemeza to regurgitate something that would stand up in court and give Zuma an excuse to fire him.

Abrahams committed hara-kiri in October 2016 when he announced – all brimstone and fire and with an aura of authority at a Hollywood-style press conference – the prosecution of Gordhan for a pension payout he had approved. He pronounced: "The days of disrespecting the NPA are over. The days of not holding senior government officials accountable are over."

Many had little doubt afterwards that Abrahams was doing the bidding of Berning Ntlemeza and Jacob Zuma. At the worst, he showed himself to be politically captured; at best, horribly incompetent.

The premise on which he wanted to haul Gordhan before a court was fatally flawed and irrational. South Africans rallied together and Abrahams was bombarded by several court applications. Three weeks later – with less brimstone and fire – he conceded he had no case.

Then public protector Thuli Madonsela dealt Zuma a second blow – the first being her *Secure in Comfort* Nkandla report – with her *State of Capture* report. In the report, Madonsela chronicled in 355 pages how much control the Gupta family wields over the country's resources and exposed a web of deceit, patronage and corruption. It showed in almost comical fashion that the Zuma cronies were at the beck and call of the Guptas: Eskom's chief executive Brian Molefe had 58 phone conversations with Ajay Gupta within the space of seven months, and Des van Rooyen visited the family compound seven days in a row before his appointment as finance minister. Madonsela's report unmasked the Zuma presidency as oozing Gupta puss from virtually every state orifice.

In dealing with the fallout of Madonsela's revelations, the ANC affirmed its confidence in Zuma and portrayed him as a victim of an overzealous public protector and an arrogant business family. Poor JZ is the perpetual victim. In the case of Nkandla, he was the victim of a "supply-chain" fiasco; something he knew nothing about.

*   *   *

The estimable Advocate Shaun Abrahams, the president's gatekeeper at the NPA, also finds himself at gunpoint. It is not inconceivable that the courts might force Zuma to reinstate former NPA head Mxolisi Nxasana. In such an event, the June 2015 appointment of Abrahams will be declared unlawful.

Corruption Watch and Freedom Under Law (FUL) have brought a court application to declare Nxasana's departure and his payout unlawful. Nxasana has publicly expressed his desire to return to the crucial post as well as to pay back the R17 million he received in a golden handshake. This is bad news for Zuma, because the High Court has already ruled that the charges against him should be reinstated. The case is on appeal.

Corruption Watch and FUL say that the settlement was a contravention of the NPA Act and the Public Finance Management Act. The NPA Act provides for very limited grounds for the removal or resignation of the director of public prosecutions, which is seen as a crucial position in the functioning of the criminal justice system.

Zuma has responded in an affidavit that Nxasana wanted to leave and was not forced out. He said senior management was divided and the NPA was "destabilised and haemorrhaging". The president added that "it was plain to me that Nxasana was no longer willing to continue . . . and the only outstanding issue remained the financial aspects relating to his vacating his office. Nxasana made the request to me to vacate his office."

In his replying affidavit, Nxasana said: "The president's version in this regard is false." He said it was Zuma who wanted him to vacate the office. He didn't want to leave and maintained that he was fit and proper to hold the office and would serve again. He said there was an "intractable, undesirable and ongoing dispute" between himself, Zuma and then justice minister Jeff Radebe.

Nxasana said that after FUL and Corruption Watch had filed their application, state security minister David Mahlobo arranged a meeting between him and Zuma's legal adviser, Michael Hulley. "Mr Hulley proposed that I should work with the president on the matter and he offered to pay my legal costs." He said he told Hulley that he couldn't do it. "It was evident to me that Mr Hulley wanted me to say on oath that I had made a request to the president to vacate my office. I advised Mr Hulley that I am not prepared to make that statement since that was not what had occurred factually."

There can be only one truth: either Nxasana had asked to leave and requested the settlement, or he was forced out by Zuma and his cronies. If the latter is true, Zuma has lied – under oath. That is called perjury and is a crime. It would also mean that Michael Hulley attempted to persuade Nxasana to lie under oath. That is a serious offence that transgresses the ethical code of attorneys.

More important: if the court reinstates Nxasana as the director of public prosecutions, he will be in charge of the prosecution of Jacob Zuma for the 783 fraud charges that he has cunningly managed to evade for a decade.

* * *

Zuma's bloodied-nosed keepers' brigade were determined to make a comeback. The man they entrusted to dent the enemy's armour was Prince Mokotedi, the former integrity head of the NPA, who was appointed by Ntlemeza and Phahlane as Gauteng Hawks head without any police experience.

Mokotedi, an ally of Jiba, resigned from the prosecution body in 2014 under a cloud of controversy after he was charged with gross insubordination and bringing the NPA into disrepute. The charges were dropped after his resignation.

Mokotedi decided to net the whole rotten rabble – Robert McBride, Shadrack Sibiya, Paul O'Sullivan, the Democratic Alliance and AfriForum – in one swoop. He made an affidavit alleging a Mad Max-like plot. It starts on a balmy night in December 2016 in Johannesburg's north-eastern suburbs – Bedfordview, to be more precise. The suburb has an (unfair) reputation as a haven for gangsters, where they shop, live and shoot. Its name has been flaunted in headline news, often for the wrong reasons.

Stripper boss Lolly Jackson was assassinated in his walled mansion in Kloof Road. An associate, Kevin Trytsman, was shot dead at the Bedford Centre. Gangster Sam Issa was gunned down at the intersection just across the road. Czech mobster Radovan Krejčíř is currently on trial for his murder. The view that Krejčíř owned in 54A Kloof Road – all paid for with the proceeds of crime – was worth millions. You stand on top of the City of Gold with spectacular views from the north and the east. After Krejčíř had swapped its comfort for a prison cell, the house went on auction after it was seized by the state to settle his substantial tax bill. The property was reportedly bought by Krejčíř's arch-nemesis, forensic investigator Paul O'Sullivan.

It was at O'Sullivan's new pad that the early December 2016 meeting was alleged by Mokotedi to have taken place. Present were, he claimed,

O'Sullivan, Robert McBride, Shadrack Sibiya, a crime intelligence captain, followers of the Afrikaner rights group AfriForum, and members of the Democratic Alliance (DA). It was a gathering of some of Jacob Zuma's fiercest enemies.

The talk was of South Africa's own Arab Spring – the series of protests and demonstrations that swept across the Middle East and North Africa in 2010 – that would destabilise the security forces, lead to a popular uprising and ultimately oust President Jacob Zuma.

Imagine that the talk around the fire reverberated from 54A Kloof Road to settlements on the furthest-flung hills of the Eastern Cape, to the intricate network of underground mining arteries of the North West's platinum belt, to villages set amid banana plantations in KwaZulu-Natal, to the shebeens and drinking holes of Alexandra, and all the way to depleted fishing communities along the Cape's West Coast. Imagine it ignites a popular revolution and the masses take to the streets.

In composing his affidavit Mokotedi didn't care if he made a fool of himself. It shows the nonsensical and almost death-defying measures that Zuma's keepers deploy to strike at their enemies. In the affidavit Mokotedi said that the people attending the braai plotted to oust Jacob Zuma. He claimed the plotters planned to use information they had gathered on Duduzane Zuma "to mobilise the community to revolt and pressure the president to quit office".

This is a quote from Mokotedi's affidavit: "A meeting was held at the Michelangelo Hotel in Sandton in March between former DCPI employees, members of the Zimbabwean intelligence agency and Serbian nationals." He got his own organisation's initials wrong.

It should have been DPCI for Directorate for Priority Crime Investigation – the Hawks.

Try and make sense of this: "The strategy would include according to the intelligence report, 'to implicate them to corruption to Mafia subsequently leaked it to the media including the foreign media'."

O'Sullivan commented that Mokotedi, who had referred to the mutineers as the "Black Hawks", was "nothing more than a dishonest criminal with a badge". Sibiya concluded: "The Prince is confused. He must decide if he wants to be a policeman, a politician or a pastor. All three in one confuse him and cause danger to him, because he doesn't know where he belongs." McBride said: "Prince is hearing voices." The IPID boss and his investigators were at the time probing Ntlemeza and Phahlane for charges including perjury, defeating the ends of justice and corruption.

Hours after IPID had obtained a warning statement from Ntlemeza, Mokotedi laid charges of treason, espionage, conspiracy to commit murder, corruption, intimidation and harassment, defeating the ends of justice, tax evasion and a contravention of the immigration laws against McBride, Sibiya, O'Sullivan and a crime intelligence captain.

McBride challenged the Gauteng Hawks head to a polygraph test. Mokotedi initially accepted, but withdrew because it "served no legal purpose". McBride went for his polygraph – conducted at the National Voice Stress and Polygraph Network – which concluded that he had told the truth. There was no plot.

Said the *Mail & Guardian* of Mokotedi: "It looks more like a case of flinging as much kak (shit) as he can find and hoping some gobbets stick. We're bewildered. And we think Mokotedi may be, too."

* * *

As 2017 dawned over the Zuma presidency, Berning Ntlemeza and Shaun Abrahams were still stalking Pravin Gordhan, but, much like Prince Mokotedi, they couldn't get any gobbets to stick.

Zuma suffered another setback when a full bench of the Pretoria High Court ruled that Ntlemeza lacks the requisite honesty, integrity and conscientiousness to occupy any public office, let alone headship of the Hawks. The judges also slammed Nathi Nhleko for ignoring the findings of the 2015 judgment against Ntlemeza that he was dishonest and lacked integrity.

The disgraced Hawks head hissed and stamped like a speared bull and initially refused to leave his office, saying he was going to appeal. The High Court turned down his application and said there was no chance of success.

The loss of Ntlemeza meant that Zuma had to do his own dirty work. At the end of March 2017, Zuma ordered Gordhan to cut short an investor roadshow in London and come home. He ordered Gordhan's deputy, Mcebisi Jonas, to cancel a similar trip to the United States. Everybody knew that Zuma's axe was about to be bloodied. But before he could guillotine his rivals, ANC stalwart Ahmed Kathrada passed away. Great men don't go quietly, and in the case of comrade Kathy, he spoke from the grave. The family told Zuma to stay away from his funeral and subsequent memorial services became a rallying point for ANC comrades to speak out against Zuma.

In the dying minutes of 30 March 2017, Zuma emptied his cabinet of his critics and replaced them with collaborators and keepers. He fired five ministers and six deputy ministers, among them Pravin Gordhan and Mcebisi Jonas. The president also got rid of police minister Nathi Nhleko – his undignified and self-degrading defence of the Nkandla upgrades having been in vain – and replaced him with sports minister Fikile Mbalula.

In what was called his midnight massacre, Zuma produced an "intelligence report" that implicated Gordhan and Jonas in a plot to undermine the government, with the assistance of international financial firms. ANC chief whip Jackson Mthembu called the report "plain rubbish" and said the only crime Gordhan and Jonas had committed was being "incorruptible". Deputy president Cyril Ramaphosa said it was "unbelievable" that Gordhan and Jonas were fired on a "dubious intelligence report" while secretary-general Gwede Mantashe said he was "uncomfortable" with Zuma's decision.

Days later, tens of thousands of South Africans of all ages, sexes and colours converged on the street corners of villages and in sweeping masses in the administrative, economic and parliamentary capitals of our nation. The message was unequivocal: Zuma, *voertsek*! Zuma brushed off the marches as racist.

Zuma lost his second police keeper within two months when Mbalula, who had been making noises of independence, suspended acting police commissioner Khomotso Phahlane. Phahlane and Ntlemeza have been replaced by acting officials, but it is doubtful if policing will improve –

which is not necessarily a bad thing for Zuma and his cronies. The rot is deep and wide.

* * *

It hasn't been plain sailing for Zuma's detractors either. In September 2017, their arch-nemesis, Robert McBride, found himself on the wrong side of the law when he was charged with child abuse and assault with the intent to do grievous bodily harm. He was released on R10,000 bail.

McBride's 18-year-old daughter claimed that he had assaulted her. She said: "It happens all the time. From the time I started living with him, almost every night, every second night . . . whenever he's got a chance to argue with me or fight with me, he would end up hitting me, and not just like hiding . . . throwing me against things or banging my head into things or whatever."

In turn, McBride denied the allegations and said he had merely "admonished" his daughter because of her rebellious behaviour and bad school marks. He suggested that the person who opened the case was linked to an IPID investigation into former acting commissioner Kgomotso Phahlane, and that a "normal family disagreement" was being used to create a public spectacle to get at him.

McBride is a survivor, and he has vowed to return from the brink once again. This time, however, he's up against the testimony of his child who said she wanted him in prison, to pay for what he had done to her. You can bet on it that the case against McBride will be immaculately investigated and prepared and he will be up against one of the NPA's best prosecutors.

In the meantime, the NPA has refused to prosecute former acting commissioner Phahlane. In a letter, McBride accused Abrahams and the NPA of deliberate inactivity that has enabled high-profile suspects to evade the law.

It was also a devastating blow to the anti-Zuma camp when Advocate Busisiwe Mkhwebane replaced Thuli Madonsela as the new public protector in 2016. A former SSA employee, she has proven herself to be a shadow of the courageous and incisive Madonsela.

She shamed herself as a lawyer when in June 2017 she released a report that instructed Parliament to institute a process that would result in a change to the Constitution to make the Reserve Bank focus on the "socio-economic well-being of the citizens" instead of inflation.

Amid a flurry of criticism that she had overstepped her mandate, she agreed that she had made "honest mistakes". It then emerged in court papers that she had consulted with the Presidency and the SSA prior to the writing of her report. The Reserve Bank said in a supplementary affidavit that these meetings were not disclosed in Mkhwebane's final report – as she was supposed to have done. According to notes provided to the Reserve Bank by the public protector, Mkhwebane discussed the "vulnerability" of the bank with the SSA.

* * *

In June 2017, Passenger Rail Agency (Prasa) chairperson Popo Molefe asked the High Court to compel the Hawks to investigate pervasive corruption at the organisation. Molefe had been urging the Hawks for 18 months to investigate fraud, but, according to him, they did nothing. The figures involved are baffling and hover in the billions. Prasa-appointed forensic experts have trawled through millions of documents and uncovered R14 billion in fruitless, wasteful and irregular expenditure.

The Hawks have failed for two years to investigate two Prasa contracts valued at R9 billion, according to court papers. Molefe said the Hawks, despite their initial enthusiasm, have failed to make any progress. Molefe had written a scathing letter to Berning Ntlemeza demanding action on the more than 39 allegations of corruption Prasa had reported in terms of the Prevention and Combating of Corrupt Activities Act. The parastatal had also seconded private forensic investigators to the Hawks – who report to the DPCI but whose bill is paid by Prasa – because of a lack of capacity in the police.

We know that the police, and especially the Hawks, have been bled dry of expertise and experience. But there is a much simpler explanation for the inaction: the alleged complicity of Zuma's cronies in the plunder at Prasa.

Treasury's chief procurement officer has recommended that the former chairperson of the Prasa board, Sfiso Buthelezi, face prosecution for alleged repeated violations of the Public Finance Management Act. Treasury concluded that "crippling mismanagement and criminality" at Prasa had reached systemic proportions under Buthelezi's tenure.

Treasury found that only 13 of the 216 Prasa contracts – worth a combined R19 billion – under investigation were above board. It was during Buthelezi's term that his brother's company was reportedly awarded a R150 million shipping and logistics contract. Both Buthelezi and his brother have denied any wrongdoing.

One would thus assume that Buthelezi would be in the Hawks' cross-hairs. There is, however, a small problem. Jacob Zuma has elevated Buthelezi – a known Zuma ally – to the position of deputy minister of finance.

The NPA confirmed in July 2017 that the Specialised Commercial Crimes Unit (SCCU) had been handed 60 files by the Hawks regarding the Prasa corruption. Prosecutors were directed to furnish the head of the SCCU with a report about possible prosecutions.

It is at times like this that one tends to play a game from childhood called "What if . . .?" As children, we would sketch scenarios, sometimes outrageous situations, and then among ourselves speculate about answers and laugh our heads off at each other. "What if you become a Springbok rugby player?"; "What if you get a million rand?" What if?

What if the Hawks, SARS, crime intelligence, the Asset Forfeiture Unit, the SSA and the NPA were still intact and headed by credible, competent and independent leadership?

What if Anwa Dramat, Shadrack Sibiya and Johan Booysen were still at the Hawks and unleashed the likes of Colonels Kobus Roelofse and Piet Viljoen on Sfiso Buthelezi?

What if Ivan Pillay and Johann van Loggerenberg were still at SARS and had ordered their investigation units to poke around Buthelezi's financial affairs and conduct lifestyle audits on both him and his brother?

And what if the intelligence chiefs – Gibson Njenje, Jeff Maqetuka and Moe Shaik – had been allowed in 2011 to continue their investigation into the influence of the Guptas on the government and the president?

What if?

* * *

As Fikile Mbalula took over the reins of the police, he announced himself at a press conference as the "new sheriff in town". He was all his usual bluster and puff as he threatened, warned and just about verbally terrorised criminality in South Africa into oblivion. Nobody took him too seriously because citizens know that the last thing criminals in this country fear is the police. They are far warier of neighbourhood vigilantes and street law.

Mbalula revealed that former Hawks head Berning Ntlemeza had gone rogue and was hiding in safe houses in Gauteng, plotting his revenge against those whom he perceived to have engineered his demise. He said: "This illegality that has been going on in this country must come to an end. We can't allow rogue police officers using state resources to undermine the state. We can't allow that."

Throughout the writing of this book, I was told about a rogue police unit – sometimes more than one – that is roaming the land and that is implicated in dirty tricks like break-ins at state institutions, illegal interceptions and intimidation. I heard more than once that Hawks and police units, under the leadership of Berning Ntlemeza, have gone rogue and were making sure that all "sensitive dockets" land up with him to stash away.

In April 2017, the Johannesburg mayor, Herman Mashaba, said that reliable sources had informed him that Ntlemeza had ordered that any cases the city opened should not be pursued and should instead be taken to him. According to the mayor, the city had opened many cases with the Hawks, but it appeared no investigation had taken place. The Hawks denied this vehemently.

The Independent Police Investigative Directorate is investigating the existence of the rogue police units. An impeccable source told me that Robert McBride's investigators have identified two groups of rogue cops. The one is the remnants of Ntlemeza's group and is known as the "Eastern Cape group". Although he has left the police, they still exist. This group operated from rooms in the Sheraton Hotel opposite the Union Buildings in Pretoria for nine months in 2016 and the beginning of 2017. The account was paid in cash that probably originated from the crime intelligence secret account. The source told me that IPID investigators have visited the hotel and confirmed the group's existence. They have the names of policemen in the group.

The second group is a mixture of crime intelligence and Hawks policemen, and they have skulked for several months in the Court Classique Hotel in Arcadia, Pretoria. The names of the two commanders of the second group are known to me. They are both generals.

I am going to leave you with a transcript that I received of a conversation with a Hawk policeman with intimate knowledge of at least one of the rogue groups. I believe that this transcription has found its way to IPID and that investigators have spoken to him. McBride wouldn't say anything about the inquiry.

> "There is a group of Hawks . . . put together by General Berning [Ntlemeza]. They move secretly . . . and most of them come from Limpopo or Eastern Cape. He handpicked them. A small team. They have everything: equipment to bug phones, a grabber, guns, cars, fancy stuff, power, everything. Some are very senior and even in the Hawks people are scared of them. They have been in the Sheraton Hotel in Tshwane. This is Pretoria, now, okay? They pay the hotel with secret funding. This is Ntlemeza's hit squad. They clean up for him. They only report to him. If there is a case that is a problem, they go to the witnesses and threaten them, assault them, klap them. Then they change their testimony and things. They take affidavits out of dockets. They change the evidence. They kill the cases. If this doesn't go down, then they sign for the dockets. They take the dockets away from the IO [investigating officer]. They say they are from head office and report to the General and he wants the docket. So, they take the dockets away from the offices in the regions and the cases are killed like this. These are dockets which implicate politicians and people who need protection. Tender cases, even murder cases. This makes the General very powerful. Because he provides protection to many people like this. These people are dangerous . . . they do dangerous things for the General . . . any-

body who goes against him will feel them. They will know them. They can even make cases against anybody who they want to take out. They go for anybody who is an enemy of the General. Some Hawks and politicians have suffered like this. They live on a whole floor there at that hotel. I don't know if they are still there or if they have safe houses now. Maybe they now have safe houses. I think they do. But they were in the hotel in 2016. Definitely in 2016. Here is a list with some names . . . you will see, all Hawks. On weekends, they party with strippers and whores, they booze, drink a lot, it is like a party there on weekends. They earn extra money because they are not based in Gauteng so they can claim extra travels. They can fly around the country, rent cars, they have so much power, they are like his own hit squad. They will take you out, they bring cases against anybody who goes against the General. Just ask around, people in the Hawks know of these guys . . . they know . . . but everybody is too scared to say anything . . . "

Epilogue

————•————

Most people expect the Guptas to leave South Africa soon. They've announced before that they're packing their bags. In April 2016, just hours after an emotional meeting with his executives, when he told them he was resigning from his business empire, Ajay Gupta, his brothers, their wives and assistants boarded their jet and took to the skies. Their destination: the laundromat of international financing, Dubai, where the brothers Gupta have reportedly stashed the billions they have siphoned from South Africa's state-owned enterprises.

It was all a charade, and two months later, they were back, saying they had gone to attend a wedding. Their spokesperson said: "They are very much South Africans and they continue to stay in South Africa." It probably wasn't time to go yet. They've managed to worm themselves into the sanctum sanctorum of the president and there were still juicy morsels to be mopped up. Once they've robbed us blind and there's nothing left, they will scatter for their paradise on the desert sand.

Everyone I have spoken to agrees that they will be leaving sooner than later. If Cyril Ramaphosa is elected as ANC president at the next elective conference, their departure will be imminent.

Many have asked me: are the Guptas also bankrolling Nkosazana Dlamini-Zuma, Number One's choice to keep the state within the state alive? I think it is plausible, but I have no evidence.

A new troop of hyenas, keepers and benefactors are already circling, enticed by the lure of a promised carcass should Dlamini-Zuma become

ANC president and possibly future head of state. Sponsoring and funding her campaign is an investment, much like the investment the Guptas made in Jacob Zuma, Duduzane Zuma, Ace Magashule, Des van Rooyen, Brian Molefe and Mosebenzi Zwane. I don't think the Guptas give a damn about Zuma's policies or in which direction he steers the ANC and the country. Their investment in Zuma is purely about money. Dlamini-Zuma's sponsors are in all likelihood no different.

We have already met Adriano Mazzotti, a South African of Italian descent, born in 1966. He is a flamboyant yet controversial character that has dabbled in the murky world of tobacco smuggling and has implicated himself in a host of crimes. He has emerged as a sponsor and financier of Dlamini-Zuma's campaign to become ANC president. Remember Mazzotti's name because he may well be a future Gupta, an enabler, a keeper. He probably hopes that if she comes to power, his business empire will bloom and blossom. He probably has aspirations of acquiring mines while filtering his money to an overseas bank – in his case Singapore, where he already has an account.

Zuma did not come cheap. Ask Roy Moodley, who allegedly employed Jacob at a million rand a month. Or Yusuf Kajee and Azeem Amodcaram, who had to pay tens of thousands a month to Edward. Or the Guptas, who had to cover for Dudu, by dealing with an alleged sex scandal and the killing of a woman with his Porsche and paying his housing, water and electricity bills. This is in addition to a salary of hundreds of thousands every month.

It is too early to say if Dlamini-Zuma is going to follow the Zuma kinfolk on the dirty road to sleaze, but associating with Mazzotti is a bad and ill-fated decision. He is a self-confessed tobacco smuggler, money launderer, tax evader, attempted briber, racketeer and fraudster. He admitted so much in an affidavit he made to SARS in May 2014. I have a copy of this affidavit, which is a devastating indictment of his integrity and her judgement.

I also find it odd that Dlamini-Zuma associates herself with a tobacco manufacturer. She lists as one of her achievements that when she was health minister in the 1990s, she spearheaded legislation to ban smoking in public places. And while Dlamini-Zuma's supporters have raged about the dangers and evils of "white monopoly capital", Mazzotti's company Carnilinx is almost lily-white. Only one of its directors is not white.

Dlamini-Zuma must also be aware that Mazzotti is a long-standing benefactor of the leader of the Economic Freedom Fighters (EFF), Julius Malema. Mazzotti has admitted that Carnilinx made a "donation" of R200,000 to Malema to enable the EFF to register for the May 2014 general election. What is more, when SARS withdrew its 2015 High Court application to sequestrate Malema, the court papers alleged that he used a R1 million loan from another Carnilinx director, Kyle Phillips, to pay his tax debt.

Mazzotti said in an interview with *City Press* that he used to be an ANC member but now believes the party needs to move left in its economic direction – towards the EFF. In doing so, he has positioned himself beautifully to ingratiate himself with Dlamini-Zuma.

In Chapter Ten, I told you that the State Security Agency (SSA) had approached Mazzotti for information on Malema. (I also believe that this is one of the reasons why SARS has done very little to collect the R600 million in taxes that Carnilinx owes.) Very little was forthcoming from Mazzotti about Malema. The SSA got reports that, instead, Mazzotti was bragging about his friendship with state security minister Mahlobo, which made him "untouchable". The SSA then started investigating Mazzotti. This was when they discovered that Carnilinx had moved on to a bigger league and had gained access to Dlamini-Zuma. While monitoring the offices of Carnilinx in July 2017, agents saw Dlamini-Zuma and her entourage entering the premises, where Mazzotti presented clothing for her political campaign under the banners "radical economic transformation", "NDZ" and "www.nkosazana.com". Since August 2017, Dlamini-Zuma's rallies have been flooded with her new, yellow "NDZ" T-shirts and black "NDZ" caps.

Agents have since been told to abandon their surveillance of Mazzotti but not before, said my source, the agency warned Dlamini-Zuma against Mazzotti. She apparently brushed them off with a "he-hasn't-been-convicted-of-anything". Does Dlamimi-Zuma realise that at least some of her "gift" may have been acquired with the proceeds of crime?

Although I am sure that Dlamini-Zuma would want to keep her relationship with Mazzotti confidential, the flamboyant tobacco man has allegedly been going around flaunting photographs of him and his new friend. My source said that Mazzotti and Carnilinx are pumping serious money into their relationship with Dlamini-Zuma and would obviously want something in return in future. "They believe their tax problems are something of the past," said my source. "If she becomes [ANC] president, they expect their business to blossom. And I'm not talking about cigarettes; I'm talking about mining and international financing."

Mazzotti has already ventured into mining. In February 2017, he became a founder member and director of Dithabeng Mining, an opencast mine in Mphahlele, 45 kilometres south-east of Polokwane in the Limpopo Province. The area is rich in chrome, iron and vanadium.

The company's statement on the website could as well have been written by mineral resources minister Mosebenzi Zwane, a devout Gupta acolyte. The website says that "now, more than ever before, a shift through radical economic transformation is required". The directors declare that the company "subscribes fully" to Zwane's 2017 mining charter, which requires all mining companies to have 30 per cent black empowerment shareholding within 12 months and that 50 per cent of all board members and executive management must be black. Dithabeng Mining has three directors. Once again, only one is not white.

Mazzotti and his directors say their relationship with the Ga-Mphahlele community is based on "mutual trust, respect, and inclusivity" and they pledge "clarity, transparency, participation, and accountability". This is rich coming from a self-confessed fraudster who shielded hundreds of millions of rand in tax from SARS – money that should have benefited an impoverished community like the Ga-Mphahlele.

My source believes that Mazzotti might be earmarked for something even more important: to bring together Julius Malema and Dr Nkosazana Dlamini-Zuma.

Many analysts have predicted a defeat for the ANC at the 2019 general election. If Dlamini-Zuma is elected ANC president at the next conference and Jacob Zuma stays on as president, a trouncing at the ballot box is in the offing – unless Malema either returns to the ANC or enters a coalition with Dlamini-Zuma. This despite his having said that she is even worse than her ex-husband and has "legitimised" the Guptas. Dlamini-Zuma and Malema have much in common politically and both believe, for example, in the nationalisation of the Reserve Bank and the expropriation of land without compensation.

"Mazzotti sees himself as a kingmaker," said my source. "I will be surprised if a meeting between Dlamini-Zuma and Malema has not already taken place. The one smiling is Mazzotti."

I wish I could have ended on a cheerier note. In the words of Richard Poplak, "countries are no longer countries, but fiefdoms run by tiny hyperelites, exclusively for their own benefit".

Perhaps the greatest wound that Zuma has inflicted upon our Republic is that he has buried decency and accountability under rubbish heaps of sleaze and corruption. He has made it possible for the Adriano Mazzottis of this world to don themselves in linen suits and garble sweet words and embrace the future leaders of this land. This is because the South Africa that Zuma has created has rendered sleazebags blameless, guiltless and even righteous. There are no consequences for those who evade tax or launder money or do corrupt deals.

Who knows if Mazzotti has any intention of benefiting the people of Ga-Mphahlele? It doesn't matter because he is, for now at least, armoured and untouchable.

Many more will eventually join the line and squawk for their share of dirty money, power and influence – all eager to join another army of keepers.

Acknowledgements

————•————

When I left journalism towards the end of 2014, it was to escape the psychosis of journalism that had engulfed my life for more than three decades. I thought that owning a restaurant, bar and guesthouse on the *platteland* would allow me the peace and quiet I longed for. How wrong I was: I jumped out of the frying pan into the fire when I attempted to try my hand at cheffing. The food held promise, but I was a far cry from Giorgio Locatelli or Gordon Ramsay. I was still pondering the wisdom of my decision when the opportunity to write this book presented itself.

I leapfrogged from the fire back into the frying pan. It has left my wife, Sam Rogers, with an enormous burden to run the Red Tin Roof on her own as I retreated into my writing shell. I am allegedly not a very nice person when I do so.

I will forever be grateful to Sam for affording me the time and support to write this book. And for her love during trying times.

So too the chefs in the kitchen and the other Red Tin Roof staff for their care and support. The same goes to the wonderful residents of Riebeek-Kasteel – especially those who took to the streets to search for my laptop after it was nicked from my office.

For those who have read the manuscript or advised me – Anneliese Burgess, Peter Thompson, Peter Bruce and Max du Preez – thank you so much.

I had a brilliant team at Tafelberg, and thank you especially to publisher Gill Moodie and editor Russell Martin. When I met Russell before his edit, he asked me what I expected from him. My mind was by then already cluttered and in ten different places. Clarity, I said, bring us clarity. I think he did it brilliantly.

A special word of gratitude to attorney Willem de Klerk. Legally vetting this book was a minefield. His 13-page legal report bears testimony to the difficult task he faced.

Old and new journalist friends gave me numbers, documents and leads, and I am deeply grateful to them.

I have relied heavily on the published work of some of this country's most distinguished journalists, among them Sam Sole, Marianne Thamm, Pieter-Louis Myburgh, Abram Mashego, Pauli van Wyk, Ferial Haffajee, Pieter du Toit, Angelique Serrao, Barry Bateman, Richard Poplak, Stephen Grootes, Marianne Merten, Mandy Wiener and Thanduxolo Jika.

I am grateful to the Taco Kuiper Fund for Investigative Journalism based at Wits Journalism for a generous grant that enabled me to do extensive research for this book.

The vast bulk of my information and material came from a host of officials, officers and administrators in our law enforcement agencies. Some were former employees; many were still employed. They spoke to me on condition of anonymity, and they will remain anonymous.

I am deeply indebted to them and honour their courage for putting their jobs on the line by divulging the dirty secrets of Jacob Zuma's keepers to me. I hope I have done justice to their pursuit for a better South Africa.

Bibliography

---•---

Books

Jane Duncan. 2014. *The Rise of the Securocrats*. Jacana Media: Johannesburg.

Martin Plaut. 2012. *Who Rules South Africa? Pulling the Strings in the Battle for Power*. Jonathan Ball Publishers: Cape Town.

R.W. Johnson. 2015. *How Long Will South Africa Survive? The Looming Crisis*. Hurst: London.

Pieter-Louis Myburgh. 2017. *The Republic of Gupta: A Story of State Capture*. Penguin Random House: Cape Town.

Adriaan Basson. 2012. *Zuma Exposed*. Jonathan Ball Publishers: Cape Town.

Jessica Pitchford. 2016. *Blood on their Hands: General Johan Booysen Reveals his Truth*. Pan Macmillan: Johannesburg.

Alec Russell. 2009. *After Mandela: The Battle for the Soul of South Africa*. Random House: London.

Johann van Loggerenberg and Adrian Lackay. 2016. *Rogue: The Inside Story of SARS's Elite Crime-Busting Unit*. Jonathan Ball: Cape Town.

Justice Malala. 2015. *We Have Now Begun our Descent: how to Stop South Africa Losing its Way*. Jonathan Ball Publishers: Cape Town.

Publications and online

Gareth van Zyl. 15 November 2016. *Shaun Abrahams rejects claim of R50bn market loss over Gordhan charges*. Fin24.

Dirk Kotze. 8 November 2016. *Step-by-step: how Zuma has used state institutions to stay in power*. Fin24.

Ralph Mathekga. 16 November 2016. *Useless Abrahams being fed to the wolves*. News24.

Marianne Thamm. 8 February 2017. *Selective prosecutions: for NPA, some cases are more equal than others*. Daily Maverick.

Jessica Pitchford. 15 September 2016. *Phiyega's war on Booysen led to an unlikely – and surprising – alliance with McBride*. Daily Maverick.

Hanlie Retief. 18 September 2016. *Vingeralleen teen die kabal*. Netwerk24.

Mandy Wiener. 18 September 2016. *Hollowing out the state: Johan Booysen speaks out*. Daily Maverick.

Johan Burger. 8 August 2013. *Johan Booysen: hero or villain?* Politicsweb.

Sam Sole. 8 December 2016. *Zuma's treasonous alliance with the Guptas.* amaBhungane.

Sam Sole. 13 May 2016. *Booysen attacks NPA 'abuse'.* amaBhungane.

Sam Sole. 9 October 2015. *How Panday wriggled off the hook.* Mail & Guardian.

Sam Sole. 2 October 2015. *Jacob Zuma and the untouchable Mr Panday.* Mail & Guardian.

Marianne Thamm. 10 April 2016. *State capture: keeping up with No 1, Hawks boss asks for a jet and more money.* Daily Maverick.

Cunningham Ngcukana. 9 July 2017. *Charge Zuma with treason.* News24.

Abram Mashego. 11 June 2017. *Crime intelligence gets a new boss.* City Press.

Save South Africa. 12 June 2017. *Allegations of new 'security police' should be looked into.* Politicsweb.

Glynnis Underhill. 8 November 2013. *Policing: the ghosts in the machine.* Mail & Guardian.

Abram Mashego. 25 June 2017. *Crime intel boss has a dodgy past.* City Press.

Abram Mashego. 9 July 2017. *Did intel boss dip into slush fund?* City Press.

Sipho Masondo and Abram Mashego. 2 July 2017. *Rogue cop a suspect in airport heist.* City Press.

Mzwandile Kabizokwakhe. 21 July 2013. *Dirty cops rule by fear in Soweto.* Sunday World.

Abram Mashego and Athandiwe Saba. 3 May 2015. *Charge Dramat, McBride and Sibiya over illegal renditions – report.* City Press.

Investigation staff. 23 October 2011. *Sent to Die.* Sunday Times.

Pauli van Wyk and Jessica Bezuidenhout. 13 December 2016. *'McBride, Sibiya, O'Sullivan planned to assassinate Hawks boss Ntlemeza'.* Mail & Guardian.

Sally Evans. 29 January 2016. *Case against Hawks boss Ntlemeza resurfaces.* amaBhungane

Sally Evans. 17 March 2016. *Hawks chief 'helped oust' Dramat.* amaBhungane.

Greg Nicolson. 6 September 2016. *McBride wins the battle as the war rages on.* Daily Maverick.

Rebecca Davis. 22 April 2015. *Blackened Hawk Down: the fall of Anwa Dramat.* Daily Maverick.

Marianne Thamm. 19 July 2016. *Political trials: David vs Goliath and the high cost of taking on a well-resourced state.* Daily Maverick.

Thanduxolo Jika. 31 May 2017. *Livin' it up: Guptas helped Zuma's son buy luxury Dubai flat.* TimesLive.

Mpumelelo Mkhabela. 26 May 2017. *Does Duduzane Zuma know what he's doing?* News24.

amaBhungane & Scorpio. 1 June 2017. *#GuptaLeaks: Duduzane Zuma, Kept and Captured.* Daily Maverick.

Pauli van Wyk. 20 June 2017. *Scorpio: SA's spy boss implicated in massive tender fraud at Prasa.* Daily Maverick.

Setumo Stone. 30 April 2017. *Spies Cry Foul.* City Press.

Sam Sole. 5 February 2010. *Zuma's new Spy Purge.* Mail & Guardian.

Pearlie Joubert and Adriaan Basson. 9 April 2009. *They spy who saved Zuma.* Mail & Guardian.

Jacques Pauw. 19 October 2014. *Spies plunder R1bn slush fund.* City Press.

Swedish government information service. 2 September 2015. *New Ambassadors to Sweden.*

Sam Sole & Karabo Rajuili. 27 February 2015. *Who is going to spy on the spymaster?* amaBhungane.

amaBhungane reporters. 30 March 2012. *Mdluli report's shocking revelations.* amaBhungane.

Bianca Capazorio. 8 November 2016. *Barely functional - office of the inspector general of intelligence.* TimesLive.

News24. 8 June 2017. *#GuptaLeaks: Guptas tipped off about SARS investigation unit.* News24.

Stephen Grootes. 14 February 2016. *Analysis: NPA's Kafkaesque charges against Glynnis Breytenbach.* Daily Maverick.

Sam Sole. 21 August 2015. *She's the boss: Jiba's stunning comeback.* amaBhungane.

Pauli van Wyk. 15 September 2016. *NPA's Nomgcobo Jiba and Lawrence Mrwebi struck off the roll of advocates.* Mail & Guardian.

Ra'eesa Pather. 30 January 2017. *NPA's Jiba and Mrwebi to launch fightback in Supreme Court of Appeal.* Mail & Guardian.

Stephen Grootes. 15 September 2016. *Advocate Jiba, Advocate Mrwebi: Not Fit, Not Proper.* Daily Maverick.

Karabo Ngoepe. 8 December 2016. *Why you should care about Jiba and Mrwebi's court bid.* Huffington Post.

Adriaan Basson. 24 November 2016. *SARS at war over 'underworld' figure Mark Lifman.* News24.

Marianne Thamm. 20 March 2017. *The usual suspects: Ntlemeza, Nhleko, Dlamini – Zuma's serial legal delinquents.* Daily Maverick.

Marianne Merten. 30 March 2016. *Analysis: under David Mahlobo, state security plays an increasingly powerful role.* Daily Maverick.

Mahlatse Gallens. 17 May 2017. *R2K challenges Mahlobo to provide regime change evidence.* News24.

Richard Poplak. 13 December 2016. *2016 Dr Strangelove of the Year Award: Take a bow, Team Zuma.* Daily Maverick.

Jan Gerber. 16 May 2017. *'We are monitoring everything' - spy minister Mahlobo.* News24.

Marc Davies. 4 July 2017. *David Mahlobo: beware forces seeking to undermine our gains.* Daily Maverick.

Tony Weaver. 15 November 2013. *Man Friday.* Cape Times.

Marianne Merten, 17 May 2017. *Parliament: Ipid and SAPS in open war.* Daily Maverick.

Pauli van Wyk. 15 December 2015. *McBride's 'treason plot': the events leading up to the Hawks' charges.* Mail & Guardian.

Marianne Merten. 5 May 2017. *McBride: Ipid investigators 'targeted for doing their jobs'.* Daily Maverick.

Marianne Thamm. 15 February 2017. *House of Cards: gloves off as head of Ipid alleges police minister protects corrupt cops.* Daily Maverick.

Mandy Wiener. 29 August 2017. *Robert McBride's daughter: 'assaults happen all the time'.* EWN.

Alex Mitchley. 30 August 2017. *McBride in court over daughter's assault.* News24.

Greg Nicolson. 8 May 2012. *Richard Mdluli: Zuma's Waterloo?* Daily Maverick.

Angelique Serrao. 3 April 2017. *Mdluli has earned a full salary during suspension.* News24.

Stefaans Brümmer. 1 February 2013. *Breytenbach hearing lays bare Mrwebi's strategy.* amaBhungane.

Naledi Shange. 3 February 2017. *Mdluli trial: 'my brother died for love, died at the hands of the police'.* TimesLive.

Sally Evans. 26 June 2015. *Mdluli lives in comfort, while murder trial witness lives in fear.* amaBhungane.

Sam Sole. 20 March 2015. *Mdluli ever at the heart of the carnage.* amaBhungane.

amaBhungane reporters. 5 April 2012. *How Mdluli got job back despite spy inspector's doubts.* amaBhungane.

Sam Sole. 27 September 2013. *Wrestling with facts and fiction in the strange case of Richard Mdluli.* amaBhungane.

Jeff Wicks. 18 August 2013. *Marimuthu still on police payroll.* IOL.

Adriaan Basson and Jacques Pauw. 22 April 2012. *Mdluli Inc in top gear.* City Press.

Ray Hartley. 18 June 2016. *Jacob Zuma: the rise and near fall of South Africa's President.* The Independent.

Pauli van Wyk. 15 December 2016. *McBride's 'treason plot': the events leading up to the Hawks' charges.* Mail & Guardian.

Marianne Thamm. 2 June 2016. *Shadow play: State Security, Marikana and a bogus union.* Daily Maverick.

Ferial Haffajee. 3 April 2017. *Sars special report: an institution in crisis as South Africa faces junk status.* Huffington Post.

Pauli van Wyk. 3 March 2015. *Spioene help SAID.* Beeld.

Marianne Merten. 28 March 2017. *Parliament: a combative Tom Moyane slams 'unwarranted attacks to sabotage SARS.* Daily Maverick.

Marianne Thamm. 17 March 2017. *Analysis: Tom Moyane, Zuma's kingpin.* Daily Maverick.

Craig McKune. 19 February 2016. *Sars wars: Moyane's empire strikes back.* amaBhungane.

Pauli van Wyk. 12 September 2016. *Sars mystery payments: Tom Moyane could face jail time.* Mail & Guardian.

Marianne Thamm. 8 June 2017. *Analysis: Moyane, the Gupta R70 million windfall and the trouble with SARS.* Daily Maverick.

Genevieve Quintal. 11 April 2016. *Zuma's late wife Kate was not my sister – Moyane.* News24.

Onkgopotse JJ Tabane. 28 May 2015. *Frank talk: Minister Nathi Nhleko and the scum-filled police service he leads.* Huffington Post.

Phillip de Wet. 3 July 2015. *Nutty Nhleko and the Qunu firepool.* Mail & Guardian.

Pontsho Pilane. 31 March 2016. *Six bizarre explanations for the Nkandla 'fire pool'.* Mail & Guardian.

Asha Speckman. 6 August 2017. *Fears grow of capture at SARS.* BusinessLive.

Rob Rose. 3 October 2016. *Just come clean, Moyane.* Financial Mail.

Rob Rose. 9 March 2017. *Fear and loathing in Sars.* Financial Mail.

Ranjeni Munusamy. 6 May 2013. *From our vault: the top spooks' Gupta warning – which cost them their jobs.* Daily Maverick.

Siphiwe Sibeko. 1 February 2017. *Is this why Gerrie Nel left? 9 reasons the NPA is screwed – to put it mildly.* Huffington Post.

Pieter-Louis Myburgh. 8 March 2017. *Exclusive: Molefe slammed Hawks boss over Prasa probe.* News24.

Stephen Grootes. 14 September 2015. *Op-ed: Ntlemeza's appointment as head of the Hawks is absurd.* Daily Maverick.

Glynnis Underhill. 30 March 2016. *State capture: Nhleko's secret cabinet memorandum unlocks mystery of Ntlemeza's appointment to lead the Hawks.* Daily Maverick.

Jeff Wicks. 13 December 2016. *Mokotedi hits out at O'Sullivan, McBride and Sibiya.* News24.

Andisiwe Makinana. 23 October 2016. *Mbete versus Nhleko versus McBride.* City Press.

Mondli Makhanya. 30 October 2016. *It's amateur hour again.* City Press.

Abram Mashego. 8 January 2017. *Ipid battles SAPS, Hawks.* City Press.

Abram Mashego. 22 January 2017. *How Nhleko gave Ntlemeza his job.* City Press.

Marianne Thamm. 6 December 2016. *House of cards: General Ntlemeza – the Hawks head, a one-man wrecking ball.* Daily Maverick.

Lizeka Tandwa. 7 December 2016. *Committee that appointed Hawks boss was 'ill-equipped', court hears.* News24.

Angelique Serrao. 4 April 2017. *Exclusive: Mashaba alleges Ntlemeza is blocking Joburg corruption case.* News24.

Sam Sole & Sally Evans. 16 October 2015. *Cloud over new Hawks boss ignored.* amaBhungane.

Ernest Mabuza. 9 June 2017. *Ntlemeza's bid to return as Hawks boss dismissed by SCA.* TimesLive.

Graeme Hosken. 23 July 2017. *Guptas seek to shift billions.* Sunday Times.

Kyle Cowan. 4 August 2017. *SARS chief financial officer resigns.* TimesLive.

Marianne Thamm. 3 April 2016. *House of cards: what does the Sunday Times SARS apology mean for the rest of the pack?* Daily Maverick.

Marianne Thamm. 2 December 2015. *SARS rogue unit controversy: Investigative journalist claims Sunday Times was part of an 'orchestrated effort'.* Daily Maverick.

RDM staff. 3 April 2016. *Sunday Times editor admits to errors in reporting on SARS 'rogue unit'.* Rand Daily Mail.

Antoinette Slabbert. 14 December 2015. *Gordhan reacts angrily to Sars rogue unit 'rumour'.* Moneyweb.

Jacques Pauw. 10 August 2014. *Sex, Sars and rogue spies.* City Press.

Piet Rampedi, Mzilikazi wa Afrika, Stephan Hofstatter, Malcolm Rees. 12 October 2014. *SARS bugged Zuma.* Sunday Times.

Marianne Thamm. 24 January 2014. *SARS Wars, season two: how can we trust the KPMG report?* Daily Maverick.

Piet Rampedi, Mzilikazi wa Afrika, Stephan Hofstatter. 9 November 2014. *Taxman's rogue unit ran a brothel.* Sunday Times.

Belinda Walter. 8 February 2015. *Right of reply: you got it all wrong about me.* City Press.

Graeme Hosken. 25 January 2015. *What's in the police commissioner's garage?* TimesLive.

Angelique Serrao & Pieter-Louis Myburgh. 23 November 2016. *This is police chief's controversial house.* News24.

Marianne Merten. 1 June 2017. *Mbalula's top cop chop shop: first Ntlemeza, now SAPS acting commissioner Phahlane out too.* Daily Maverick.

Graeme Hosken. 28 April 2017. *Phahlane 'fix-it squad' warned off by Ipid.* TimesLive.

Greg Nicolson. 31 May 2017. *Ipid trades blows with SAPS while calls grow for acting police commissioner to step down.* Daily Maverick.

Angelique Serrao. 29 March 2017. *Exclusive: dramatic new information on police chief's spending.* News24.

Stephen Grootes. 30 January 2017. *Pravin Gordhan: 'systematic and highly organised campaign by the Gupta family'.* Daily Maverick.

Will Jordan. 24 February 2015. *Inside the battle for intelligence in South Africa.* Al Jazeera.

Thanduxolo Jika. 12 June 2016. *Top spy comes in from the cold - R6m later.* Sunday Times.

Marianne Thamm. 2 June 2016. *Shadow play: state security, Marikana and a bogus union.* Daily Maverick.

Marianne Merten. 31 March 2017. *Reshuffle chronicles: 'intelligence' reports – No securocrat's toolbox should ever be without them.* Daily Maverick.

Marianne Thamm. 22 March 2017. *Analysis: happy Human Rights Day – 57 years later, political thugs threaten fragile democracy.* Daily Maverick.

Caryn Dolley. 9 December 2013. *The day Mandela got lost in a crowd.* IOL.

Shaun Swingler. 29 May 2014. *Fighting the gangs of South Africa's Western Cape.* The Guardian.

Marianne Thamm. 4 November 2016. *State capture: Vytjie Mentor and the affidavit that caused all the trouble.* Daily Maverick.

Jenna Etheridge. 13 December 2016. *Mystery of the 'missing' record in top cops' transfer.* News24.

Tammy Petersen. 8 July 2015. *Guns sold to Cape gangsters meant for destruction, court hears.* News24.

Warda Meyer. 20 June 2016. *Row after two top Cape cops 'demoted'.* IOL.

Marianne Thamm. 4 July 2016. *When hell is not hot enough: a top cop who supplied weapons to country's gangsters and right wingers.* Daily Maverick.

Pieter-Louis Myburgh, Angelique Serrao, Monica Laganparsad and Amanda Khoza. 24 March 2017. *Exclusive: fake numbers, addresses for Mogoeng break-in suspects.* News24.

Sunday Times investigations. 28 September 2014. *Exposed: how arms dealer Thales bankrolled Zuma.* Sunday Times.

Rapula Moatshe & Lionel Faull. 2 November 2012. *JZ's decade of destruction.* Mail & Guardian.

Media24 Investigations. 8 December 2013. *Krejčíř's arresting colonel has a past.* City Press.

Paul Trewhela. 15 February 2009. *Jacob Zuma in exile: three unexplored issues.* Politicsweb.

Justice Malala. 8 April 2014. *The big read: Old goons protect No 1.* TimesLive.

Kenneth Good. 19 November 1989. *How the killing of Thami Zulu contradicts Zuma's claims.* Politicsweb.

David Beresford. 25 February 2009. *Hints of a darker past.* News24.

Marianne Thamm. 29 August 2016. *Gexit? Not so fast, Guptas.* Daily Maverick.

Ismail Lagardien. 8 February 2016. *Jacob Zuma and the rise and fall of the ANC.* Daily Maverick.

Mark Heywood. 5 March 2017. *Jacob Zuma and the rise and fall of the ANC.* Daily Maverick.

Marianne Thamm. 12 July 2017. *Corrupting the country's soul, Zupta style: South Africa, you are on your own.* Daily Maverick.

Richard Poplak. 5 March 2017. *Trainspotter: Jacob Zuma, and how the state breaks when you're otherwise occupied.* Daily Maverick.

Pieter-Louis Myburgh. 14 August 2016. *Exclusive: Zuma friend's R550m bonanza.* News24.

Ranjeni Munusamy. 2 March 2015. *Information = Power: Jacob Zuma's shrinking circle of trust.* Daily Maverick.

Liesl Peyper. 21 June 2017. *SARS' Makwakwa on paid leave for 9 months as investigation stalls.* Fin24.

Pauli van Wyk. 15 September 2016. *Sars' second in command Jonas Makwakwa suspended over mystery payments of R1.2m.* Mail & Guardian.

Susan Comrie, Craig McKune, Sam Sole. 11 September 2016. *Sars chief's mystery stash.* amaBhungane.

Marianne Merten. 16 August 2017. *Parliament: SA's crime-intelligence fighters, at war with themselves.* Daily Maverick.

Zukile Majova and Mbuyisi Mgibisa. 29 June 2007. *Agliotti and the Cuban 'drug lord'.* Mail & Guardian.

Marianne Thamm. 10 February 2017. *SARS wars: suspension of the last remaining key official jeopardises 'Tobacco War' cases.* Daily Maverick.

Sibongakonke Shoba. 12 April 2015. *Where did Malema get the money? Sars reveals why deal collapsed.* TimesLive.

Pearlie Joubert. 12 April 2015. *How SARS bust Lifman.* City Press.

Marianne Thamm. 12 January 2017. *SARS wars: Moyane/Gordhan cold war to reach breaking point in 2017.* Daily Maverick.

Amanda Khoza. 15 April 2015. *I never hid anything from SARS – Lifman.* Fin 24.

Sam Sole. 7 January 2011. *Ex-con is Khulubuse's link to Chinese deals.* Mail & Guardian.

Sam Sole. 10 July 2015. *Zuma crony linked to Swazi fraud and bribery scandals.* Mail & Guardian.

Angelique Serrao. 16 November 2016. *Senior SARS employee involved with Zuma family-linked company.* News24.

Gertrude Makhafola. 12 May 2016. *Khulubuse Zuma and Co lose appeal, must pay Aurora workers.* Mail & Guardian.

Pierre de Vos. 19 October 2016. *The law, Gordhan's tactical move – and those 72 suspicious transactions by the Guptas.* Daily Maverick.

Ray Hartley. 30 March 2017. *The story of the very political funeral of Ahmed Kathrada.* Rand Daily Mail.

Qaanitah Hunter. 29 March 2017. *Zuma to justify Gordhan axing with intelligence report – sources.* Sowetan.

Jan Gerber. 22 May 2017. *Zuma refuses to answer questions on Nkandla tax, 'intelligence report'.* News24.

Jeff Wicks. 28 February 2017. *Suspended KZN Hawks head Johan Booysen calls off fight.* Business Day.

Documents/reports published online

Freedom Under Law court application, *Case no 87643/2016*. Pretoria High Court.

Johan Booysen. 20 February 2017. *Second Supplementary Founding Affidavit*. Durban High Court.

SAFLII. 15 September 2016. *General Council of the Bar of South Africa v Jiba and Others*. Pretoria High Court.

JCPS Cluster Report. 17 May 2013. *Landing of a chartered commercial aircraft at Air Force base Waterkloof.*

Ipid. 22 January 2014. *Case investigative report on alleged renditions.*

Stephen Ellis. April 1994. *Mbokodo: Security in ANC camps, 1961-1990*. African Affairs.

Nadja Manghezi. 2008. *They were part of us and we were part of them: The ANC in Mozambique from 1976 to 1990.*

Index

About the author

Journalist and author **Jacques Pauw** was a founder member of the anti-apartheid Afrikaans newspaper *Vrye Weekblad* in the late 1980s, where he exposed the Vlakplaas police death squads. He worked for some of the country's most esteemed publications before becoming a documentary film-maker, producing documentaries on wars and conflicts in Rwanda, Burundi, Algeria, Liberia, Sudan, the Democratic Republic of Congo and Sierra Leone, among other countries. When he left journalism in 2014, he was the head of investigations at Media24 newspapers. He has won the CNN African Journalist of the Year Award twice, the Daniel Pearl Award for Outstanding International Investigative Reporting in the US, Italy's Ilaria Alpi and the Nat Nakasa award for bravery and integrity in journalism. He is the author of five books: four nonfiction and one fiction. They are *In the Heart of the Whore*, *Into the Heart of Darkness*, *Dances with Devils*, *Rat Roads* and *Little Ice Cream Boy*. Three of his books have been shortlisted for major literary awards.